National Acclaim for *For the Glory*

" . . . an utterly candid book . . . about dreams, both dashed and realized. This book will change the way you watch college
football."   —*The South Bend Tribune*

" . . . a fascinating look at what big-time college football involves for
those who play the game."   —*The Washington Post Book World*

"Anyone who cares about young men and college football should
run, not walk, to a bookstore."—David Kindred, *The Sporting News*

"Ken Denlinger's ambitious new book . . . should be mandatory
reading."   —Michael Moran, *The New York Times*

"Denlinger's reverence for Paterno suffuses the book, as does his
kindness and respect for the young players. *For the Glory* is a solid
look at the pleasures and pressures of playing for a major college
program."   —Robert Lipsyte, *The New York Times*

"A thoughtful and compelling book . . . Denlinger captures in equal
parts the frustrating pain and the adrenaline-pumping thrill of playing college football at the highest level."   —*Kirkus Reviews*

"You don't have to be a Penn State fan to enjoy *For the Glory*, even
Pitt fans and graduates will like it."   —Beano Cook, ESPN,
                             University of Pittsburgh,
                             Class of 1954

   "If a person wants insight into any big-time college football program, *For the Glory* is the only book to read. This book should be
   required reading for any and every high school athlete who wants
   to know what to expect in college athletics. The best part of *For the
   Glory* was following the dreams of the freshmen into the realities of
   the senior class."   —Matt Millen, FOX Sports Commentator,
                             Penn State Class of 1980, Former San
                             Francisco 49er

"*For the Glory* gives you the rare opportunity to get an all-encom-
passing perspective on college football players."
                             —Roger Staubach, Hall of Fame Quarterback

FOR THE GLORY

College Football Dreams and

Realities Inside Paterno's Program

KEN DENLINGER

St. Martin's Griffin ✦ New York

Design by Sara Stemen

"A Thomas Dunne Book"

Library of Congress
Cataloging-in-Publication Data

Denlinger, Ken.
For the glory : college football dreams and
realities inside Paterno's program / Ken
Denlinger.
    p. cm.
    ISBN 0-312-13496-7 (pbk.)
    1. Pennsylvania State University—Foot-
ball—Case studies. 2. Football players—
Pennsylvania—Case studies. 3. Student
aspirations—Pennsylvania—Case studies.
4. College orientation—Pennsylvania—Case
studies. I. Title.
[GV958.P46D466 1995]
796.332'63'0974811—dc20   95-22203
                                            CIP

First St. Martin's Griffin Edition:
September 1995
10 9 8 7 6 5 4 3 2 1

*To the 29 Nittany Lions
and coach Joe Paterno,
who took a chance
on themselves—and on me.*

Contents

FOR THE
GLORY

Introduction

The only sound of their coming together one final time before the home fans was the clickety-clack of football cleats on concrete. This was late afternoon on November 21, 1992, under the south stands of Beaver Stadium, whose customary population of 91,000-plus once again had become the fourth largest in all of Pennsylvania. The crowd had bucked a cold, hard rain to watch the annual grudge match against Pitt and, not insignificantly, to honor these Penn State seniors about an hour before kickoff.

Was it time to leave already? Yes. College football allows its hired hands five years to complete four seasons of eligibility, and the oldest of the young men pacing nervously in their blue and white uniforms had arrived in early August 1988. Truth be known, the end seemed far removed in those first several months at Penn State and too quickly at hand during the most recent several months.

Nine of the soon-to-leave Nittany Lions were both lonely and not alone. Lonely because so many who had started with them were not around to share this unique moment of glory. Each player would be introduced on the public-address system and, as he soaked in the applause, trot to midfield; the final player to hit the 50 yard line would trigger another ovation, this one for the group. But the unit that mattered most to this ninesome had long ago been broken. Quickly. Dramatically. Sometimes tragically.

There had been twenty-eight of them at the start, twenty-eight scholarship players who had come from as close as a ninety-minute drive and from as far away as New Mexico, twenty-eight dreamers for whom the journey to this day was wilder than they could possibly have imagined. Out of those twenty-eight, only nine were still on the Penn State roster. The fortunate ones. The survivors.

Joining them for this full-dress review were a few players who also had arrived five seasons earlier but without scholarships. Walk-ons, they were called. Long shots for even a few minutes of playing time. Impossible dreamers. And the lanky player wearing number 70 hadn't even walked on. He was Bob Ceh (pronounced Check), who had come only expecting to be a team manager, a semi-servant, but who, by circumstances close to miraculous, had ended up with more precious minutes of playing time than many of his highly heralded classmates.

As they started to line up alphabetically, several shook hands and a few hugged. John Gerak's face was a collection of raindrops and tears. Chris Cisar swung an imaginary bat, reaffirming his belief that his athletic future was in baseball. Mark Graham winked. He had vowed on at least half a dozen occasions over the years to escape this sweaty, frenetic, incredibly pressurized rat race where any result less than the national championship was deemed a failure. Once, after intercepting a pass on the last play of a home game against Rutgers, he sought me out in the fenced-in reception area near the dressing room and declared: "And I'm *still* not coming back." Of course, he did.

Had Donnie Bunch stayed—and not been kicked out of school more than four years earlier after a series of drinking violations and then all but dropped out of sight—he would have been first on the field. Bunch had so craved attention that he had even worn uniform number 1. Instead, Todd Burger was the first to be introduced, the first to high-five the team mascot near the goalpost and then dash to midfield.

The pattern continued. For every player who followed Burger onto the soggy field, an absent friend was far from the celebration—either in body or in spirit. Cisar made it all the way, though he had played far more as a freshman than any season thereafter; Chad Cunningham did not, a terrible knee injury suffered in high school having cost him the quickness so necessary for a running back. And so on. Mark Graham, yes. Anthony Grego, no. Adam Shinnick, no. Derek Van Nort, no. Tom Wade, no. Brett Wright, sort of.

Wright was a team captain in 1992, yet he neither wore his uniform nor ran to join his buddies at midfield. As had happened to so many others, a knee injury two weeks earlier had caused a premature end to his career. Dressed in a suit and tie, shivering even with a topcoat, Wright walked to midfield from the bench area. So did Bob Daman, done in by back misery after his sophomore year and not sure he really ought to be here. He said: "My mother made me feel guilty."

The odd and unsettling fact about high-level football is that unless a person contributes in some very obvious way, he is not considered part of the team. Or, perhaps more accurately, the player does not think of himself as a full-fledged member. Daman in his imaginatively impish fashion had meant a lot to morale in the three years after his playing career ended. The last two seasons he also had worked on the practice field each week, with defensive players acting the part of the opposition. Even so, Daman was not sure he belonged here this special day. This perception helps explain why Eric Renkey and some others still in school at Penn State had decided to pass on this formal goodbye.

By senior day, five years after they had arrived at Penn State, classmates once as close as a brief walk down the first floor of Nittany Hall were miles apart in nearly every way possible. Van Nort was living near Los Angeles, happily married and involved

4 FOR THE GLORY

in a work-study program related to chemical engineering. Tony Sacca was a back-up quarterback with the NFL Phoenix Cardinals. He and cornerback Leonard Humphries had been the only members of the class to complete their four years of eligibility at Penn State without an inactive season. Humphries had gotten his degree; Sacca had not.

Like Daman, Rudy Glocker and Rich Rosa had maintained their scholarships by working as untitled coaching aides. During games, Glocker helped Penn State's full-time assistants in the booth high above the field; Rosa was active near the sidelines with a wide-receiver corps that included his best friend, O. J. McDuffie. Glocker in his dark blue jacket and dark blue trousers chose to join the class for its pregame processional; Rosa did not, preferring to keep his quasi-coach distance—of the class but not with it just now.

By this time, Todd Rucci had come to a simple conclusion about Penn State football, which he also passed along to recruits: "I tell 'em, sometimes you'll want to be somewhere else. But you'll be with a bunch of guys you want to hang out with." Rucci shrugged. That was all anyone really needed to know. It also was the best endorsement coach Joe Paterno could ask for.

To understand the comfort level among Penn State football players, one need only watch McDuffie in the near-empty locker room after a winter workout. Out of deodorant, he walked to Matt Nardolillo's locker, opened the door to a small compartment and got some. Out of lotion, he walked to Rucci's locker and got some. Had he needed a pick, he would have gone across the room to an upperclassman's locker.

I watched this and must have looked skeptical about McDuffie's familiarity with the locker room and his teammates. He may have thought that I was thinking: Everybody has deodorant; everybody has lotion; everybody has some sort of comb. Ah, but everybody doesn't, and McDuffie took it from there: "Ritz crackers. [Underclass fullback] Brian O'Neal keeps 'em in that little cubicle in his locker." Two steps, a slight stretch, and McDuffie was dining at the Ritz.

The fans were passionate about Penn State football but knew very little about the Penn State football players passing in front of them. They could match most of the names and numbers and recognize most of the faces. They knew the dollars-and-cents cost of big-time football but had no clue about the price that young men pay to play it.

The frightening, almost sick side of college football is the danger. Of this recruiting class of twenty-eight, half suffered an injury serious enough to require an operation. And although Eric Renkey and Ron Fields never underwent surgery, their careers ended when neck trouble made playing not worth the risk of serious injury.

Nearly everybody in the sea of colorful rain costumes and umbrellas inside Beaver Stadium could recall a particular play by the All-American McDuffie; his reception was the warmest. Almost no one had realized that Cisar's route to midfield had taken him across the very part of the end zone where, three years earlier, he had suffered a broken wrist during a preseason scrimmage.

Out of sight for the moment was the man who dominated Penn State football and whose many-sided personality both lured all twenty-eight scholarship players here and caused all twenty-eight, every last one, either to want to quit or to actually do so: Paterno. Oh boy. Did these kids ever get a dose of JoePa. Sweet and sour. Tough and tender. And he got a dose of them. Many had disappointed him. A few had thrilled him.

This project—following one scholarship football class, and its magnificent, lower-than-walk-on Ceh, from beginning to end at a big-time football program—started with a phone call to Paterno. "Sure," he said. "Come on up. Maybe we'll learn something." The access that Paterno gave me was virtually unlimited. The only aspect of the program that I was not privy to was the near-endless meetings between Paterno and his staff, and that didn't matter for two reasons: This book is primarily about how players view major college football, and I soon knew how those closed-door decisions affected my class.

I say "my" class because I have gotten very possessive about
it. I would not hesitate to invite any of the players into my home
or into my family. They shared their feelings and insights—as
much as young men a year or so each side of twenty are able
to—because, I hope, they sensed that although this would be
an honest book it would not be a mean one.

To rivals tempted to blindside perspective and use the dicey
material in future recruiting battles with Paterno and Penn State,
I say: "Let me inside *your* program for five years."

I have tried to avoid being too judgmental about the players,
because not succeeding at football is hardly the worst thing that
can happen to a young man. Also, my own academic performance
at Penn State in the early 1960s was as lackluster as many in
this class, and I did not have twenty-five hours of football each
week to drag it down. So, of the charges that might be brought
against me, hypocrisy at least will be dismissed.

However, not sermonizing about at least a few subjects,
among them big-time college football and Paterno, after five
years of research and up-close observations would be dereliction
of duty. As a tease, let me say this: Artificial playing surfaces
ought to be burned, and I would dearly love to strike the first
match.

I did not find submachine guns under any pillows at Penn
State, but I do believe that "my guys" experienced nearly everything possible, positive and negative, about highest-altitude college football. An Alabama player, a Yale player, a Notre Dame
player, a Sooner, a Buckeye, a Bruin, or a Hurricane—active or
out of the game—ought to nod his head in recognition during
at least a few pages of this book.

Here's the A-to-Z of those final few moments before the class
of 1992 played its final home game: While McDuffie was waving
back to his adoring public one last time in misty Beaver Stadium
and preparing to be a first-round choice in the 1993 NFL draft,
Rick Sayles was no more than two miles away and trying to stay
out of jail.

PART ONE

IN SEARCH OF

1

The Parade Begins

E arly December is, on the surface, the quietest time in college football. By then, the eleven-game season is over, and empty stadiums, such as Penn State's, resemble gray aircraft carriers in dry dock. Starting to focus on Christmas, alumni and student fans are either grumbling about what should have been or gloating over successes that have earned for their schools an invitation to one of the bowl binges that will begin in a few weeks and end New Year's night. For most players, the ones not involved in bowl practices, this is unrippled calm, a brief national time-out from hitting and being hit.

College coaches, however, are anything but serene, their considerable energies not being recharged so much as redirected. For them, December is the most important part of a very different kind of season, one that also demands the utmost in strategic planning and persuasion techniques: the recruiting season.

The hectic weeks between the final game and the middle of February will be the culmination of a wooing process that has been going on for several years, the gathering of the next fall's freshman football players. During what amounts to a kind of two-minute drill, college coaches spring about the land in not-so-polite competition to secure commitments from a couple of dozen of the most desirable high school seniors.

Since the mid-1960s, nowhere in college football has this recruiting campaign been waged with more zest and success than at Penn State, and no coach in any sport during the late fall of 1987 was held in more esteem than Paterno. Earlier that year his Nittany Lions had won their second national championship. Paterno himself was on a run of incredible good fortune that had begun the season after his elevation to head coach in 1965. During that twenty-two-year period, his teams had compiled a record of 207–48–2, which put him in a tie for sixth on the list of winningest all-time major college coaches. Only Bear Bryant, with twenty-nine, had more bowl appearances than Paterno's nineteen. Almost surely, no other school's Creamery had dedicated a flavor of ice cream, Peachy Paterno, to its coach.

For Paterno and every other coach, the recruiting process never ends. It occupies some of almost all days and almost all of some days. A half hour into his honeymoon on May 12, 1962, then-assistant Paterno left his bride, Sue, in the car while he pitched Penn State to a player who still ended up going to Miami. For the basketball program. Paterno one Easter put in a phone call to Danny Ferry, who later chose Duke.

If recruiting is a seamless and, at times, unseemly affair for coaches, it is a dazzling, once-in-a-lifetime experience for the recruits. Suddenly, during the final two-month frenzy, an enormously gifted teenager will find famous coaches seemingly walking right off the television screen to sit down beside him on the living room sofa. They will simultaneously beg and challenge him with a pitch that goes something like: "Son, you can help us win a national championship." In December 1987 this goal was for the 1992 season, at the latest, when the group of scholarship signees would reach full fifth-year maturity.

The final sixty days are the most hectic and disjointed for the coaches. They have whittled the recruiting list to about six dozen and done as much homework as possible about each prospect's football ability and his potential as a college student. Absolutely no one can predict what will happen when each breaks away from home for the first time, and the frightening fact for coaches, Paterno included, is that their livelihood rests on the whims of teenagers.

Elite schools, such as Penn State, are hopeful, knowing they will beat out at least 80 percent of the competition for the best players. It's winning those tense recruiting games with the remaining 20 percent that determines national championships. Beating Notre Dame in the living room leads to beating Notre Dame on the field.

The pace of recruiting increases dramatically as everyone approaches the home stretch. A coach might be in New York City one day, in an obscure Midwest hamlet the next, gliding through the corridors of an unfamiliar high school in the morning, and complimenting mom on her apple pie in the evening. If his sales pitch rarely varies, the areas in which he gives it almost always do. No telling from what roots the next Heisman Trophy winner might sprout.

Paterno was embarking not only on what was perhaps the most critical part of his year but also of his future. Four days before Christmas, he would turn sixty-one. Already, recruiters from the other heavyweight schools were using age against him, planting in impressionable minds the thought that Paterno might not be around for their entire collegiate experience. Speculation was adrift that this might be his last class.

And so for perhaps the first time as head coach, Paterno was not selling from near-total strength as he left his office the snowy afternoon of December 3. Dressed in a conservative suit, with a tie whose knot seemed too wide for current fashion trends, he flew in one of the university's two small jets from almost the geographic midpoint of Pennsylvania and joined assistant coach Tom Bradley in Pittsburgh. .

He and Bradley then drove about a half hour to one of those otherwise obscure areas of the United States that become famous for their football sons: North Hills. What had drawn them there was a prospect off the charts academically and athletically, a recruiter's dream and the focal point of a parade later that evening that would end about an hour before Paterno was scheduled to make his pitch.

Of all the post-season high-school celebrations, the one for the North Hills Indians was especially significant. Unbeaten in thirteen games, having outscored the opposition by 435–20, North Hills had been judged the best high-school team in the country by the influential newspaper *USA Today*. North Hills's slightly partisan coach, Jack McCurry, who had won ninety-six games and three regional championships in ten seasons, solemnly said: "This is the best [team] that has ever been assembled in western Pennsylvania."

This was a statement to be savored, for western Pennsylvania is to big-time football what parts of the Midwest are to wheat. Many a college team has grown from marginal to majestic by recruiting players whose ferocity and manner of speech seem unique to their roots. Pro football's history starts in western Pennsylvania. One of the earliest for-pay players was a sixteen-year-old quarterback named John Brallier, who in 1895 accepted $10 to join the Latrobe YMCA for a game against the Jeannette Athletic Club.

So Paterno was in the familiar and rich territory that had produced Mike Ditka, Tony Dorsett, and such renowned quarterbacks as John Unitas, Joe Namath, and Joe Montana. And much of this night belonged to the latest heralded western Pennsylvanian, a linebacker whose eyes could switch from twinkling to terrifying in an instant, Eric Renkey.

For the North Hills parade, more than a dozen fire trucks had been borrowed from nearby towns. Climbing aboard them in their red and white jerseys and letter jackets were eight players considered big-time college prospects. The center of attention on the lead truck, as always, was the 230-pound Renkey, who had anchored the North Hills defense during most of a glorious season that included a 21–0 shutout of arch-rival Mount Lebanon for the highest possible on-the-field honor: the Western Pennsylvania Interscholastic Athletic League AAAA title.

Renkey often got more space in the Pittsburgh papers than many of the professional Steelers and Pirates. That was mostly because, at his level, he had a far superior season. But he also had a sophisticated wit rare in a youngster who would not turn eighteen until December 31. About a key reception against Mount Lebanon as an occasional tight end, he had said: "It's the first anniversary of my last catch." Renkey was the North Hills player that college recruiters from coast to coast had come to visit. And for good reason.

On a very good team in one of the most competitive leagues anywhere, Renkey had become a starter at linebacker four games into his freshman season. As a tension-bursting joke before that first start, Mel Renkey had slipped a diaper into his son's equipment bag. "In case I wet myself," Eric explained.

Some 70 pounds heavier than the 160 that he carried as a baby 'backer, Renkey at 6 feet 3 inches tall still looked rather slender. To college salesmen, he provided these gaudy career numbers: more than 300 tackles, more than 30 quarterback sacks, and a combined score of 1370 (out of a possible 1600) on the Scholastic Aptitude Test. The National High School Athletic Coaches Association chose him as defensive captain of its All-American team; that honor included a trip to Chicago, where he was joined during a television appearance by the offensive captain, a California quarterback named Todd Marinovich.

Earning such heady stature had not been easy, though Renkey early seemed to relish each step in the rugged process. As an eighth grader, he had read a magazine story in which Herschel Walker described an exercise that involved strapping a tire loaded with enormous lead weights around his waist and walking painful stretches with it.

Renkey quickly devised a similar contraption, with chunks of cement blocks substituted for lead weights. Mel, an executive with AT&T, obtained for Eric a strap that telephone repairmen used to attach themselves to poles. Routinely, Eric would lug the cement-stuffed tire down an incline behind the house, harness himself to it and stagger thirty or so yards across the lawn and then back. Again and again.

Pain, like any other opponent, was an obstacle to be played around. Or through. When he suffered a broken right shoulder playing basketball against adults, Eric said to Mel, "Why don't I play left-handed?" He did.

But Eric clearly was a football player. Though he played basketball, he once advised a Pittsburgh reporter inquiring about an upcoming basketball game, "Better get there early if you want to see me . . . I've either fouled out or been thrown out of every game this year."

Such an ornery streak is much admired in football. That prompted Renkey's coach, McCurry, to say: "Eric is the most intense player I have ever had and probably ever will have. He's very intelligent and has that drive you just can't coach. Wherever the ball is, he'll be there. Will another Eric Renkey come along? I hope so, but I doubt it."

If Renkey had been the strongest magnet that had drawn Paterno to North Hills, he was not the only one. Not long before the parade started forming in the school's parking lot, Paterno had been to the home of the most versatile North Hills senior, Chris Cisar, who could play about every position available to someone slightly taller than 6 feet and slightly heavier than 180 pounds. Penn State wanted him as a defensive back, specifically for the strong safety position it called "Hero."

This double-dip trip, to see Cisar and his family before the parade and the Renkeys after, was significant because the head coach is allowed by NCAA rules only one home visit per prospect. Because this night was theirs and he could turn every head in the crowd his way, Paterno passed on the parade and remained for more than two hours at Carmassi's, where he and assistant coach Tom Bradley had dinner.

After dinner, Bradley left for the parade. At thirty, he was the most outgoing of State's stable of assistants and had been following Renkey and Cisar for more than three years. He had tried with letters, phone calls, and all the visits to games and schools that the rules permitted to develop a brotherlike relationship with them. The closer a coach gets to him, the harder it is for a player to say no when he finally must choose a school.

Bradley's zest was such that an oil spill near Pittsburgh was reason to pitch Penn State at the expense of arch-rival Pitt. "He called one night," Renkey recalled, "and mentioned that Pittsburgh didn't have water. So he turned on some water at his place and put the phone by it. Then he took a big gulp of water and said: 'See, we always have water at Penn State.' "

During the parade, Bradley hopped from place to place, waving wildly each time the truck carrying Renkey and Cisar passed, making sure they noticed him and how much he still cared.

Even if the night had not been so nasty as to keep Marilyn Renkey back at school, she and Mel would have greeted Eric from separate locations along the parade route. They had divorced four years earlier. Ironically, Mel had come twice as far, from southern New Jersey, as Paterno had to see Eric. From the parking lot of a shopping center, Mel rifled a couple of snowballs toward his famous son.

The ninety-minute parade passed by most of the cherished spots for the North Hills players: the elementary school in the town of West View, where each week the name of a player would be strung along its six front windows, and Monte Cello's Pizza, the main hangout. The parade came within a block of the field where North Hills played its home games, which was appropriate because Renkey and the other seniors already were starting to distance themselves from high school.

"There's a house right by the field," Renkey said, "and the people who own it cut down all the trees in the backyard so they could watch the games. They put up signs with lights on them, called themselves the Rowdy Rooters. Maybe fifty fans would be there, with a couple of kegs. Rooting us on and insulting the other team. They'd also always be at school when we'd come home from away games. Our most loyal fans."

Still nearly a month shy of turning eighteen, Renkey knew this parade would be unique in his life. And while he enjoyed being the envy of men two and three times his age, he also was uncomfortable being the object of ceaseless attention. "I used to never go into Ross Park Mall," he said. "And especially if I had something that said North Hills Football on, because ten people would stop and ask me where I was going to college. Especially right after the season. A couple of times in West View I'd be getting something to eat and people would ask for autographs. All the kids know who you are."

He had not been that way as a kid. Mel coached one of the youth league teams, which featured the pass-and-catch combination of quarterback Eric Renkey and receiver Chris Cisar. But Eric had not been starstruck over the North Hills Indians, though it was obvious how special they were. "Friday night [youth league] practices had to be cut short," he said, "because everybody had to go see the North Hills game. People with no kids at North Hills would go. But my dad and I never got caught up in it."

"Caught up in it" would be a mild way of describing Eric's attitude once he became a North Hills Indian. Now and then he had been frightened by a nerve injury in the neck area. It was called a "burner" because burning was one of the immediate sensations along the shoulder area and down the adjoining arm. Worse, a good deal of the area would go numb. But the burners passed quickly, within twenty or thirty seconds, and he pressed ahead with near-fanatic devotion. "If you want to get really fired up, you have to start on a Monday to get ready for a Friday," Renkey observed. "By Friday, you're nuts. Then you calm down a little over the weekend."

Renkey's zest was matched by those who watched his game and followed his progress. Coach McCurry spoke of western Pennsylvania as others did about sizable regions of Texas and Georgia and smaller ones in most other states: "Football here is just a way of life." The player judged the best in such a place commanded immense respect, which meant that the parade for Renkey was both the end of one grand adventure and the beginning of another. Joe Paterno soon would be dropping by the house to try and coax this extraordinary linebacker to Linebacker U. And while Renkey was most important just now, he was not the only recruit on Paterno's mind. . . .

*   *   *

Woodrow Wilson High School sends off conflicting impressions about one of America's sad cities—Camden, New Jersey. At times it seems so tranquil, sitting across Federal Street from a mostly grassy park that stretches for several hundred yards. Beyond the hallway inside the main entrance is a courtyard. A portrait of the school's namesake near the principal's office looks at banners encouraging achievement.

Uniformed men with walkie-talkies patrol the halls. Quickly, the quiet can be broken by three police cars coming to a sudden halt. Officers stream out of the cars, scurry past the billboard that announces future games, and up the wide steps. Soon, they return, often with several students invited to accompany them back to headquarters.

Woodrow Wilson has a rich athletic tradition: Former Heisman Trophy winner Mike Rozier is its most famous football alumnus. With that in mind, with Nebraska and other big-time colleges offering Wilson players scholarships, coach Greg Singleton in the early fall of 1987 could not understand why Penn State had never come calling. Singleton mentioned this to a reporter from the *Philadelphia Inquirer*, and within a day of the story being printed Penn State assistant Nick Gasparato, whose recruiting territory included Philadelphia and South Jersey, phoned.

As he was venting his frustration about Singleton going public, Gasparato wondered if Woodrow Wilson had any impressive prospects. It did, an option quarterback named Donnie Bunch, who, his coach said, "could do magical things with a football." Standing about 5 feet 10 inches and weighing 160 pounds, Bunch had been a wide receiver and defensive back prior to Singleton coaxing him, before his junior season, into being the quick-thinking, run-and-pass trigger to the Tiger offense.

"Donnie was a joy," Singleton said. "He ran back punts and kickoffs. Played safety on defense. Very rarely stepped off the field. In situations that seemed almost hopeless, fourth and 30 with time of the essence, Donnie would drop back to throw, scramble, and somehow get the first down. He could pass decently." Bunch had an infectious personality and an upbeat attitude that suggested a home life far better than it was.

"His circumstances are like a lot coming up in the city through broken homes," Singleton said. "Father somewhat invisible. A nice man, but I don't see enough guidance. Not at home, and this is not a big town. It's not Chicago. Nine square miles of city. If you want to see your kid, you can see your kid. And vice versa. Donnie's mother has problems. At times, she's not around. So Donnie was the one responsible for taking care of everything [for his five younger brothers and sisters]. That's a heavy load for a young kid to bear *and* to go to school *and* to become a National Honor Society member *and* to practice football. He also ran track.

"I know of instances where Donnie came to school and maybe hadn't eaten. Had no money. He didn't complain. He knew what the situation was and made the best of it. So it became even more important to me to see that this young man had a chance. Because he'd been placed in a position where a lesser kid, a kid with not as much determination, maybe would have folded up and been a street person. There are some kids who stay in your mind constantly. Donnie's one of those kids."

Singleton thought Penn State would be ideal for Bunch. It was about four hours away and located in a smaller, less frenetic area. Troubled Donnie Bunch in Happy Valley seemed perfect, especially with Paterno there to continue the stern, academic-oriented discipline Singleton had tried to give.

Bunch had been smitten by Penn State long before Penn State heard of him. Sunday mornings, still full of pride from wonderful football work himself, Bunch would flip on the television and watch reruns of Penn State's games on a cable channel. Playing football and watching it were his great escapes. "I'd come to school," Bunch said, "and Mr. Barth, my math teacher, would treat me to lunch every day. I had him for calculus. Sometimes, I'd go to his house, watch football games."

There were secrets Singleton and Barth didn't know. "Not that much money around the house," Bunch said, "so I used to hustle to get some. This was when I was a freshman. I'd ask people, sit on the corner, make some money."

Sit on the corner?

"Sell drugs."

That stopped after his sophomore year, he said, when he began getting recruiting letters. The first was from Lock Haven, a small college not far from Penn State. "I started worrying about college," he said. "Doing the right thing."

Bunch's all-around ability excited Penn State. On offense, he was projected as a wide receiver; he was good enough to be a cornerback or free safety on defense. His quickness and speed suggested thrilling possibilities as a kick returner. His making the National Honor Society showed the sort of potential that stirred the liberal-thinking Paterno. Besides, wondrous wide receivers do not naturally gravitate toward run-oriented Penn State. From a name offered by a caring coach, Donnie Bunch became a highly valued recruit.

More and more prospects in the 1980s were like Bunch and Renkey, coming from broken homes. A slender Ohio defensive back, Leonard Humphries, had a cross-country childhood.

"I went back and forth, from Akron to Los Angeles," said Humphries. "When I was young, my mom left for California, and I stayed with my grandmother for a while. Mom would send for me, and I'd stay with her for a year or sometimes two. Back and forth. Really hectic.

"She came back in 1979, when I was nine, and got married a couple of years later. Ever since, I've lived with my mom and stepdad. I saw my real father, off and on, till five or six. Saw him a lot—and then never again. He ended up in prison in Arizona, because of something he did in Akron. I never really try to think about him, because I looked at him as a negative influence."

Looking at the 5-foot-9-inch, 159-pound Humphries his senior season in high school, the last projection would be major college cornerback. Yet he was among the most widely sought in the country. Could such a skinny fellow with such soft features survive against players a hundred pounds heavier? Penn State thought so. When Humphries called and said he'd verbally committed to Ohio State, Paterno was at his doorstep in what seemed an instant.

Unlike Humphries, Bunch was a late addition to a list of

nearly four thousand that Paterno and his aides gradually whittled to several hundred and, for the past two years, to the several dozen worth serious attention. No tip from the most casual alumni about a backwater behemoth goes unchecked, for the obvious reason that forecasting success in elite college football is as difficult as judging whether a shaky-legged foal can win the Kentucky Derby. Twenty years earlier, Penn State had reluctantly given its last scholarship to an undersized linebacker named Jack Ham, who blossomed into an All-American, led the Pittsburgh Steelers to National Football League dominance through most of the 1970s, and was elected to the Pro Football Hall of Fame. Bradley had to be brazenly persuasive to convince Paterno to take another unheralded linebacker who later became an All-American and a first-round NFL draftee, Shane Conlan.

Penn State says that it does not recruit anyone not capable of playing regularly for two seasons. Paterno usually starts the final-thrust process by deciding what positions will need reinforcing in a couple of years. Quarterbacks were a priority for this class, and he focused on five in hopes of signing two.

Towns never before touched by fame or favored by a visit from the famous become must-stops each fall. When told the recruitment parade would be passing her way, Tony Sacca's mother, Peg, exclaimed: "You mean little old Delran!" Little old Delran, New Jersey, is not far from Donnie Bunch's Camden but eons removed from Donnie Bunch's environment. The Sacca home is a large colonial; the six-member Sacca family is exceptionally tight. Recruiters were most intense about charming this household because, in no special order, the three high-school quarterbacks coveted most in the fall of 1987 were: Todd Marinovich and Brett Johnson from the West Coast and 6-foot 5-inch Tony Sacca, of 213 Sharrow Vale Road.

"Tony's family lived right behind my mom," said the Delran coach, Jim Donoghue, "so I knew him since he was a little kid. I first became aware of his ability through Pop Warner ball. Word gets around. Big and gangly. Always a quarterback." Two summers at a quarterback camp, where he met the stylish Rich Rosa, had helped Sacca immensely with fundamentals. Just as significant, Donoghue said, "was something instinctive you can't coach. When you needed something big, Tony was able to come up with it."

One of those something-bigs was a sixty-yard march in the final minute of a rain-slogged game that ended with Sacca throwing the winning touchdown pass. His progress was impeded by a broken thumb on his throwing hand suffered during practice his junior year.

"He missed the first three games," Donoghue said, "and we're 1–2. We're playing an unbeaten team the fourth game. He plays offense the first quarter, and we're down 20–0. He'd been begging me to play defense, but I'm thinking, if he hurts that thumb, we won't have him for another three weeks.

"In the middle of the second quarter, he's bugged me so much I let him go in on defense. At safety. I tell him not to take any unnecessary chances. A very good running back comes Tony's way, and he nails him. Breaks three ribs. The kid flies over the bench. It was like sticking a pin in the other team. We win, 21–20."

Sacca relished drawing attention to himself on the field; he also was not above playing the clown. Before a championship basketball game his sophomore year, he had shaved part of his head into his uniform number: 24. "My mom didn't come out of her room for a week," he said.

The difference between Sacca's junior and senior seasons was staggering. "All of a sudden eyeballs popped out," Donoghue said. "He broke the South Jersey record for touchdown passes, with twenty-four, and must have run for six or seven more touchdowns. [Notre Dame coach] Lou Holtz was in my office looking at films. Tiny and scruffy bags under his eyes. He looked at eight films. Finally, he turned to [assistant] Foge Fazio and said: 'You're right. He's the best in the country. Let's go get him.' Quick as you could imagine, Holtz got himself straightened up, looked like he was ready for the Johnny Carson show and was off for the [Sacca] home."

Holtz and most other coaches were impressive. What stuck in Peg Sacca's mind was some advice from Paterno. "Joe had stressed that if you're hearing from schools saying you'll go right in there and play, that's not really a good idea," she said. "I liked that. I remember thinking: 'There's no way you can go from high school right in and play as freshman.' "

In Cincinnati, Ohio, another facet of recruiting was going on. Greg Huntington, an offensive lineman for one of the country's legendary high schools, Moeller, was ready to grab a pen the instant Paterno or someone else from Penn State offered a scholarship. They kept waffling, knowing that he was a legitimate prospect but being bothered by his weight, 225 pounds. Could Huntington add to his 6-foot 3-inch body the forty or fifty pounds necessary to crack the Lions' O-line? Even more critical, could he remain agile with that added weight? Sensing his eagerness from several summer camps, Penn State's staff guessed it could troll for larger linemen while stringing Huntington along. He would not be a battle.

"What's a battle?" asked the Lions' top recruiter, offensive coordinator Fran Ganter. He smiled, sat back in his office chair, and saw one forming in his mind: "A battle is where it's tooth and nail and you're sneaking around. And you're watching [another recruiter] because you know he's gonna sneak in and see the kid. A battle is sitting outside the door of a kid's house, waiting to see if this other guy's gonna come over and take him to school [to sign the national letter of intent].

"I'm in Bayonne. New Jersey [in the late 1970s]. There's rows and rows of row houses—A, B, C, D, E, and so on. Kid's gonna make up his mind the next morning, and I know Bernie Wyatt from Iowa is gonna pick him up. I know he's gonna get him last [and that the final words usually win the battle]. We're all supposed to be at the school at eight o'clock in the morning. Five coaches. Kid didn't turn anybody down. I don't trust Bernie. He's a friend of mine, but I do not trust him. So at four in the A.M. I'm in this alley, watching the kid's front door. It's February.

Cold. Hours pass. The sun comes up and all of a sudden I realize I'm on the wrong street. Same house numbers; same house. Wrong street. I finally say: 'Bernie's got him.' But he didn't. Kid comes to school, crying. Can't make up his mind. We're all to come back at eleven." At eleven, Grover Edwards announced that he would attend Penn State.

Paterno never visited 10733 Old Pond Road in Cincinnati— and that bothered Greg Huntington. The coach and his aides were being lovey-dovey with other players during heated recruiting battles. Here he was, all but dying to go to Penn State and not getting much more than a polite "We'll stay in touch."

Huntington's father graduated from Penn State in 1963, when Paterno was an assistant starting to receive national attention; his mother had worked in State College. The family later spent eleven years in Alabama, and Greg's unyielding allegiance to Penn State caused some problems. 'Bama football is the biggest happening in the state, through much of the South in fact, so it always is more comfortable to switch than fight. Greg refused. "I told all my friends in Alabama," he said, "that I'd got a schol arship to Penn State. Nobody believed me."

"Never in my wildest imagination had I dreamt Greg would be a Penn State prospect," said defensive coordinator Jerry Sandusky. "He was a little runt when he first came to camp [between his eighth and ninth grade years]. His senior year, when the coaches said there's this prospect named Greg Huntington at Cincinnati Moeller. I said: 'You're kidding.' They told me to look at the film. I did, and I said: 'Yes, that's a prospect. He'll play here.' "

About twenty-five years earlier, Sandusky himself had endured what Huntington was sweating out. He was being strung along by Penn State. "Finally," said Sandusky, "we had to call. 'Are you going to offer me a scholarship?' 'Yes.' If I hadn't called, I'm not sure they would ever have given me one." So Huntington had a kindred soul at Penn State. Had he known, it still would not have brightened his mood. But he also knew the recruiting game had barely kicked off.

2

Paper Tigers

$\mathbf{B}$efore a coach sets foot inside a high-school hero's home, he bombards it with mail. Letters. Postcards. Brochures. Pictures. Saturation to the point that a mailman's gait slows noticeably from late August through the mid-February signing date. Also burdensome are phone calls from assistant coaches trying to become like brothers. They come weekly in the early going. Then, near decision-making time, usually nightly and frequently hourly. Sad is the sibling of a star player in a home without call waiting.

The routine rarely varies. The first letter almost always starts: "Dear Student Athlete." It may arrive before a player has completed his ninth grade season. How much interest a school gets back through the mail determines how personal later correspondence becomes. When Paterno and other coaches about the country are fretting over game plans in early fall, their recruiting coordinators are designing Christmas cards for the most favored recruits.

Rich Rosa's heart beat much more quickly when a letter on Penn State stationery began: "There are many student-athletes that are suggested to us each year. You have been referred as

one of the outstanding prospects in the class of 1988. . . . Rest
assured that we will be following your progress this season. . . . "

Rosa was a quarterback and defensive back at St. Joseph's Hill
School in a small New Jersey town not far from Tony Sacca's
Delran. His father had emigrated from Puerto Rico at age
eleven, never finished high school, but paid for Rich's private
school education by becoming one of the managers of a fashion-
able restaurant.

Neither José nor his wife, Sonya, was keen on Rich playing
football; they relented and also provided the best in a football
education, the summer camp for rising sophomore quarterbacks
at nearby Glassboro State College, where Rich became friendly
with Sacca.

"I was a Michigan fan growing up," Rosa said. "Bo [Schem-
bechler] and the boys." As if heaven-sent, a letter signed "Bo"
arrived in late July. It read, in part: "Your performance on the
athletic field and in the classroom has impressed my University
of Michigan football staff. . . . We will be following your
progress with great interest and are looking forward to getting
to know you better." The Big Ten school with the most letter
thunder, however, was Purdue. Coach Fred Akers was almost
military at times, one example coming under the heading:
"WE NEED MEN."

Akers needed men, he said, "who cannot be bought, whose
word is their bond, who put character above wealth," and possess
several other traditional virtues. In addition, Akers sought young
men who "give 36 inches to the yard and 32 quarts to the
bushel."

Later, Akers devoted an entire page to: "HOW TO TELL A
WINNER FROM A LOSER." There were nineteen clues in
all, among them: "A winner isn't nearly as afraid of losing as a
loser is secretly afraid of winning."

Akers even found time to send Rosa a poem:

Now this is the law of the jungle,
As old and as true as the sky.

And the wolf that shall keep it, will prosper;
But the wolf that shall break it must die.
As the vine that girdles the tree trunk;
The law runneth forward and back;
The strength of the pack is the wolf
And the strength of the wolf is the pack.
And this is the law of athletics;
As true as the flight of the ball;
And the player that keeps it shall prosper;
But the player that breaks it must fall.
As the ball and parts that it's made of
Are bound and held fast with the seam.
The strength of the team is the player.
The strength of the player, the team.

All along Rosa had considered football a game. Tough, of course. Even dangerous. But essentially fun as well as an ego blast. At next level could he be jumping into a jungle? This intrusion of doubt soon passed, for the deities of football kept wanting to be his pen pals. During a twelve-day stretch in early July, Rosa received "Dear Richard" letters from Rickey Jackson, Hugh Green, Tony Dorsett, and a "Danny Marino, #13." All spoke highly of their alma mater, Pitt, Marino saying: "Hopefully, I will have the opportunity to meet you in Pittsburgh this season." Rosa was dazzled.

Tom Osborne wrote, extolling Nebraska. The vice president and general manager of Ohio Bell was glowing, in three brief paragraphs, about Ohio State. The man from "Rapid Oil Change" thought: "Minnesota will turn out to be No. 1." The senate majority leader from Massachusetts insisted "the experience of Boston College will live with you forever." Duke mentioned that its graduates had an average income of $78,012.00, that 53 percent had four to seven credit cards, that 67 percent ate five or more meals per month in restaurants, and that the market value of their "main" residence was $204,182.00. From Heisman Trophy winner Doug Flutie's coach, Jack Bicknell, came this: "I just finished watching you on film and was very impressed with the way you play the game. From filling from free safety [on running plays] to covering your own punt to covering kickoffs and throwing a completion with a guy stuck in your throat. I have coached quarterbacks ever since I have been in coaching and I am convinced that you can be a great quarterback. . . . "

Is there ever a sense of balance during recruiting? Almost never, unless ice-water realism happens to be one way a school can sell itself. In a get-acquainted pamphlet to a gifted tight end prospect from rural Pennsylvania, Rudy Glocker, Army said: "Let's Compare the Odds." The service academy guaranteed a job after graduation; it emphasized that only one in 12,000 high school graduates becomes a pro football player.

Army in the summer of 1987 gave Glocker a position-by-position breakdown of its 1969 team and what twenty-seven prominent players had done with their lives. Defensive lineman Steve Yarnell had become an FBI agent; defensive back James McCall was involved in research and development for General Electric. Seven players had stayed in the Army and risen to the rank of major. "Give serious thought to the significance of being a West Point graduate," the summary concluded.

Although the Glockers' large brick colonial with a pond out back was not far from a turnpike exit in north-central Pennsylvania, neither Army nor all other recruiters could be trusted to find it on their own. The routine for everyone, Paterno included, was to drive to the crossroads village of Bucktown and call from the pay phone outside the Sunoco Farm Market. Usually, Rudy's father would arrive within minutes to provide escort.

Glocker's head was turning in several directions during this hectic phase, but not toward the Hudson River. Although he was highly disciplined, the military had little appeal. Besides, at a sure-handed 6 feet 7 inches tall and with a slender frame that might stay mobile with more pounds attached, he just might beat those 1-in-12,000 odds.

Glocker was the son of parents who had attended either graduate school or a professional school. One sister graduated from
Vermont, the other from Dartmouth. Wherever he went to college, Glocker would be six credits to the good before stepping
inside his first classroom, those being for the advanced place-
ment courses in history earned at Owen J. Roberts High School.

The gung-ho spirit, sense of adventure, and commitment to
team that Purdue's Akers wanted, Glocker had in abundance.
Not satisfied with 1100 on an earlier college board exam, Glocker
had taken a tutorial course and improved his score by 160 points.
Like Eric Renkey, Glocker's academic and athlete credentials
were rarefied. "I like Rudy," assistant coach Tom Bradley said
years later, "because he's one of the few people who brings the
Wall Street Journal with him on trips."

One of the fascinations for anyone able to step back and watch
the process of teenagers being courted by famous adults is how
each reacts. Eric Renkey saved almost none of his letters; a western Pennsylvania running back recruited every bit as heavily,
Bobby Samuels, kept all his letters. It took three enormous trash
bags to store them. Tony Sacca tossed the letters but used the
empty envelopes with the colorful return addresses to decorate
his room. Glocker not only kept nearly every bit of mail but also
filed it under the appropriate school. The Notre Dame section
was a half-inch thick and featured the relentless presence of
recruiting coordinator Vinny Cerrato. Here are samples of postcards, each with a scene unique to Notre Dame:

June 16—"Notre Dame is interested in serving you in your
total development. . . . We hope you will join us in search of a
rich 4-year experience."

June 22—"The Notre Dame stadium has produced many exciting victories and with players of your caliber we can keep the
tradition going." ·

June 29—"What is this place called Notre Dame? Enthusi-
asm, Commitment, Dedication, Motivation, Inquiring, Progressive, Serving, Disciplined, Structured, Excellence. We want you
to come to be a part of this remarkable place!"

July 10—"The campus is preparing for the large number of athletes, parents, coaches and spectators arriving for the International Special Olympics, July 31–August 8. As always, Notre Dame is a realm of activity and excitement. You, too, may be a part of this exciting place. Think ND!"

July 27—"Summer school is ending and our players are excited about the coming season. Our athletes report on Aug. 9, and one year from that day you also can be thinking about wearing the blue and gold of Notre Dame. Get ready for your senior year."

Aug. 6—"The campus is alive with excitement. The International Special Olympics is in full swing. This typifies the warmth and caring of our community. . . . BE A PART OF IT!"

Aug. 12—"Today, we are 31 days away from teeing it up against Michigan. The game will be televised by ABC—2:30 EST. Our freshmen arrived on Aug. 9 and the upperclassmen will arrive on Aug. 15. We trust you have already begun and wish you the best during these 'dog' days."

Aug. 24—"We hope you are as anxious to begin your season as we are ours."

Aug. 31—"The return to the classroom also marks our return to the football field. We're looking forward to a winning season—like you."

Sept. 4—"Well, the school year is in full swing, and the big opening game with Michigan is only 8 days away. Watch us on ABC—3:30 EDT. The team is looking good and all psyched up for the season opener. We hope your season is going well."

Oct. 2—"Notre Dame is on the up-swing—3–0. We hope to continue our winning ways as we travel to Pittsburgh October 10. Watch us on ESPN 7:15 P.M. EST."

Oct. 14—"There are 6,800 students enrolled at Notre Dame. There are 62,000 alumni scattered around the world, organized into a network of 176 active alumni clubs. Over 99 percent of our athletes at Notre Dame have graduated. No other university can match that remarkable figure. Become a Notre Dame man!!"

At the other end of Pennsylvania, Renkey and his North Hills

High buddy, Chris Cisar, were getting exactly the same post-cards on exactly the same days. Fourteen-cent pitches for the Fighting Irish. Only the greeting was unique. "Dear Rudy" changing to "Dear Eric" to "Dear Chris" and so on for probably a hundred or so other prospects.

Just in case a perceptive young man such as Glocker might get the idea these postcards were being mass mailed, Cerrato sent a personal note the week of the Michigan game, ending it with: "I hope you get a chance to see the game." In late September, on Holiday Inn stationery, Notre Dame assistant Tony Yelovich hand printed: "Thought of writing you. Just think, you could be writing to your parents from a road trip next year with the Fighting Irish."

"An assistant from Mississippi State used to send me a hand-written letter every week of their games," Glocker said. "Every letter usually said he wished I was sitting next to him, cause they certainly could use me. He might have written twenty of them at a time, but they were so sincere. And I never met the guy. Of all the people I never met, he had to be the nicest."

No one was more persistent than Pitt. "Every day in the mail," said Glocker, "I got something from Pitt. If I didn't get something Thursday, I'd get two pieces Friday."

Possibly by coincidence, Tony Dorsett, Hugh Green, and Rickey Jackson wrote Glocker and Rosa on the same days in July and said exactly the same wonderful things about Pitt. Quarterback "Danny Marino #13" did not write tight end Glocker; it was Mr. and Mrs. Dan Marino, Sr., who wrote, glowingly about Pitt—"To the parents of Rudy Glocker." Because Glocker was so large, former linemen Mark May (Redskins), Bill Fralic (Falcons), and Bill Maas (Chiefs) were his Pitt pen pals.

Or seemed to be. May said he never actually wrote anything that carried his signature. He told Pitt his experience had been positive and that it could write anything reasonable and sign his name. To make the letters even more authentic, the football staff designed stationery very close to that used by May's team at the time, the Washington Redskins. And Pitt played with semantics, quoting May as saying: "The University of Pittsburgh afforded me the opportunity to play college football and to earn my degree. . . . " Pitt had "afforded" May the "opportunity" to "earn" his degree; May hadn't bothered to complete the work necessary to get it.

The fluff-and-puff messages through the mail are designed to coax the prospect and his family into allowing what the windy NCAA calls "a representative of a member institution" into their home. As a practical matter, it meant that around 9 P.M. on December 3, 1987, Joe Paterno was getting his foot in Eric Renkey's door.

It would be "Joe" almost as soon as Marilyn Renkey greeted Paterno and Bradley and guided them off the foyer and into a living room mostly used for formal occasions such as this, where her ex-husband was waiting. Comfortable in the company of presidents of the United States, having been honored by Ronald Reagan at the White House less than a year earlier, after Penn State won its second national championship of the 1980s, Paterno immediately put Marilyn and Mel at ease. Upstairs, Eric had grabbed a Penn State sweatshirt while dressing in no-socks haste after the parade.

Bradley had done well in establishing a comfortable rapport with the Renkeys. He had suggested to Eric's younger sister, Melanie, that, as a tension reliever, she make more of a fuss over him than the man who within a year would be giving one of the seconding speeches for George Bush at the Republican National Convention. Melanie outdid herself. All Bradley had wanted was for her to sweep down the stairway off the foyer, rush toward him and Paterno and say something like: "Oh, Tom Bradley, I'm so glad to see you again." Which she did. Unknown to anyone else, Melanie and a friend also had tamped this snowy script into the driveway: "We love you, Tom Bradley."

Paterno was confident. Had he rapped at the door several years earlier, however, Eric would have shooed him away, if he'd been in a polite mood. Eric grew up a Pitt fan because the school was nearby and his father had done graduate work there. Reasons for his early, and rather fierce, anti-Penn State sentiment were unclear, though he recalled being among the not-so-silent minority in North Hills that rooted for Alabama during its victory over the Lions in the 1979 Sugar Bowl collision for the national championship. Ironically, there was an Alabaman, Greg Huntington, rooting that afternoon for Penn State.

Renkey's attitude began to change when he attended Penn State's summer camp before his sophomore season at North Hills. He went at about 185 pounds and as a quarterback that first year, then gained weight and an affection for Penn State his last two summers. The coaches were relaxed, a condition that Renkey would rarely see them in again. Two of his future defensive coaches, Jerry Sandusky and Joe (Buddy) Sarra, even donned wigs and danced during part of one evening's entertainment.

Summer camp is as important as any recruiting tool for Penn State. In addition to getting to know the most promising players as they mature, Penn State has over the years used as counselors hundreds of high-school coaches from the 300-mile radius it regards as its natural recruiting turf. "Originally," said Mel, "he wanted to go to Pitt's, Penn State's, and Notre Dame's camps. He went to Penn State's first, as a get-this-out-of-the way kind of thing before going to Pitt's and Notre Dame's. Once he went to Penn State's camp, he never went anywhere else."

If Renkey was going to be a linebacker at Penn State, his position coach would either be the energetic Buddy Sarra or his new buddy, Bradley. Sarra handled the inside positions in the Lions' four linebacker alignment; Bradley was in charge of the outside linebackers.

In a sense, Penn State had the Renkeys in a sort of can't-escape embrace. Bradley had become extremely close to Eric and had thrilled his sister. Mel's first piece of football equipment, a leather helmet and shoulder pads, had come from Sarra, their fathers having worked together. And Marilyn? Here was the Great God Paterno in her home, on her sofa, eager to pose with her for a picture Melanie later captioned: "Friends Forever." Paterno's personal success featured the stat that he and Penn State wanted drummed into the consciousness of each recruit: Everyone who had played out his eligibility under Paterno had experienced an undefeated, untied season or played in a bowl game for the national championship or played on a team that won the national title.

Could Paterno still lose Eric?

He could.

One way was his age. That night Paterno was eighteen days shy of sixty-one. He looked fifty-one and recently had acted forty-one by leading a university financial drive that had raised more than $350 million. Paterno had personally pledged $150,000, earmarked for the library, which he figured was about what it would have cost him to send his four children through Penn State. As a tenured professor in the phys ed department, Paterno had free educational privileges for his family. Of course, given Paterno's stature in sport, $150,000 also amounted to about six speeches to organizations wealthy enough to afford his fee.

Mel broached Joe's age rather early in a forty-five-minute meeting more relaxed than the elder Renkeys had imagined. He knew to get to the critical points as swiftly as possible, for Eric had scolded him for being too chatty during an unofficial visit to Pitt. When Mel asked Joe about his plans, the coach realized he meant: "Will you be at State as long as Eric will?"

He'd be there five years, at least, Paterno assured. This meant that Eric could be redshirted, held out of competition for a year, and still complete his four years of eligibility with Paterno around. Redshirting was not on Eric's or Mel's mind. Players accustomed to being the best—by far—in high school almost assume the next step will come quickly, if not easily. To play as a true freshman is the ultimate early merit badge in college.

Could Eric do this? Given that nearly everyone had projected him as the best linebacker prospect in the country, might he even be good enough to start? "Joe said there weren't guarantees," Mel said. "Then he went through the names of every player who had played his freshman year," Marilyn added.

So playing time was possible, maybe even likely, "Joe said he would rather play someone one week later than he should rather than one week sooner," according to Mel. "He said the worst thing he could do was play someone one second before he was ready. He also said he expected Eric to be a leader."

Then Paterno did something that a year or so earlier would have cost him twenty-five cents: He swore. Sort of. Paterno loathes swearing, to the point where for years he had a Profanity Box in the locker room area. If a player got caught swearing, he dropped a dime in the Profanity Box. Cussing cost a coach a quarter. (One exception had been a since-retired, colorful-talking assistant, J. D. White, who was given three-for-a-quarter dispensation.)

Lately, the Profanity Box had disappeared, in part because Paterno thought that using its contents to finance a team party might be a violation of NCAA rules. Even without knowing the background, it was more than a minor surprise when, according to Mel, Paterno said: "I apologize for saying it this way, but I want players who knock other guys on their ass. I feel Eric is one of those people."

Still forceful, Paterno said he regarded Eric as a cornerstone recruit around whom another national championship might be forged in four or five years. Other prospects, knowing of his reputation, would be inclined to commit to Penn State if Eric said yes tonight.

Most players under such sweet circumstances might have jumped off their chair immediately and into Paterno's waiting arms. Mel and Marilyn felt Paterno's compelling persuasion more than Eric. Never had they imagined being in such lustrous company, let alone seeing St. Joseph not only turn mortal but practically beg for their son's services. Having achieved so much so soon, having been inordinately praised for so long and having been flattered in letters by famous folk he'd never met, Eric resisted Paterno's appeal to sign on the dotted line. "He didn't really respond," Mel said. "He kind of ignored it."

And Paterno backed off. Even though Eric had worn a Penn State T-shirt under his North Hills jersey that final glorious season, he was going to wait. He would take the five official visits that he was permitted under NCAA rules, meaning the schools could pay for transportation and lodging.

One of those trips would definitely be to Penn State. Mel figured the recruiting process the next couple of months would be a lot like the summer-camp experience years earlier, that each visit to some other school would be compared unfavorably with Penn State.

Still confident when he left, Paterno also was disappointed. Even the most positive vibes can change, he knew. Also, what with alums and school officials also tugging at his sleeves for appearances at extremely worthy causes, Paterno's time is precious. As Greg Huntington realized, he does not visit the home of every recruit Penn State hopes to sign. And when Paterno does come calling, he expects to close the deal. This night, the scholarship forms he'd brought along remained blank.

The official-visit procedure has been the same at Penn State for decades. Whether the prospect is as coveted as Eric Renkey or not yet offered a scholarship, as happened with an enormous lineman from northern New Jersey, Anthony Grego, he bunks in with a couple of varsity players. Only parents get hotel comfort during the Penn State look-see, at the on-campus Nittany Lion Inn, where live chamber music in the lobby usually accompanies dinner. Their sizable sons, upon whom Penn State depends to keep its multimillion-dollar program thriving, experience dorm life at its rawest. No sense giving false impressions, Paterno reasons.

Thorough to a staggering degree, Penn State even keeps statistics on what weekends have resulted in the greatest number of signees. Over a nine-year period, the second weekend in December (54 percent) edged the first weekend in February (53 percent). The overall percentage was 45, high considering prospects are permitted just five college-sponsored visits.

In late January, nearly two months after Paterno had failed to get a commitment during that home-visit pitch, Renkey and his parents got together again, this time at Penn State. The weekend tour began for Renkey with places familiar from two summers of camp: Beaver Stadium, expected to swell to more than 90,000 seats by the early 1990s, the indoor practice site (Holuba Hall), and the east locker area with its weight-lifting apparatus and study hall rooms.

The 1980s had been a decade of immense change for Penn State football. The 1968, 1969, and 1973 teams had gone undefeated but, to Paterno's increasing frustration, had failed to win the mythical national championship. Even more vexing, Penn State until perhaps the mid-1970s was not recognized much beyond the East. This became evident to a former sports information director, Ernie Accorsi, while he was advancing a game at Kansas State in early October 1969.

On New Year's night in the Orange Bowl that year, Penn State had beaten the University of Kansas by 15–14. Victory only became possible when Kansas, during Penn State's missed try for a two-point conversion, was caught with 12 men on the field. The winning points immediately followed the penalty. In Manhattan, Kansas, about eighty miles away from KU and just ten months later, a veteran sportswriter bid Accorsi good day with a cheer: "And good luck this season in the Ivy League."

By 1980, there would be no more mistaking Penn State for Penn. And by the mid 1980s, Penn State had grown rich enough from the blood and sweat of hundreds of oversized undergrads to move its football operation all the way across campus.

Slowly, a sort of theme park had sprouted. The east locker room included the training facilities, a mirror-lined weight area, and, on the second story, rooms for study hall and the no-nonsense academic advisor, Don Ferrell. Less than a hundred yards away was Holuba Hall, an indoor practice facility that resembled an airplane hangar. Holuba was so massive that players and coaches sometimes turned it into a golf course, smacking low-compression balls toward holes and hazards on the artificial turf built with large pads and other football gear.

The centerpiece of the new football operation was the Philip M. and Barbara E. Greenberg Indoor Sports Complex. The lower level, set into a hillside, housed an ice-skating rink. Above were offices for Paterno and his staff. Attached was an indoor facility soon too small for football and used mostly by other Penn State teams and groups after Holuba's construction. Even though he and Paterno had been friends for years, Greenberg still asked the very obvious question: Why should I bankroll this grand building? "Because," said Paterno, "I need it and you can afford it."

There was one unexpected hitch: The interior of the building that would partly bear her name also had to be overseen by Barbara Greenberg's decorator. The high-toned fashion fellow even had to do Paterno's office.

Why?

"Because you have terrible taste," Barbara told as prestigious a sportsman as the 1980s would produce.

What do you mean? Paterno countered.

"Well," she snapped, "look at those uniforms."

Indeed.

Dark blue and white, Penn State's play duds were a sorry sight to an artsy person's eyes. No names on the jerseys; no numbers on the helmets. And most definitely no lightning-bolt or lions-head decals. Early 1950s fashion in the early 1980s, which also happened to be what some alumni were growling about Paterno's offense. Oatmeal in a yogurt world.

Because Phil Greenberg was opening his wallet so wide, Paterno was more than happy to give Barbara's decorator fairly free—and expensive—rein. A football coach would not think of the enormous action-montage that filled most of one wall off the reception area.

The money-tackling reality of college football suggests a lack of stability about Penn State that could not be farther from the truth. On the door of each of the prominent offices is the name not of the aide who occupies it but of the people who put up the funds for it.

The door to Tom Bradley's rather spartan office has two small nameplates. One says: "Coach's office." The other: "Donor: Mr.

and Mrs. Gerald C. Romig '27." And so on. The one exception is the door adoring Penn State fans would give so much—and often do—to walk through. The top nameplate there does identify the occupant, reading: "Coach Joe Paterno's Office." Underneath is: "Mr. and Mrs. Charles W. Shaeffer '33."

Apparently, assistant coaches could come and go without any change in the office landscape. But football aides at Penn State also happen to be like those nameplates; they get attached to the place. Bradley in the fall of 1987 had completed his ninth year on Paterno's staff. The top offensive and defensive coaches, Fran Ganter and Jerry Sandusky, were in their eighteenth and twentieth years respectively. Paterno had finished his twenty-second year as head coach and his thirty-eighth at Penn State. Continuity and success were what State's salesmen emphasized, the often-spoken bottom line to worried parents being: "You can trust us with your son."

Paterno's office seemed surprisingly small to the Renkeys. From a light brown leather chair behind a desk of sturdy dark wood, Paterno could see all that mattered most: his family, through a portrait on a wall near a shelf, and his signature accomplishments, through pictures of the 1982 and 1986 national championship teams on a far wall. A couch and straight-backed chairs were done in a blend of blue and white and red and green. Conversation pieces, two Dodgers baseball caps, stood atop a row of books. Players who wore the B-cap were the heroes of Paterno's youth in Brooklyn. When Paterno was seven years into assisting Rip Engle at Penn State, Dodger players started wearing caps with L.A. stitched to them.

Paterno's reading material included *The Last Great Wilderness*, *Careers in Sport*, *Paul Robeson: The Great Forerunner*, *The Fitzgeralds and the Kennedys*, *Sports Psychology*, and *An Athlete's Guide to Agents*.

Near a Fiesta Bowl trophy were two pieces of inspiration, each done in needlepoint. One was Robert Browning's "A man's reach should exceed his grasp or what's a heaven for?" The other was something that Penn Staters hoped recruits would read and think of Paterno: "Once in a while we meet someone who stands out from the flock . . . Someone who flies higher and faster and further than we ever thought possible and helps us to do the same."

Much more showy, and exciting for Eric, was the Penn State Hall of Fame. Through a sliding panel that connects it with the main reception area, an ambitious athlete can walk into 100-plus years of history—and imagine joining it some day. Plaques of Penn Staters in the National Football Foundation and Hall of Fame are prominent, along with certificates presented to Penn State's academic All-Americans. The two national championships are celebrated through magazine covers and elegant trophies. Featured in the center is State's Heisman Trophy winner, John Cappelletti.

In one of the side cases is a letter to Paterno from former President Gerald Ford, which reads in part: "I am most grateful for your friendship. I love the game. It taught me a great deal and gave me an opportunity for an education. You have done a superb job in coaching but more importantly in building character. It thrills me to see how everyone loves and respects you."

Tucked in a corner are game balls: from the 1–0 victory over Ohio State in 1912, from the 45–3 victory over Bucknell in 1916, from the 0–0 tie with Notre Dame in 1925. Naturally, there is no mention of the most lopsided game in Penn State history, the 106–0 loss to Lehigh in 1889. To the obvious question of how such a shellacking could happen, team captain Charlie Aull had said: "We couldn't get at the son-of-a-bitch with the ball."

During his visit, Renkey roomed with another western Pennsylvanian, junior linebacker Brian Chizmar. Saturday afternoon consisted mostly of chitchat. No cosmic questions about reality at Penn State got asked. The twenty dollars Chizmar was allowed by NCAA rules for spending money disappeared at a junk food joint. Sunday's schedule ended with a pizza party at Paterno's ranch-style home at the end of McKee Street. At one point the coach directed Mel and Eric into his office and again pressed Eric for a commitment. The signing date was closing in fast. Once more, Eric put Paterno off.

*　　*　　*

Three of the major 1987 battles were being waged along a front that extended from Wilkes-Barre, in north central Pennsylvania, through Farrell, near the Ohio border, to the Cleveland suburb of Warrensville Heights. The treasures, running from east to west, were Raghib (Rocket) Ismail, Bobby Samuels, and O. J. McDuffie. All were touchdown machines, runners with astonishing ability but fragile enough so that wide receiver might be their eventual football home. Such similar styles meant they were not likely to attend the same college.

One-for-three also would be a tremendous batting average in this game; Paterno wanted two hits. He sensed Ismail was the highest-magnitude star, as gifted as any prospect ever; he also knew that Lou Holtz and Notre Dame were solidly entrenched, close to impossible to beat. So he concentrated even more energy on the runner who had beaten Ismail in four of their five state championship sprint races, Samuels, and the Ohioan who had scored seventy-two touchdowns, McDuffie.

Like Renkey, Samuels was from western Pennsylvania, which meant that Pitt also caught his eye first and held it until gunshots, perhaps five in all, burst out only a few steps from where he was standing inside the Pitt student union four days before Christmas. Those crazy, frightful few seconds eliminated the Panthers.

"Pitt had a tailback position open," Samuels said in the clinical manner in which he and his family had evaluated schools. "I'd gone to their summer camp; they knew what I could do." So did everyone else, it seemed. Three Hefty trash bags were filled with recruiting mail, a great deal of it unopened. The Pitt players who had written Rich Rosa and Rudy Glocker also found time to direct the same message to 407 Lincoln Avenue in Farrell. Matters were so hectic that once at school Samuels found himself talking with Holtz in a history classroom while Paterno waited outside. When Holtz left and Samuels had begun chatting with Paterno, Tennessee's Johnny Majors happened by. "Majors showed up unannounced," Samuels said. "I told him he didn't have an appointment, but he stayed around. I talked to him after Joe left. Maybe 10 minutes. I kinda laughed about it. Joe said it was just like him."

Paterno's style was low-key aggressive. If he wasn't pushy, neither would he be pushed around. During his visit to the Samuels home, he dominated the conversation, from the blue hardback chair at one end of the living room, but also rolled about the floor briefly while playing with two of Bobby's young cousins. St. Joseph also was an Ordinary Joe.

"Joe was more at ease than any coach that came by," said Bobby's father, Robert. "A lot of 'em, a lot of coaches when they go in black families' homes feel sort of intimidated, I think. And they sort of shy back a little bit. Joe wasn't that way. He was really down to earth."

"Not so uptight, like he'd rehearsed his lines," Bobby said. "I figured it would be very hard to be that at ease if you really had something to hide."

Although Penn State nationally is pegged Linebacker U., it also is a runners' school. The 185-pound Samuels considered himself next in a tradition of rugged rushers. In his mind, he was going to follow Blair Thomas, who had followed D. J. Dozier, who had followed Curt Warner, who had followed Matt Suhey, who had followed Heisman Trophy runner John Cappelletti, who had followed Lydell Mitchell and Franco Harris.

Penn State has a theory that a prospect makes up his mind about a school long before he makes his intentions public, perhaps even before he takes his visit or allows a head coach into his home. The youngster attaches himself to a college years earlier, for who-knows-what reason. The recruitment process then becomes a way to eliminate schools who intrude on that longstanding romance.

Although not obvious to Paterno, the theory was being proven once more. Donnie Bunch had become enamored with Penn State by watching its games on cable television; the best player in South Carolina, linebacker Ivory Gethers, had fallen in love with, of all things, Penn State's uniforms. He thought anyone who wore such no-nonsense clothes to work had to mean business. When Penn State staffers hadn't contacted him, he called them.

Eric Renkey had been influenced by summer camps, Greg Huntington by family ties, and Tony Sacca by Penn State being the closest significant big-time school to his home. Samuels became infatuated with the Nittany Lions at about twelve, when he lost an age-group sprint at Penn State. "He stood on the track and cried," Robert recalled. "He always said he'd go back there and win." (The state championship races his junior and senior years, that rivalry with Ismail, were held at other colleges.)

Robert Samuels and Bobby's stepmother, Patricia, were more concerned with academics than football, the father having been acquainted with the major college scene at Bowling Green before dropping out after his sophomore year. "I had a girl at home who I was missing," he said. "And I didn't want to study. Simple as that. I turned the switch. Otherwise, I should have stayed in school; I was playing. I don't want him to do the same darn thing. He's not going to talk about leaving, or him and I are really going to go around." Samuels and Renkey also shared an inclination to avoid studying as much as possible. "I didn't do a damn thing in high school," Renkey said. "I wasted about four years of academics, actually five if you count the eighth grade. Didn't do anything in high school. I never did homework. Didn't get that good a grade considering what I got on my SATs."

Renkey was referring to that 1370, which should have translated into all-As at North Hills. Instead, he graduated with slightly better than a B average. He captured Samuels, and the official visit to Notre Dame that both happened to take at the same time, by saying: "It was so boring Bobby Samuels actually did homework. Bobby Samuels wasn't too big on homework."

Paterno also knew the academic numbers on Renkey didn't fit, and why. But lots of his former players had needed a go-to-class butt kicking. His brain coach, Don Ferrell, was relentless at that. Besides, Renkey seemed so serious about an eventual career in medicine that, during his official visit, Paterno had arranged a meeting with a prominent official at the hospital that Penn State runs in Hershey.

Samuels was different. He might go to all his classes at Penn State and still not survive. Paterno was stern with him. "I said: 'Bobby, don't come unless you're gonna go to class. If you don't go to class, you're not gonna make it. You're not that good a student. And I'm not gonna play you.' We took a shot with him. His high-school people said he was a good kid. I like the dad. Maybe the acorn won't fall far from that tree. He comes here, gets some character. Maybe he'll grow out of it." So Samuels was set for Penn State. Paterno was batting .500. His next task: getting O. J. McDuffie.

McDuffie's initials were no accident. He had been named after the magnificent Southern Cal runner and member of the Pro Football Hall of Fame, O. J. Simpson. McDuffie's birth was December 2, 1969, about a year after Simpson had won the Heisman Trophy. "But my grandmother didn't like Oranthal," he said. "So I was Otis James. My mother, who was fifteen at the time, had nothing to do with naming me." McDuffie grew up with his mother, Gloria, and her parents. She had twelve brothers and sisters, and all of them were athletic. Before he was walking, McDuffie was dealing with sports. But he hated football at first, probably because it had been forced on him so soon. Uncle Homer had him running from the house to a stop sign and back— a total of about a hundred yards—to get in shape. That was at age two. Also, there was lots of change in his life at an early age. Seven or eight different schools. When Gloria first enrolled in college, he stayed with her parents. Later, Gloria could go to school and have him with her. Each was a tough adjustment for O. J., but he eventually enjoyed every new setting.

Gloria and O. J.'s father never married. "I saw him my senior year in high school when our baseball team went down to Florida for spring break," O. J. said. "My last contact—and nothing major. He knew I was coming down to where we were playing. I spent a couple days with him. No bitterness."

When he and Paterno were talking one day, McDuffie mentioned a preference for playing wide receiver in college. Paterno couldn't have been more pleased. *Voilà!* Samuels wanted to run the ball; McDuffie wanted to catch it. They could come to Penn

State together after all. When McDuffie brought up Penn State's well-deserved reputation for running the ball, Paterno insisted that would change, that he was recruiting a terrific passer from New Jersey, Tony Sacca.

Still, McDuffie was no sure thing. UCLA, Ohio State, Notre Dame, and Michigan State were strong contenders. The day before the national signing date in mid-February, when he was going to announce his choice of schools, McDuffie received by express mail Paterno's final pitch. It was the most flattering, ego-soaring recruiting letter of them all. The ultimate football valentine.

One of the most famous men in the United States, *Sports Illustrated*'s Sportsman of the Year in 1986, hobnobber with presidents past, present, and future had taken the time to fill ten pages of a classroom notebook with reasons why McDuffie was vital to his future.

Most of the early pages were routine, thinking-about-you chat-up, the soup before an eye-popping main course. On page six, however, was this: "If we could get O. J. McDuffie, we would have all the pieces in place to go after a national championship . . . the only other wideout we've signed is a quarterback [the reference being to Donnie Bunch]."

To make sure McDuffie knew that he was not dealing with just any very good football school, Paterno wrote: "We have never recruited a young man in the twenty-two years I have been head coach who has not played on an undefeated team or played for the national championship." Wow! That, after Paterno had said McDuffie was a vital piece to another national championship. To emphasize what he'd said earlier, Paterno wrote: "I have made a commitment to coach five more years at Penn State." No way could McDuffie refuse such a proposal.

In eastern Pennsylvania, Rudy Glocker also was being flattered by Paterno. "Joe sat in my living room," Glocker said, "and told me, 'You know. I think you can play for us next year.' Looked me right in the eye. And he said I could be a heckuva first-round pick for somebody some day."

That eliminated the other finalist, Dartmouth. Given Paterno's reputation, it was not unusual for a prospect's last two choices to be Penn State or an Ivy League school. "I thought about it," Glocker said, "and figured there would be a major time commitment to football either way, Ivy League or Penn State. Twenty hours a week at Penn State; maybe sixteen to eighteen at Dartmouth. I figured if it was going to amount to about a thousand hours a year for football, I'd rather for it to be for something more important than to play at a 5-and-6 school."

When Rudy had made his decision, his mother, Maryann, looked back at recruiting and said: "Unless you become president of the United States, you never will get this treatment again."

Meanwhile, back at 10733 Old Pond Road in Cincinnati, Greg Huntington was getting antsy. "Joe's not visiting was really a disappointment," he said. "I'd been recruited hard by lots of schools. Pitt was really high on me. Same with Michigan, Alabama, and Boston College. All these teams Penn State played wanted me so bad. Penn State was so nonchalant."

Huntington was sitting in one of Penn State's several football meeting rooms as he spoke. It was early September of his sophomore season of eligibility. The blocker that Penn State didn't especially want had blossomed to 265 pounds and become a starter at short guard. Looking back, still sour, he said: "I came here for a visit. Didn't even really talk to Joe. I wasn't offered a scholarship. That almost changed my view. I almost didn't want to come here. It made me mad, knowing this was the school I wanted to go to all my life and not to be heavily recruited by them.

"About a week after the official visit, Craig Cirbus [the Penn State assistant assigned the territory that included Cincinnati] called. I told him, 'Listen. I don't know what you're thinking. I really want to go there—and I think you know that. But if you don't offer me a scholarship, I'll probably end up going to a school that plays you guys.' They knew they had me. They might have figured they could get me to walk on [pay his own way, thereby saving a scholarship]. I wasn't going to play that game. Craig said he'd send a letter of intent in the mail."

By early February 1988, everything was falling into place. The most hectic part of dozens of young lives, perhaps what eventually would prove the apex, was coming to a close. Penn State and Paterno had done their judging—and had been judged.

Handicapping high-school athletes is inexact work. That's one reason college rosters are so huge, more than twice that of NFL teams. If a highest-magnitude star in high school plummets, maybe a less glittering one will ascend. Colleges at that time were allowed ninety-five total scholarships but could give no more than thirty-five in one year. Another reason for so many players: College football is dangerous. Paterno and every other college coach like to have at least two players of equally exceptional ability at each position.

For the recruits, the interlude between the final high-school game and the first collision in college is for dreaming. Late at night, the ceiling serves as a screen for the mind's projector. Nowhere in those glory scenes is there a brief pause to consider reality—that someone somewhere else may be superior and that the college crooking its finger toward you might be doing the same to him. And three others at your position. No high school hero fully realizes that football is not forever and that out of those ninety-five scholarship players only eleven trot into combat at a given time.

Penn State did not get every prospect it wanted. Although it did get an exceptional core around which to build in a few years, Paterno admitted: "We took some chances. We've got some shaky kids."

Rich Rosa was the first to commit. He'd decided defensive back, particularly the strong safety position Penn State calls Hero, would be his best bet in college. That's why his early first choice, Michigan, was eliminated. "They'd recruited six D-backs," Rosa said. "Too many for me. Penn State was losing everybody. I visited, and the depth chart was very thin. They'd just lost two guys to academics and were bringing in just two safeties [the other being Chris Cisar]."

As his father expected, Eric Renkey eliminated Stanford, Notre Dame, and Pitt. So sure was he that a scheduled trip to Ohio State got scrubbed. His announcement was featured on a Pittsburgh television station's six o'clock news and played prominently in both major papers. Renkey lately had been adding weight at a rapid rate. That did not concern Penn State too much, because he could easily be moved from linebacker to the line, possibly to the nastiest position of all on defense, nose tackle, where a player hunkers almost on his hands and knees and frequently gets attacked from two angles and straight-on. To Renkey, that prospect was scary. "I am trying," he said, "to avoid the four-point stance."

Sacca also seemed to wait longer than necessary to commit, possibly because not everyone close to him thought Penn State was the wisest choice. His Delran coach wasn't sure Sacca ought to even be playing quarterback in college. "I told Tony's father, prior to his senior year," said Jim Donoghue, "that if you're talking long-term pro career he'd have a better shot as a defensive player. First off, the number of big time quarterback positions is limited. There were a number of defensive positions he could play. What it boiled down to were numbers: one quarterback versus two safety and two inside-linebacker positions."

Tony's heart was set on quarterback. Even so, Donoghue was none too excited about the choice of official visits. Penn State and Michigan were run-run-run schools. Florida was fine. Donoghue suggested considering other pass-oriented schools, such as UCLA and Duke. Or Maryland. The Terrapins' new head coach, Joe Krivak, had been Donoghue's coach at Syracuse. Starting with Boomer Esiason when he was Maryland's top offensive aide, Krivak had been sending a steady stream of quarterbacks to the pros. "Joe [Paterno] emphasized to Tony that, with Todd Blackledge, Penn State had been the first team to win the national championship by passing more than it ran," Donoghue said. "Everybody thinks he'll be the one Joe changes for. Ultimately, it was Tony's decision. All I could do was make sure he knew everything up front."

Shortly after South Jersey's Sacca said yes to Penn State, the best quarterback in North Jersey, Matt Nardolillo, said he wanted to sign up. He was surprised at Fran Ganter's response. In his welcome was a warning. You do know, Ganter said, that Tony Sacca has signed. That was Ganter's way of saying: "Tony's our top choice; he'll get every chance to succeed." Not quite sure he did, Nardolillo said he understood. His team also had been 11–0 perfect. "No matter where I go," Matt said he told himself, "there is going to be competition."

When Penn State's interest in Donnie Bunch was not as keen as he had hoped, coach Singleton knew how to rekindle it. Only five words were necessary: "Donnie might go to Pitt." Paterno and Gasparato were at Woodrow Wilson High the next day, Singleton said, and Bunch signed.

There was one below-the-belt twist to the final decision days: a packet thick as a small town telephone directory and packed with unflattering newspaper stories about Paterno and Penn State was mailed to more than a dozen recruits. The one that Bob Daman received was tucked inside an oversized brown envelope with an obscure postmark and addressed to his high school in suburban Harrisburg.

One of the stories concerned Paterno pushing a lineman, Paul Gabel, too hard during an early 1970s practice and causing an asthmatic attack. Several others dealt with Penn State players being arrested for sins that ranged from bounced checks to drinking to assault to burglary. Paterno even confessed to a recruiting violation, appearing at the home of a New Jersey prospect when he signed his national letter of intent.

Especially useful, the anonymous donor thought, was the wire service story quoting one of Penn State's co-captains, Carmen Masciantonio. The piece appeared after the Nittany Lions ended their 1984 season with a 31–11 loss to Pitt, and Masciantonio commented, "We had plenty of talent this year but still got killed. Joe kept trying to fix something that wasn't broken." He said Paterno called the players "babies" after the Pitt game.

The smallest clip was the most intriguing. It was a portion of a 1987 story in the *Washington Post* in which Paterno had said to reporter Michael Wilbon: "I did bad stuff [as a youngster]. I just never got caught."

When Wilbon asked what might qualify as bad, Paterno said: "Robbing a laundry, just for the sake of it. You know how it is. You're twelve or thirteen, and you go along with it because your buddies say: 'Let's do it.' " Not to discriminate, clips about recent racial tension at Penn State also were sent to white recruits Daman, Renkey, and Glocker.

When the final maneuvering was over, Penn State had offered fifty-one players scholarships and gotten commitments from twenty-eight. An unintended bonus was Eric Renkey's girlfriend, Wendy Frank, also choosing Penn State. She had been impressed by Paterno during that December 3 visit. Three signees were from outside Penn State's natural recruiting area: linebacker Gethers and tight end Derek Van Nort from South Carolina and linebacker Tom Wade from New Mexico.

There were no Proposition 48 recruits, meaning that everyone had achieved the proper rank in high school, scored at least 700 on the SAT, and could play his first year. Still, it had taken a linebacker prospect from an apartment project in the Bronx, Ron Fields, three tries to crack 700. And Paterno had to personally go to bat to get Samuels and Gethers admitted.

These young Lions were an extremely diverse collection of personalities and backgrounds. In early August 1988 they gathered their dreams and other necessities of life and made off for close to the geographic center of Pennsylvania, which for nearly twenty years had also been central to college football.

PART TWO

HELLO AND GOOD-BYE

3

Little Pit

T he first official sound that a Penn State football player hears is the gawdawful blare from an airhorn around six-thirty on an early August morning. Decades ago, the horn was removed from a Volkswagen and placed inside a deep rectangular box painted with the shade of dark blue that Penn State favors. Before the nearby chicken houses were boarded over, it was a toss-up as to which irritating wake-up call would arrive earliest in the east campus dorm used for summer camp: a rooster's or that piercing VW *beeeeeeep* activated by a team manager outside each room.

"That sound is the worst you've ever heard," said Eric Renkey, "because you're always in some good dream. You suddenly get jolted awake and you say: 'Damn!' "

"The scariest thing," said Tony Matesic, a barrel-chested defensive lineman from New Jersey, "is that you fall asleep—and you're so tired you almost can't fall asleep right away. Your legs are killing you. Finally, you fall asleep. You feel like you're asleep for two minutes, and you gotta get up. That thing is deadly. That thing is unbelievable."

"We would have to physically pick Rick Sayles out of bed,

try and get him on his feet," said Brett Wright, referring to a lanky linebacker prospect from near Pittsburgh.

Wright also was a linebacker, from an area of southern Maryland not far from Washington, D.C. Of the scholarship players who arrived on August 9, 1988, he and Renkey could be considered veterans. Anxious for a head start, they had enrolled at Penn State for its summer session. Renkey even experienced the odd feeling of having to leave college to attend his high-school graduation.

Wright and Renkey roomed together in the relatively new Nittany Apartments, located about a hundred yards from the east locker room and about the same distance from the building where training table meals were taken.

Each had signed up for two summer school classes, with little success. Wright got an F and a D in his English and math courses, in large part because he missed two weeks to participate in a high-school all-star game. Renkey took a biology and an English course, dropping the latter "because I didn't go to a couple of classes and it was getting out of hand. My tremendous high-school study habits got me in a lot of trouble."

The freshmen had started measuring themselves against each other the night they arrived, specifically during a pick-up basketball game. More than a dozen of them after dinner had piled into, and onto, the brown 1983 Toyota pickup that Wright had brought along to summer school and slowly rocked to the ancient, near-empty building that Penn State still used for its varsity games: Rec Hall.

Some of the new classmates had become acquainted before coming to Penn State. And not always in traditional ways, although a few had taken recruiting trips to the same college at the same time. When their highly touted teams had played in high school, Renkey was amused that the running back he'd just tackled hopped off the ground and said: "Hi, my name's Eric Lewandowski." For his official recruiting visit to Penn State, Donnie Bunch had no ride, so he went with the Sacca family.

Because everybody wanted to establish quickly at least a wee bit of macho turf in this new setting, the language in Rec Hall that first night tended to be as raw as the basketball. Rich Rosa chose one of the teams, and little did he know that a lasting bond, almost a brother-brother relationship, would start when he looked at O. J. McDuffie and said: "I want that curly-haired motherfucker right there."

O. J. could play. Could *really* play. At 5-feet 10, he could dunk with ease. Also impressive with a well-rounded game was the brash Sacca. Surprisingly agile were two oversized linemen from near Philadelphia, 310-pound Brian Dozier and 6-foot 7-inch Todd Rucci. Dozier had gained thirty-some unnecessary pounds after his senior season at Chester High by drinking great quantities of beer. Rucci was a late-blooming prospect from Upper Darby who was going to try out for the defensive line. Several Penn State coaches, however, considered him a possible pro prospect on the other side of the ball, at offensive tackle.

Renkey and Wright had become familiar with what, in the early days of summer camp, was fresh and somewhat daunting to their new classmates. Except for parts of some evenings, when they could explore the limited social possibilities of State College, their lives were consumed by football. A tougher, more sophisticated, more competitive, more corporate, and more intimidating brand of football than any of them had ever experienced—or, for that matter, had ever thought possible. "Even the smells of the locker room, that whiff of liniment, make you a little uneasy," said Greg Huntington.

Renkey's father noticed another of his son's high-school habits not serving him well at Penn State. Simply put, Eric was eating himself out of linebacker. "At the end of his senior season," said Mel, "he was about 228. By the time he went to Penn State in January [for his official visit], he was 248. In late June, he was 265." When Mel asked how the two dozen or so upperclass Penn State players also enrolled for summer school viewed this quick expansion, Eric said: "They laugh when I tell 'em I'm a linebacker."

In fact, Eric soon was placed where, months earlier, he'd

vowed to avoid—the defense line. His new position, nose tackle, was the most thankless and dangerous on either offense or defense. The considerable potential for injury came from so many blockers charging from so many directions. If the nose tackle, the enormous anchor, gets rooted out, a defense is vulnerable up the middle, and, because of that, everywhere else. Also, lots of quarterback sacks come from pass rushers benefitting from a nose tackle occupying two or three blockers. The attitude necessary to be successful at nose tackle was expressed by one of Renkey's upperclass competitors, Jim Deter, who once told a timid autograph seeker: "I'm not a nice person."

"In high school," Mel Renkey said, "I had no trouble picking Eric out on the field. When I walked into Holuba Hall [Penn State's indoor practice facility], I had trouble finding him. He was the second-smallest defensive lineman."

The blue carpeted locker room dominates the ground floor of a nameless two-story building in which football players spend more time than any other at Penn State. They suit up there. They have meetings with Paterno and their position coaches there. They lift weights there. All through their freshman year, and later if their grades remain shaky, they study in two large rooms on the second floor there. They gossip there. Sometimes, for football's universal facial expression is a yawn, they nap there. Often, they leave there, for practice or a game, in perfectly fine health and come back a few hours later with some body part severely damaged.

Football is the only sport that comes with a warning label. It's attached to the least obvious part of the most vital piece of equipment, the helmet, and says: "Do not strike an opponent with any part of this helmet or face mask. This is a violation of football rules and may cause you to suffer severe brain or neck injury, including paralysis or death. Severe brain and neck injury may also occur while playing football. . . . You use this helmet at your own risk."

Any glance at any locker room at every level of football indicates a lot of players lead with their helmeted heads. Almost always, it is possible to tell what position someone plays by the number of gouges on his helmet—and how deep they are. Linemen and fullbacks have the ugliest helmet scars. Defensive backs and receivers have very few. Quarterbacks rarely need helmets repaired.

The first floor reception area and the hallways that lead to Penn State's locker room are lined with achievement—and achievers. Two banners, each about the size and width of a beach towel, remind anyone walking through the main entrance that the Nittany Lions won the national championship in 1982 and 1986. There is not enough convenient space for pictures of all the prominent Penn State players, because more than fifty during Paterno's era alone became All-Americans. And Paterno, as is celebrated in the framed copy of the story, was *Sports Illustrated*'s Sportsman of the Year for 1986.

Not far from the team meeting room, a reproduction of a distinctly designed ad reads:

The bruises
The pain
The mud
The pulled muscles
The chalk talks
The long hours
Are all worth it
Because when you are part of a team, you are better than you ever could be alone.

The halls are for dreaming, and one of the grandest dreamers among the new freshmen in the summer of 1988 was Ron Fields. He could see one of his bright smiles, by the mid-1990s, when he was a rich and famous NFL linebacker, hanging next to the rather stern expressions of former heroes Lionized here in his new workplace. "I want to be the best outside linebacker, next to Shane Conlan," said Fields, referring to the two-time All-American linebacker and first-round draftee of the Buffalo Bills in 1987. "I want them to talk about me like they do him." Here Fields's soft features turned wide-eyed, and he assumed a fan's awestruck whisper: "Ron Fields. Always aggressive. Always around the ball." As himself once more, Fields said, "I have Lawrence Taylor's number [56]. I want to go pro—and get that degree."

That degree also would be a mighty stretch. "He didn't make the 700 [on his college boards] Penn State wanted right away," said his mother, Dolores. "He made 640 the first time, then 630. He went to classes weekends in high school. I bought the [practice SAT] books. Then we got this paper [after his third crack at the SAT] in the mail. I wouldn't look, figuring he didn't make it again and this was his last chance. I told him to read me the bad news."

"He said, 'Oh, Ma, I made it'. He went up 90 points. Up 80 in verbal and 10 in math. He picked me up in the living room and turned me around. I told him: 'You don't have to be separated from the team [as a Proposition 48 player, he would not have been allowed to participate in practice or in games]. You made it on your own.' "

Dolores and Fred Fields separated when Ron was two; Dolores later met Walter Miller, and they had been living together in a small, tidy project apartment on Randall Avenue in the Bronx. From a roly-poly sixth grader who, to avoid being seen, would crawl from his bedroom into the kitchen for late-night snacks, Ron had become sensible—and a sensational linebacker prospect.

Although Dolores tried to protect him as much as possible, Ron said, "I've seen people getting shot in the street. In my building complex, there was a girl, pregnant with twins, who got stabbed in the stomach by her boyfriend with a big butcher knife. Got thrown off the roof and landed in front of my window. I looked out. The body was right there. I was a junior in high school."

As a senior at Adlai Stevenson High, Fields was relentlessly pursued by Penn State assistant Joe (Buddy) Sarra. "He called me at least once a week," Fields said. "Also came by my school numerous times. The faculty noticed. Some of my friends would see him and run to me and say: 'Your father's here.'

" 'My father?'

" 'Yeah. Joe Sarra.' "

Of her family, Dolores said, "We were always go-getters." That was obvious when Walter's car broke down the day before she and Ron were to make their official visit to Penn State seven months earlier, in January. Sarra said no problem, come sometime again, when the car is fixed. Insistent on fulfilling that obligation, Dolores and Ron arose at 2 A.M. and made off for a Port Authority bus. Later, they changed buses in Philadelphia and Harrisburg and arrived at Penn State at the appointed hour.

"It's not gonna be an easy [academic] time," Walter said. "He's in there with kids who got eleven, twelve hundred on their SATs and finished high in their class. Who around here knows Mozart? He hasn't been exposed to that kind of thing. This is not our culture. He needs help, but he's gonna be a professional football player."

"All I hope," said Dolores, "is that he survives."

The initial act of survival for a college football player has nothing to do with football. Right away, before any tackles, a teenager away from home for the first time must deal with money and a roommate.

Before she left, Dolores had opened a checking account for Ron at a downtown bank. In less than a week, Ron had written the first check of his life. For $50. To himself. That had reduced by 20 percent the allowance Dolores had given him. Ron also applied for, and received, a charge card issued by the university, shiny blue and white plastic highlighted by a small Nittany Lion. "Makes you feel good," he said. "Makes you feel grown up. This is my money. I got to handle it. No help from mamma."

The roommate deal started badly. As he always had over his twenty-two years, Paterno with this class frequently matched a black player with a white player. One of those 1988 arrangements was Fields, a black linebacker from a project apartment in the Bronx, and Tom Wade, a white linebacker from wide-open New Mexico. When they met, each almost immediately thought, "This is not gonna work. No way."

"You're a field-hand cowboy, and I'm a city slicker," Fields said he told Wade. Gradually that first day, the tension began to ease. Their ideas on how to arrange the rather small room in Porter Hall meshed. They thought the room could use a plant and soon went downtown and bought one.

"He hates to get up in the morning; I hate to get up in the morning," said Fields. "He complains about practice; I complain about practice. He said he was The Man in high school; so was I. So we really didn't have to work real hard. Plus both of our study skills were poor."

Once they decided to be friendly, they could ride each other about their backgrounds:

Wade: "How can you live in a rat-infested place with millions of people, a filthy town?"

Fields: "How can you live in a barren desert with nobody around for miles?"

Wade: "At least the air is clean. And it's pretty at night."

Wade's use of smokeless tobacco bothered Fields. And New Yorker Fields always locking his door irritated the more trusting Wade. "He always forgot his key," said Fields. "He'd be sitting outside the door when I came back. Finally, he got to remembering to take it with him."

Football survival crept into the minds of Fields, Wade, and the others early in their first workout, when one of their new teammates, Ivory Gethers, suddenly was lying on the artificial turf of Holuba Hall and holding his right knee. Wearing little more than a T-shirt and shorts and doing nothing more strenuous than running around a series of orange-colored cones, Gethers had torn the anterior cruciate ligament. No more than ten steps into it, his college career seemed in jeopardy.

Hard luck had swooped down on Ivory Gethers very early and then lingered. From a distance, his 6-foot 1-inch body seemed sculpted, so defined were his features. Up close over the next two-plus years, that still-taut frame was looking both flawed and flamboyant. For in addition to the scars from two serious operations, to his right knee and left shoulder, there were two horseshoe-shaped brands he'd been required to suffer through to join the service fraternity Omega Psi Phi. Gethers taped soft poetry to a locker loaded with other necessities to withstand punishment.

Behind his helmet and neck brace was this from Edgar A. Guest:

When things go wrong, as they sometimes will,
When the road you're trudging seems all too uphill,
When the funds are low and the debts are high,
And you want to smile, but you have to sigh,
When care is pressing you down a bit,
Rest if you must, but don't quit . . .
Don't give up though the pace seems slow,
You may succeed with another blow.
Often the goal is nearer than it seems to a faint and faltering man;
Often the struggler has given up
When he might have captured the victor's cup.

A decade or so earlier, the sort of injury Gethers suffered during that seemingly harmless no-contact drill would have ended football for him. So improved were the surgical techniques that a return to action was possible, but no sooner than a year.

So common was a torn anterior cruciate ligament that everyone close to football referred to it as "ACL." Copies of the early, sixteen-week rehabilitation phase were, like aspirin, available upon request. "Postoperative Rehabilitation Protocol" is what the sheet called four months of misery. As a practical matter, it meant his first-ever serious injury and first-ever fall without football would largely be spent on crutches and in the Jack Hulme Training Room.

His academic background also was weak, so Gethers once a week limped into Paterno's house, though not to see the coach.

He was there to be tutored in writing by Sue Paterno, who had been doing that sort of thing for a few players each season since 1983. A familiar scene would be Sue nursing a Diet Pepsi and preparing for guests later in the week while Gethers and Bobby Samuels did writing exercises at the kitchen table.

Neither Samuels nor the hobbling Gethers realized Sue Paterno's own long-term suffering. She had endured three back operations since the mid-1970s to ease, if not totally correct, disc problems.

She was nearly fourteen years younger than Joe and had grown up in a western Pennsylvania family dominated by sports. Still, nothing ever fully prepares a woman to be a football wife. Joe and Sue had planned a honeymoon in Europe, but recruiting intruded. Recruiting also was the reason plans to Jamaica, then to Bermuda, then to Sea Island, Georgia, got altered. "A month or six weeks in Europe," she said, "ended up as five days between Williamsburg and Virginia Beach."

Forty miles into that shortened honeymoon, after their wedding May 12, 1962, Paterno stopped the car to visit a prospect— who chose Miami anyway. "He went in; I read," Sue recalled, "And it hasn't changed. At that time, there were few restrictions on recruiting. So on our honeymoon we bought salt water taffy for his recruits' mothers, sent postcards to his recruits. It was fine. It better be fine. You have to roll with the punches. When we got home from the honeymoon, he left two days later with [fellow assistant coach] Earl Bruce to go recruiting. I thought he was married to Earl Bruce for the first two months of our marriage."

Sue's degree from Penn State was in English, and she taught the first year of their marriage. Then came the kids, two girls and three boys. In the last five-plus years, with everyone mostly grown, she was able to help Nittany Lion football players with these part-time tutorials.

"Do you know how many kids come out of high school who have never had to write a paragraph?" she said. "They have no conception of how to start. They'll come here, say, before an essay final, so they won't panic. I've had kids here while I was icing Christmas cookies."

Since the early 1980s, Paterno has been referred to as JoePa by Penn State students. To her small flock of football players, Sue became known as Mrs. Pa. Gethers in his deep voice called Sue "sincere and very caring. And hard."

In Penn State's locker room, all freshmen, even the fortunate few granted playing time, are tucked off to one side, segregated in a conscious way from the upperclass elite. Rich Rosa called their home "Little Pit." From the door everyone uses after most practices, freshmen get to Little Pit by taking about twenty to twenty-five steps and hanging a right at either of two entrances separated by a small row of lockers. Alphabetically, from Donnie Bunch to Brett Wright, the scholarship freshmen resided there with assorted walk-ons and upperclass outcasts.

"An experience, good for freshman," Rosa called Little Pit. "When you walk in from practice, all the upperclass guys are checking out the unfamiliar guy who'd made that play maybe a half hour earlier. Walk into Little Pit and it's almost an escape. Upperclassmen don't ever come back and bother you. Once you get outta there, seems like you never return. Kinda weird. Like a sacred ground for freshmen."

By the second week or so of preseason camp, the freshmen had learned that their locker number was far more important than their uniform number, for so much flowed from it. A player's locker number also was his seat number in the team meeting room, which, with its rising rows of soft seats, resembles a small lecture hall. Managers had copies of the seating chart of that meeting room, so two glances—one at the empty seat and the other at their seating chart—told them who was tardy. Or AWOL. One of the Little Pit routines was assistant coach Buddy Sarra dropping by. The white-haired inside linebackers coach would say: "How ya doing, men? Everybody all right?" Then he would move on, a no-nonsense man whose stride suggested someone constantly boring into a powerful wind.

Rarely was everybody in Little Pit all right at the same time.

Frequently their first weeks at Penn State, however, everybody was down in the dumps together. Homesickness had set in. Tony Sacca and John Gerak slapped a small strip of adhesive tape to a pole near their locker and marked off the days until they figured it would be possible to go home: the season opener at Virginia in about a month. Players redshirted, held out a season to learn the system and mature, do not make trips. Sacca and Gerak thought they surely would be redshirted, Sacca especially, because he was a quarterback; no true freshman ever had been given that position at Penn State.

After every practice, 5-foot 8-inch cornerback Mark Graham would all but sprint to the phone in the Nittany Hall lounge and usually have to wait in line until some other lonely teammate finished his sad tale. Phone bills of several hundred dollars that first semester were common; most of Graham's came from talking with the girl he'd left behind in northern Jersey.

Sometimes, several freshmen would turn off the lights in Little Pit before practice and go to sleep. That was the rich and rare commodity. Sleep. Conversation almost always included young women and how many of them were gravitating toward the coverboy-handsome John Gerak. That and the other terrific topic: drinking.

Being exceptionally healthy and virile, the freshmen football players very quickly took to doing what comes naturally on and off this campus of about 28,000. They partied. Make that PARTIED. Popular myth suggests that Paterno runs a sort of monastery where players during the week are devoted to the highest academic discipline and gather only to discuss noble and pure thoughts.

In fact, Nittany Lions can hang out, hang loose, hang dangerously, hang tipsy, and hang together in times of alcohol-induced trouble with anybody in any conference. And, much to their delight, the freshmen soon knew that the welcome mat for them started at the dorm door and led to nearly all merriment. Fraternities? Don't bother calling ahead or having somebody put your name on a list. Walk right in. Keg's over there.

"Everywhere you go, people just accept you, because you're a Penn State football player," said Fields. "They see you as a football player first and a person second. Your ego starts to inflate. You've got homework, but somebody says: 'Come on and drink. Come and do this.' You say you'll get to the homework later. There are things you never get to."

Chris Cisar explained a routine: "Me, Chad [Cunningham], Sacca, [Todd] Burger, Nardo [Matt Nardolillo], and a couple of others went out almost every night after class. Got a couple of cases of beer [ID cards were never a problem]. Or went to parties. Five nights a week. Pretty heavy. That lasted through the season and winter workouts. Something new for us. Something different."

"Around two or three o'clock in the morning," said Gerak, "people would pop into rooms. Lots of times, it was to see if any girls were there." Of those who drank, the most troubling to his new buddies and to Paterno was the wide receiver from Camden, Donnie Bunch. Said his roommate, Gerak: "He'd practice every day with a buzz on. He had two forty-ounce pops of beer every single day before practice and three after. A great athlete, but he never practiced sober."

The serious matter of having fun got to the point where the mere mention of a number—611—brought all-knowing smiles and a cancellation of previous plans. Six-eleven was the apartment number of a building two blocks from campus on Beaver Avenue. Occupied by some friends of Brett Wright, it got stretched to structural limits many nights and all weekends by eager crowds. The all-time one-night record for quarter-kegs was thirty-three.

News of the naughty behavior during one party at 611 reached Paterno. "A girl wrote a letter to him that said she couldn't believe football players carried on that way," said Graham. "Drinking. Womanizing. She was so flabbergasted, shocked. Joe even brought it up in a squad meeting, and I thought: 'Jesus Christ. We're human, just like everybody else.'"

There was gossip in Little Pit, about the fuss created when a slightly sauced Nardolillo tried to escort a chicken leg outside the downtown Roy Rogers restaurant without paying for it. There was intrigue, over items they deemed insignificant but Paterno went ballistic over: earrings, hats, and facial hair that the coach in his high-pitched voice called "chin whiskers."

Innocently, New Yorker Ron Fields had arrived wearing an earring, and Sarra had all but ripped it off. Joe can't stand 'em, Sarra said. Once in a while, a freshman would get bold enough to sport an earring about campus, then quickly take it off when Paterno or an assistant came into sight.

The earrings went underground because everyone knew that Paterno learned about all mischief thirty seconds after it took place. Hell, he even knew about the young woman with whom Brian Dozier was keeping company in his room.

Fields, as he was starting to grow a goatee, happened along the same path as Paterno. As Fields recounted it, the conversation went:

Paterno: "Shave that off."

Fields: "Why?"

Paterno: "Because I don't allow any chin whiskers."

Fields: "Why?"

Paterno: "I just don't like 'em."

Fields shaved.

Paterno seemed to mount a crusade against wearing hats inside a building. And he didn't limit showing his displeasure to the players. Grown-ups, respected citizens, would be scolded by Paterno for not removing their hats in, say, the football office. The only time anyone could recall Paterno not demanding that a hat be removed in the football office was when, as a favor, he spoke with the visiting son of an influential alum.

Five minutes into the conversation a buzz began among the secretaries: Can you believe it? The kid still has his hat on. Twenty minutes later, Paterno bid a polite so long. And the young man walked out the door, still without even touching his hat.

To each outside door of the building that housed the lockers, study hall, and meeting rooms was attached a brass-plate reminder to remove hats. Four years into his Penn State life, during his academic senior year, Tony Matesic walked into the locker room and nodded to assistant coach Fran Ganter. Sternly, Ganter snapped: "Anthony!" Immediately, instinctively, Matesic grabbed the baseball cap perched on his head and snatched it off.

This seemingly irrational rule was unsettling to the freshmen but of no great consequence in the grand scheme of their existence at Penn State. The residents of Little Pit had come to play football and get to know the coach for whom they had planned to deliver another national championship. From day one, they had been getting huge and unexpected doses of both.

Esteem among football players at Penn State is measured by the color of their practice jerseys. Ironically, the range from elite regulars to obscure scrubs called foreign teamers spans the school colors, blue and white. Blue denotes the first string and others likely to see significant playing time. Dark blue is worn by the renowned defense; light blue is worn by the offense. Second teamers on defense wear red; second teamers on offense wear green. Third teamers on defense wear maroon; third teamers on offense wear yellow.

White may be fashionably equal to blue everywhere else on campus; it is repugnant to all football players. Freshmen tolerate white because most figure to take a redshirt season. An upperclassman wearing white either is in disfavor at the moment or might not ever play for more than a few mop-up seconds his entire Penn State life. White is nightmarish: blue the theme of dreams.

"A big mental thing, that blue jersey," John Gerak would say a year later, after he'd earned one. "You see a guy in white and in your mind you're better than he is; you see a guy in blue and you automatically respect him. Take a tackling drill: You see a guy in a white or maroon jersey and you run him over. It's in your head. He could be better than the next guy, in red, but that doesn't matter. Guys demoted to white [for a sin such as failure to make prescribed times in preseason running drills] just do not practice as well as they do in blue."

At 6 feet 5 inches and 235 pounds, Gerak was among the most versatile freshmen. He was projected out of high school in eastern Ohio as a linebacker or tight end. Penn State thought he was fast enough and tough enough to be a terrific fullback. Being so tall, Paterno thought, Gerak could fall down at the line of scrimmage and still gain two yards.

No longer were Gerak and any of the others the obvious standouts in their new environment, however. As Mel Renkey had observed about Eric, the competition often was much larger and more physically mature. The playbook was thicker and more thorough than any they'd seen. And adding to this new and often sudden humility was a militarylike regimen and the dark, driven side of their head coach.

The Paterno they had been drawn to on television, the Paterno who had charmed them and their parents, the Paterno who had enthralled much of the country with his wit and enlightened thinking about big-time sport was not the Paterno they were now seeing up close and very personally.

This Paterno was a screamer. The calm voice that had inflated their egos several months before was very quickly cutting to the core of their self-esteem. His voice was high-pitched and distinctive; his manner was anvil-hard and blunt, as when he told the overweight Dozier in a full squad meeting: "You should have gone to [Division III] Widener." The coach also could be generous. A few weeks later, when Dozier had lost 25 pounds and gotten to 285, Paterno pulled him aside after practice and complimented him on working so hard.

"As soon as the upperclassmen came [about a week after the freshmen reported], everything changed," said Brett Wright. "We were pushed into the background. We weren't even looked at. Most of us. Joe starts screaming at the top of his lungs. I'm like: 'Who is this guy?' "

This man was progressive in many ways, publicly candid earlier than most coaches about colleges exploiting athletes and calling for a playoff system, similar to the NCAA basketball tournament, to determine the national football champion. Shortly after assuming command from Rip Engle in 1965, Paterno talked up what he called his Grand Experiment, insisting his players could excel academically and still become number one on the field.

During a late 1960s interview with *Sports Illustrated*, Paterno pushed the fact that some of his players had class the day of a home game, that a linebacker majored in physics, and that a defensive line grunt played classical piano. (The fellow who could play Mozart and make plays in the opponent's backfield was Mike Reid, who, after a short but successful career in the NFL, became a massively popular country-and-western songwriter and singer.) There also was the practical side to Paterno, as when *SI* writer Dan Jenkins looked down the roster and pointed to a prominent player in the usual jock major, phys ed. Paterno replied, "What God had in mind there was a football player."

In his approach to playing football and to those who play it, Paterno was rigid and old-fashioned. As conservative and as loud as Vince Lombardi. Every bit as sarcastic as Bobby Knight, but without the swear words or furniture throwing. An equal-opportunity screamer, as likely to blow off a blue shirted starter as a non-factor in white, and close to paranoid about who watched practice. A new manager on the lookout for suspicious persons once dashed toward the otherwise empty stands inside Beaver Stadium during a scrimmage and asked the dignified man in suit and tie walking toward midfield to identify himself. It was Penn State's associate athletic director for communications, L. Budd Thalman.

Paterno's worrisome eyesight had caused periodic examinations at Johns Hopkins University in Baltimore. Once at practice, he charged toward an unfamiliar figure on the periphery, only to discover, on closer inspection and to his considerable embarrassment, that it was the husband of his administrative aide, Cheryl Norman.

70   FOR THE GLORY

"I didn't think he'd be quite as hands-on as he is," said Tom Wade. "He's more hands-on than some of the position coaches. It's funny when he gets down with the offensive linemen and takes off his glasses. He gets down there, shows 'em how to block and then wanders around trying to find his glasses."

Eric Renkey was among those newcomers trying to find their way around. "I'm never going to learn this thing," he said of his playbook. "Everything is so accelerated," Brett Wright added. "In high school, you put in a play a week and went into a game with maybe ten plays. We're getting whole offensive and defensive schemes in one gulp."

"My fourth system in two months," exclaimed Rudy Glocker. "The first was high school. I was on two all-star teams and now this."

Fields and two other freshman competing for the two inside linebacker positions known as Fritz and Backer were shocked to realize that a football class at Penn State began before an academic one. Their position coach, Buddy Sarra, was the only assistant to call a meeting *before* breakfast—at 6:30 A.M.

A half hour earlier than anyone else ever arrived for morning chow, Fields, Brett Wright, and Ivory Gethers (even while recovering from reconstructive knee surgery) would join a dozen or so other inside linebackers in the dining hall. The football menu almost always was the tape of the previous day's practice and served by the assistant who had recruited Fields.

"You say to yourself: 'This man is crazy,'" said Fields. "He has this portable VCR in the dining hall. No one is even half awake, either from studying or partying till about 3 A.M. Sleep still in your eyes. Teeth not brushed. And he's yelling"—here Fields imitated Sarra's gruff manner—"'Your drop's not far enough. What was that? Get back in the curl.'"

Only the Fritzes and Backers at Linebacker U. got such a sleepy-eyed start on the day. Every other assistant could manage to work in a review of the most recent practice during the meetings that preceded each late-afternoon workout. The white-haired Sarra seemed the most devoted of Paterno's

single-minded staff—and also the most paranoid. The harmless
act of a student raising the hood of a car near an always-closed
practice would suggest conspiracy to Sarra.

"When he was an assistant at a small college," said Brett
Wright, repeating one of the hand-me-down stories about Sarra,
"he and a couple of others on the staff were sent to scout another
team. Told to get all the information they could. At halftime,
Buddy disappeared from the group. No one knew where he was.
At the end of halftime, out comes the team they're scouting—
and with them trots Buddy. Jogging on the field with them. He'd
gotten into their locker room—and stayed on the field with them
for the third quarter."

Sarra was tough and relentless. He would gather his troops at
an uncivil time; he would interrupt small-talk moments in the
locker room with advice or to hand out a small card with defensive signals to be taped to each Backer's wrist. Players joked
about Sarra and with him. It was only when an upperclass leader,
All-American Andre Collins, led a rebellion that Sarra after a
couple of weeks stopped his sunrise services.

Bad enough was that horn-honk wake-up call. Bad enough
were the morning meetings followed by morning practice followed by lunch followed by some rest followed by more meetings, more practice, dinner and, of course, more meetings. Worst
of all were the scrimmages in Beaver Stadium.

Going to those full-pads affairs, the players resembled troops
on some forced march into battle. Alone or in small groups, they
walked in a strung-out line from the locker room, across University Drive, through a weedy area and two parking lots before
arriving, about half a mile later, for as long as three hours of
serious hitting. After battle, around sunset, came the much
slower return.

"Even if you're not tired and beat up," said slender cornerback Leonard Humphries, carrying his helmet and soaked shoulder pads, "this walk back is no joke. Joe's gone off. Players on
the sideline have been saying: 'Joe, just shut up.' Joe doesn't
look at it logically, we think. We know we're tired; he pushes

us more. Our legs are gone. And we have to walk back. The march from hell, I call it. The man is crazy."

Rich Rosa was dreamy his first scrimmage, though not in the way he'd hoped. "I'd been intimidated by [junior tailback] Sean Redman," he said. "Just his name, because he's also from South Jersey and I'd heard about him all through high school. It was like: 'Wow, Sean Redman! Sometime I'm gonna have to tackle him.' It turned out to be the first tackle I ever made. In the stadium. Scrimmage all day. Hot as blazes. I was playing Hero [the position that combines some attributes of linebacker and strong safety]. All of a sudden here comes Sean Redman. Me 'n' him. One on one.

"I took two reaction steps. Saw him come around the corner and then froze for a second. 'What am I going to do? Here's my chance.' I just went out and did it. He's about 210; I'm about 190. I tackled him by the thighs, and it didn't tickle. Some guys you'd hit in high school and black out. See spots and stuff. Hitting him was like hitting a brick wall. I had a splitting headache that lasted the whole scrimmage. But I got up and got back to the huddle. My first taste of it."

Always, no matter how tired they were—and frequently *because* of how tired they were—the freshmen made time for gripe sessions. Up to a dozen of them at a time would congregate in one room. What with fake identification and other resources, a keg of beer sometimes was on hand and helped animate the talk even more.

"I don't like to play football," Gerak said. "I like to talk about it. Between the guys. Complaining actually in the best part of this place. Just bitching about Joe. That's what we enjoy most. And we do it constantly."

Fairly soon everybody was trying to imitate Paterno in full fury. That shrill voice and abrupt manner. The city kid, Donnie Bunch, was the quickest to catch the coach's voice and gestures. One of the most gifted players, Sacca, also was among the grumpiest. Said Renkey: "Once Sacca's done bitching, you really don't have anything to talk about."

Running contrary to his new teammates was Rudy Glocker, who said of Paterno: "I don't think Joe yells that much." Glocker was coming off an experience with another Joe, his high-school coach, known as Jumpin' Joe Edwards. "I remember when I was a junior," Glocker said, "I watched the same play about seventeen times in a row. Each time, there was a new insult about me." Glocker's mind moved ahead from high school, and he said: "Paterno did say I ran like a duck; it was valid criticism."

The afternoon the veterans reported was, as always, picture day. Newspapers from around the state, around the East in fact, sent staffers for interviews with Paterno and the players. That is about as open as Penn State ever gets with the press. Every other phase—practices and the locker room during weekdays and after games—is off limits. As the players were trooping back to the locker room from Beaver Stadium, a car stopped along University Drive and the driver asked Tony Matesic for directions to Nittany Hall. It was Anthony Grego's uncle answering a get-me-out-of-here phone call.

Grego was a 275-pound offensive lineman from northern New Jersey who had caused even the heads of several upperclass starters to turn in mild awe. Such a prospect, strength coach Chet Fuhrman had thought. Grego's father had made a $765 deposit to reserve hotel accommodation for Penn State's seven home games when he'd dropped Anthony off for freshmen camp ten days earlier. Now, Grego was packing his belongings in the parking lot and leaving.

Paterno only a few days earlier had predicted such a scene. To the freshmen during a meeting in the squad room, Paterno had become very blunt very quickly. Everything will be done my way. Academics *will be emphasized*! How you perform in the classroom affects whether you play in games. He told each player to look around at his new classmates. Look hard, he said, because lots of them aren't going to be around here four or five years from now. Some might quit; some might flunk out.

Bobby Samuels thought the coach couldn't be right. Not

with this class. This class had talent. Paterno had said it was the most gifted class he'd ever had and the best prepared academically, even though Fields had barely made 700 on his SAT and Samuels and Gethers were marginal admits. Samuels on the field showed as much potential as anyone. The first time he touched the ball during a scrimmage he ran it more than half the length of the field for a touchdown. There was glory ahead, Samuels thought, for him and for everyone seated around him.

Brett Wright said to himself: "We're gonna stick together. Be a group. Be the best class ever around here. All twenty-eight. Like a family. There can't be a better class than us."

Paterno knew better, although he had no idea the class would diminish so quickly. However, if someone had asked Paterno to guess which of the new recruits would leave first, he would have said Grego. Even in his brief summer camp period at Penn State as a high schooler, Grego had become homesick.

Watching Grego, Mark Graham thought: "You've got to be strong to make a decision like that. Because you know people are going to be saying all kinds of stuff. People are going to label you a quitter, you can't handle this and that. But I'll never quit. I have plans. Big plans."

As the car carrying Grego was pulling away, an especially promising linebacker prospect, Eric Lewandowski, walked into the parking lot. He said to himself: "I could do that." For the moment, however, he dismissed the thought and soon was participating in a part of football orientation that involves freshmen entertaining the entire squad after dinner.

The entertainment can include several freshmen at a time or one. It can be as involved as skits or as brief as a song. If the performance is judged terrible, the flustered newcomer is given rowdy thumbs down and required to sing the kid ditty: "I'm a Little Tea Pot."

Lewandowski was part of a group that included Eric Renkey and Chris Cisar. They had given some thought to a skit based on a popular quiz show, and one of the items was a mild jab at Paterno: "[Who] wears the bottoms of Coke bottles for glasses."

Still, the fun for Lewandowski by now had all but ceased. Two days after watching Grego leave, the slender player that recruiting coordinator John Bove had seen as a future team captain left a note for his roommate, Eric Renkey, and also quit. Lewandowski was the sort of player Penn State covets—a straight-A student with immense athletic ability. "I was impressed," Bove said. "We lined him up [at an inside linebacker position] and I said: 'Wow! He's gonna be okay.'"

Even before he arrived at Penn State, after that stellar career at Cathedral Prep in Erie, Lewandowski had not been okay with football. "All my goals were around high school," he said, "so there was nothing more for me to go for. I never thought about the college level until it was right on me. Then I didn't know if I wanted it.

"In the eight grade, I went to a Prep game with my dad. I saw number 7. His name was Chris Filipkowski. He was quarterback for Prep. I said: 'Dad, I want to be that one day. I want to be number 7; I want to be quarterback.' He thought I was blowing steam. Next year, I went to Prep. Dad said there would be a lot of competition, but I was put at running back because that's what I was in grade school. When I couldn't get 7, the next best number was 25. You know, two plus five."

Lewandowski was sitting in an Erie restaurant about a year later. Nearby, two young waitresses gave him a curious, didn't-you-used-to-be-famous look as he continued: "My sophomore year, I played quarterback. And wore number 7. It was like a dream come true. I never spoke to Chris Filipkowski. I just saw him. That's what I wanted to be; that's what I wanted to accomplish. And it happened. I was the quarterback for two years, until I got switched to running back as a senior."

Lewandowski suffered a shoulder injury the last game of his senior season, but thought little about it until the Big 33 game—Pennsylvania's best high-school seniors against Maryland's best. During a practice, the whistle blew, but his future teammate at Penn State, Bobby Samuels, didn't hear it and kept going full speed with the ball. Tackler Lewandowski slowed some, and both players landed on that left shoulder. Even though the shoulder quickly improved once again, Lewandowski became concerned. Two weeks later, he reported to Penn State.

"There were only two freshmen inside linebackers at one point. Me and Brett [Wright]," he said. "The others got hurt. So neither of us got a break. On blocking drills, I'd be the linebacker and he'd be the guard for a while, and then we'd switch. Not full speed. We were so wet from sweating one time that my arm slid off his chest and went off his pads. I'd really hurt the shoulder that time."

Surgery was a possibility. Two operations might be necessary, the first being exploratory. Already confused about whether he wanted four or five years of high-voltage football, this seemed the signal to walk away.

"My sister, who's a nurse, understood best," he said. "My mom also understood; my father, who might have been living a little bit through me, kinda didn't understand at first. He thought it was my girlfriend. He didn't want me to give up all this for her. I didn't."

Paterno talked with Lewandowski before he left, tried to coax him into giving Penn State a try for a semester, without football. The assistant who recruited Lewandowski, Tom Bradley, later called and offered one final—and futile—pitch.

"If I could play my lifetime, at Prep and in a high-school atmosphere, I would," Lewandowski said. "That was the best. You could play football for three months, and it would stop. Then you'd lift and play basketball. And you wouldn't think about football till the next July or August. College is like five years. Year around. I played for fun. It was a great game, but I didn't want the game to control me. Up to then, I controlled it. If I wanted to play, fine; if I didn't, I could stay in bed. No problem. I couldn't stay in bed anymore."

There was some guilt. "It seemed like in high school I always got handed things," he said. "My coach would need an outside linebacker. I never played defense. Never even practiced defense. Ever. He would say: 'Eric, go in.' I wasn't going to go out for football as a freshman. Finally, I did, and they had pads my size reserved for me."

Determined to graduate from college, Lewandowski enrolled at Mercyhurst. That was close enough for him to walk to class and where, perhaps by coincidence, his girlfriend, Lisa, was attending. With jobs and a few academic scholarships, he was paying his own way by his sophomore year. He declined Mercyhurst's invitation to try its Division III brand of football.

"It kinda made me happy," he said, "because I knew I was working for this. Nothing was handed to me. Things always had fallen in front of me; all I had to do was pick them up and go. I didn't have to work for it. I have a loan to pay back when I'm done. That's fine. I can do that. I was confused [at Penn State], I think, because I didn't want to admit to myself what I wanted to do. I kept thinking, 'Everyone else wants me to play.' Then I just said, 'I want to do this. I'm going to have to live with it. They're not.'"

4

Reading, Writing, and Sleeping

Nearly two weeks after football practice began, on the Wednesday before Labor Day, Penn State swung open its academic doors, and Ron Fields couldn't find the first one. "Chambers Building," he said. "For anthropology. All the way on the other side of campus. At least a mile."

Like Chris Cisar, Fields had gotten a map. But Cisar had taken the time to highlight the exact route to each of his classes. Where he would make the right to get to the left that led to . . . bingo! Yellow marked the paths for Monday, Wednesday, and Friday; green would lead him through Tuesday and Thursday. Fields failed to plan ahead. Soon that map was useless, so he resorted to a tactic tourists in his native Bronx found useful: Follow the crowd and ask directions.

"Where's Chambers?"

"Well, you walk past the HUB [the student activities center] and keep going till you get to Wartek."

"Where's Wartek?"

"Tall building on the corner. There you make a right, go past Patee Library."

"Where's Patee Library?"

"You're new here, right?"

"And totally lost."

Anthropology 1 was about five minutes old by the time Fields arrived.

"Then comes the second shock," he said. "You're over the fact that it's not one big building for all your classes, like high school. You're in the room and it hits you: 'Oh, Lord, lecture class. Huge.' You don't want to sit up front, because it's your first time there and you're shy. So you slip in the back. You just want to be a number. You sit in the back, and you hear the teacher lecturing.

"High-school teachers usually write on the board; you just copy it. Lecture class, they don't do that. So you're sitting there. You hear the teacher speak and you look around and see all the people writing. You think: 'What's going on here? What did I miss?' You pick up some key words; you glance over at some other person's paper. You don't know that person and you're too shy to ask what the teacher said. So you look. Sometimes, the person will shove a book over the paper, so you can't copy.

"Difficult."

Fields at least found his class. During that erratic adventure, he had bumped into the even more bewildered Bobby Samuels and O. J. McDuffie. Some seventy-five minutes after leaving room 208 of Nittany Hall, they still had not located English 1. Worse, nobody was left to ask directions. They walked back to the HUB and plotted how to get to the second class of their college careers. In less than a week, Fields and the others were oriented to the point of even knowing the shortcuts and how to manage the bus system necessary for a campus of 28,000 students.

Back in Little Pit, someone mentioned Schwab Auditorium. Anyone ever seen such a place! More than 900 seats for Bi-Sci 4, or about twice the number necessary for every student in Rich Rosa's southern New Jersey high school. Schwab was theater-like, frequently used for campus plays, with lush red seats and a balcony. For the football weary, that balcony was Schwab's alluring feature.

"If you sit in the balcony," Rosa said, "forget it. Bi-Sci 4 my first semester. The one D I got. Everything else was As and Bs. I just slept." Later, for an economics class, slumber in Schwab became sophisticated. One day, Rosa would sleep and O. J. McDuffie would take notes to be shared that night; next time, McDuffie would sleep and Rosa would take the note-writing shift.

"The first couple of weeks," said Eric Renkey, "classes are great, because they're the only times you see people other than football players. For a while, class is the only way to stay sane. You go to class till the first game. Then you go to a party after the first game, you see a bunch of people and that's the end of it for class. You don't usually miss the first three weeks of class. After that, it's sleep time." Breakfast is mandatory. But that can be little more than a brief intrusion, a short walk, some nourishment, and a hop back into the sack. As Renkey put it: "The factors were how tired I was versus how much I needed to go to class. Usually, the tiredness factor won out."

For a football player, there is only one trouble with going beddy-bye during class time. Unless some sort of academic osmosis takes place, whereby a player somehow snores in knowledge or he coaxes enough from more conscientious students, he gets caught. Grades flow from professors to academic advisor Don Ferrell's office and eventually to Paterno. In one form or another, at one time or another, the player with slumping grades is awakened.

"If you're supposed to be in class," said Renkey, "you never answer the phone. Or you disguise your voice. I've done that a couple of times. It works."

One morning Tony Matesic rolled over in bed and, still in a daze, recognized the stern figure of Ferrell hovering over his bed. This was a nightmare but no dream. Ferrell had seen Matesic at breakfast, figured he would slip back to bed, and walked through the open door to his room. Within a few days, Matesic was summoned to Paterno's office, and he decided to make this scolding a memorable one. He was going to tape it, record the

coach in high-volume disgust, and play it later for the amuse-
ment of his closest and most trusted friends.

It was a bold plan. Outrageous for a freshman. But not totally
unexpected for a Jersey Guy. To conservative, buttoned-down,
watch-your-tongue Penn State, the Jersey Guys were unique.
Jersey Guys almost always were the loudest in the locker room,
were the most profane and daring, and also played with the most
abandon. It was an upperclass Jersey Guy, linebacker Mark
D'Onofrio, who once was kicked out of practice *before practice
even began.* For no special reason, he started going after a startled
Rudy Glocker during a drill before the stretching routine that
signals the official start of practice.

When Paterno had gathered the full squad in mid-August, he
introduced each freshman and told him to recite his honors. The
walls outside the team room were filled with achievers and
achievement; the coach wanted that attitude inside as well. It
was a Jersey Guy, the 5-foot-8-inch Mark Graham, who stole the
show. Freshmen before and after would get up and mention
being All-State, or All-American, being in the National Honor
Society, blah-blah-blah. Graham stuck out his chest and said: "If
I told you all my honors, we'd be here all night."

Hmmmmmmmmmmmmmmmm.

Matesic and another North Jersey defensive lineman, Todd
Burger, also backed down to no one. The 270-pound Burger
quickly became king of the weight room, bench-pressing 225
pounds, a team high, twenty-seven straight times. An unnerving
and energizing early sensation for him was the first day in pads.
He said: "I saw all this fighting. I was like: 'Wow!' There'd
never been competitive practices in my high school. There were
only thirty to thirty-five guys on the whole team. But I liked
what I was seeing. It was great. I think I was the first kid in our
class to get thrown out of practice. I was fighting all the time.
With [upperclassman] Tim Freeman mostly, because he kept
holding me. Joe would tell me to get out of there, go to the
locker room, take a shower. Next day, I'd be [promoted to] second or third team."

Matesic never violated Paterno's chin whiskers rule, though he rarely was clean shaven. There was this locker room dialogue between him and junior offensive lineman Dave Szott, who later became a starter for the Kansas City Chiefs.

Szott, in Matesic's face: "You're only a freshman. Keep your mouth shut."

Matesic: "Hey. I'm still part of this team." Later, Matesic's features softened and he said: "I take the most abuse."

To a small group of friends that included roommate Bob Daman, whose small tape recorder he borrowed, Matesic the night before his meeting with Paterno said: "If Joe goes off on me, I want you guys to hear it."

Next morning, Matesic slipped the tape recorder among some books in a sack and soon was crossing the road that separated the dorm area from the football offices. Nervous, he greeted the receptionist, Mel Capobianco, and walked slowly down the row of four offices, each occupied by a veteran Paterno aide. Here was a freshman trying to pull off a stunt an All-American might back away from.

This was during the season, so the assistant coaches were in suit-and-tie uniform. In the off season, open collars, even jogging gear is permitted. Games here are serious—and serious business. Matesic was bent on folly. Past Tom Bradley's office Matesic went; past the office of the man who supervised his recruitment, John Bove; past the office of the man who had recruited him most heavily, Fran Ganter; past the office of his overall defensive coach, Jerry Sandusky; finally, into a small reception area where secretary Cynthia Ault said to go right in. Paterno was waiting.

Inside, Matesic fumbled through his sack and activated the recorder. All went well, except Paterno was not quite as entertainingly nasty as Matesic had anticipated. There was a fine kicker, however. When Matesic mentioned that his parents, first-generation immigrants from Yugoslavia, were on a cruise, the coach said: "Keep what you've been doing up and you'll be joining them."

That night, Matesic gathered his friends and reported: "Successful mission." He played the tape and then very quickly erased it, fearful that Paterno would get wind of the merriment.

"After what happened with Tony," said Renkey, referring to Ferrell walking in on Matesic, "I always made sure the door was locked. Whatever it took, I never was caught. I considered sleeping in the closet a couple of times I thought he'd try and come get me. He never did."

Renkey had encouraging priorities that gave a misleading tilt to his cumulative average, a pathetic, barely-above-a-D 1.31 his first semester. He would get an A in something difficult but stimulating, such as chemistry, but that success would be undermined with an F in some twinkie course, such as gym. He flunked tennis the only way that was possible—by almost never attending class.

Assistant coach Bradley, who had recruited him, once told Renkey to make up some sort of excuse about not going to class; perhaps the tennis instructor would cut him a break. A week or so later, Bradley asked if Renkey had followed his advice.

"No."

"Why?"

"It would have been lying."

In room 204 of Mifflin Hall, there was no mischief from Rudy Glocker. He brought from high school the disciplined habits that had earned him six credits in history before he attended his first class at Penn State. Part of his routine each morning was to buy a *New York Times*, which, he said, "is great to read between class and also serves as a raincoat. You can hold the *Times* over your head and not get wet at all."

Glocker tried to fill his mornings with back-to-back-to-back classes, reasoning: "If you have to go back to your room, you're mighty tempted to go back to sleep. What I'd do [during an open period] is come back, shower to keep awake, read the paper, and then be ready for my Shakespeare class."

Shakespeare? Indeed. Paterno's ability to attract superior student-athletes was living on, through Glocker and another tight end candidate, Derek Van Nort, whose academic goal was to be accepted in a major that included no more than a hundred or so of the 28,000 undergrads: Engineering Science.

"My favorite class was Shakespeare," Glocker said. "I liked the professor, John McAdams, really identified with his way of teaching. Plus I made friends with some of the class. There were maybe fifty kids in all, only two or three of us freshmen. We read six or seven plays. Of course, I'd already read *Othello* in high school." Glocker got a B-plus for the course, which was balanced by a C in Oriental Philosophy.

Ever the one to go against popular thought, Glocker said football players had too much free time. "Twelve credits is tops [each semester]," he said. "That amounts to three hours a day. At the most. Even if you have eight hours for football, that leaves thirteen hours, Sleep takes eight of those hours, so that leaves five free. Maybe if we had another class, making it fifteen hours instead of twelve, they'd have to study." Glocker did carry fifteen credits that first semester. Fortunately for his snoozing buddies, that extra-course heresy never went farther than Glocker's mind.

Glocker also found a way to get around a system that he and the other freshmen thought stifling. Permission for almost every non-football act, even something as simple as leaving campus for a tragedy, had to come from the football office.

"Around Easter," said Brett Wright, "on the morning of a Saturday practice, I got a call that a friend of mine from home had been killed by a drunk driver. I had a hard time dealing with it. I wanted to go home, talk to the family, sort things out. I called [administrative assistant] Frank Rocco. He said: 'How can you think about missing practice?' I went to Jim Caldwell [the assistant who had recruited Wright], and he said: 'It may not be in your best interest.' So I went to Joe, and he finally gave his permission, like it was some big thing to miss one spring practice. That hurt me a lot."

By then, the spring of his freshman year, Glocker had learned how to save time and frustration in such situations. "I always viewed this as a corporation and Joe kinda like the CEO," he said. "I figured every time I had a problem, I don't tell the CEO; I tell one of his subordinates and he'll pass the message along.

"I had to testify in court right around Thanksgiving. It involved my high school and its former basketball coach, and I told two or three aides that I'd be missing a squad meeting. At the meeting, Joe asked where I was and Chet [Fuhrman] told him. Joe said he still wanted to see me, and it basically turned out well. Because what I learned was that anytime something comes up, I just go see Joe. It's that easy, I have connections with the CEO."

5

Blue and the Blues

Knowing Penn State's pecking order and his own limitations, it came as something close to a sun-rises-in-the-West shock to Rick Sayles when, fairly late in preseason practice, he was given the dark blue jersey that means first team defense. Most freshmen not only accept scrub-gang white, they expect it, judging a redshirt season and its indignities to be part of the apprenticeship of big-time college football. All of a sudden, one of the lowly residents of Little Pit was bedecked in the color that signifies royalty.

Sayles one afternoon received what amounted to a series of quick battlefield promotions. He'd left the locker room in white. Quickly, there was an injury, and he switched to the red jersey that means second team. Then Quintus McDonald got hurt, and Sayles slipped into a blue jersey. Just like that. Bam-bam, from white to red to blue.

Here was the 6-foot 5-inch Sayles, skinny as a sideline marker and only days out of boot-camp football, thinking about manning the outside linebacker position called Willie for the season opener at Virginia. "I have an uncle, George Little, who went to Iowa and later played with the Dolphins and 49ers," he said.

"I exceeded his postseason honors in high school. I love football, the challenges. All the ambitions that I have are for the game, I really want to go professional."

High school for Sayles was McKeesport, a potent pocket of the vast and football-rich western Pennsylvania area from which Penn State also had mined Eric Renkey, Bobby Samuels, and Chris Cisar. Sayles was neither as famous as those players in high school nor projected to play as early, if at all. The concern among Paterno and his staff was whether Sayles would add enough weight to keep from being blown off the field by blockers nearly a hundred pounds heavier.

"I was a dollar eight five," Sayles said, meaning 185 pounds. Over time, the coaches thought Sayles might be able to gain enough weight to resemble a similarly constructed former outside linebacker from the University of Miami who later became a Hall of Fame player in pro ball: Ted (The Mad Stork) Hendricks. It was going to take years for Sayles to become prominent among the other young Lions—or was it?

Players never are certain about their status until they see the color jersey hanging from the oversized safety pin that also holds their shirts, shorts, and socks. In Penn State's corporate structure, orders pass from the football office to the equipment staff—usually by word of mouth, sometimes by memo—about the color jersey to be issued each player for each practice.

Sayles was in blue again the day after that hectic jersey switching. "I was having to go against Steve Wisniewski [a future Pro Bowl guard with the Los Angeles Raiders] and [325-pound] Eric Jonassen," Sayles said. "When I hit somebody, I'd run right at 'em, and the hit would go from my toenails all the way up through my head. I was worried all the time, cause I was getting mauled, manhandled.

"Brett Wright and I shared a room during two-a-days. Every time after practice we'd come home, lay on our beds, and moan like old ladies. 'This is hell. We're getting killed.' But I was always motivated. I won't quit. Unless you disable me, I will come back. My strength is my inner determination. Some guys get licked one time, and it messes up their entire game. You gotta lick me till that last buzzer goes off."

Sayles sometimes got in a loud lick of his own. "One time in a pass-rush drill I bull-rushed Jonassen all the way back to the quarterback. He was 325 pounds; I was 185. Bill Kenney [the offensive line coach] was highly impressed. Jonassen was embarrassed. So next time he set up for the bull rush. I changed, spun around, and beat him again."

Those highs were the exception. During a practice on the field adjacent to Holuba Hall one afternoon, Sayles was unnerved enough to draw the wrath of Paterno. "I get vocal when people cut me or hold me or a coach tells me something that doesn't make sense just then," Sayles said. "I'll either not do it or ask questions. Joe kinda got on my case about thinking on my own, talking to teammates, and being just a freshman. He said I hadn't even got my feet wet." Boiling, Sayles turned his head and half-whispered, so Paterno could not hear, "Haven't got my feet wet? Hell, I'm drowning. Quintus is over there lollygagging and I'm getting killed."

The gang in Little Pit was happy for Sayles but also envious. A few towels once were laid end to end, so his feet would not have to touch the carpet during those final steps to his locker. But Rudy Glocker admitted: "I was kinda jealous. I'm a competitor by heart. I see almost everything in terms of advantage-disadvantage. You're happy for the person, but you dislike him because he's doing better than you. I don't dislike people who start, but you wish you were like them. That's all there is to it."

Glocker and Sayles had been thrown together as roommates in 204 Mifflin Hall. Theirs also began as an uneasy relationship, for reasons beyond Glocker being white and from a small-town part of eastern Pennsylvania and Sayles being black and from a broken home in an urban area of western Pennsylvania. As he had with Donnie Bunch and John Gerak, Ron Fields and Tommy Wade, and Ivory Gethers and Derek Van Nort, Paterno arranged this black and white room matchup, "because I've got to find out about that sort of thing in a hurry."

Glocker had scored 1260 on his SAT, Sayles 760. But Glocker admitted: "I also took a tutoring class [after scoring 1100 in his first crack]. He couldn't afford that. If he had, maybe his score also would have gone up 160 points.

"We were the odd couple. I like a room cold; he likes it hot. It got to be funny, what would happen almost every night. I'd come home before him, and that window would get slung open. Even in the winter. I'd be sleeping. I'd be fine. He'd come home and close the window. He'd go to sleep. I'd wake up in the middle of the night, usually because I was hot. Open goes the window. Then he'd get cold. He'd get up and close the window. Sometimes, this would go on three or four times a night. Comical. A Laurel and Hardy type thing. We never compromised. It was never: 'Like, let's have the window halfway open.' That was never enough. We went from extremes. Back and forth. We never argued. It was just kinda accepted after a while that if you wake up, you get to set the temperature of the room—until the other guy does.

"Then there's music. I like classical; he likes rap. If he's listening to music I didn't like, I'd leave. If I was in the room listening to music he didn't like, he'd leave. The only near-fight we ever had was when I left once and ended up asleep in the study lounge. I'd put chairs together, with a blanket and pillow. He and the guys in the room with him at the time ended up throwing water on me."

While Glocker and Sayles were getting used to each other off the field, they were becoming equals on it. Sayles gradually was moving back down the jersey ladder. Quintus McDonald was returning to good health and to starter status. Sayles was never quite sure McDonald was as hurt as he'd claimed.

"He never really broke his tail at practice or whatever," Sayles said. "Come the week before the game, he starts practicing a bit. And I just slid back down the hierarchy. Over a two-week period, I was with the elite. I would have been excited if I'd stepped in and found out I could play. The one time I called home was when I was getting beat up.

"The Monday before the Virginia game Quintus came back. I was upset at first—me getting beat up and him getting to play. I slid down to nothing. Just faded. Monday I was in red, along with [upperclassman] Keith Goganious, but not getting any repetitions. I went to red and then got redshirted. After I thought about it, I was like: 'Okay, fine. I shouldn't have been there.' When I satisfy myself, the joy will come." For many others, joy was at hand.

September 10, 1988. Charlottesville, Virginia, 1 P.M. Finally upon them was a game, what cornerback Mark Graham called "the first taste of everything." Meaning the hoopla of college football, heroes and heroics, the reason everyone endures all those marches-from-hell practices and the stinging abuse from Paterno. Before going off to sleep, less than twelve hours earlier, Graham had played the game against Virginia in his mind, anticipating situations in case he actually got to play.

A year or so earlier, the thought of the 158-pound Graham even getting a scholarship to Penn State, let alone playing in the first game of his first season, would have been a stretch. Paterno admitted: "If I had had my way, we wouldn't have recruited him. So thin, just a little guy from Clifton, New Jersey. My assistants kept telling me how good he was."

Graham's cockiness had become evident early on, during that if-I-told-you-all-my-honors-we'd-be-here-all-night   introduction to the squad in early August. Also, Graham was drawn toward finance, specifically the high-wire area of junk bonds. And he was bold enough to tweak the football system.

"Sometimes, you get rebellious," he said. "You go out to a party or something after study hall. Sometimes I'd say: 'I'm not gonna play anyway. Let's go to a party.' Coach [Ron] Dickerson would watch me in practice next day and say: 'You getting enough sleep?'

"No."

Penn State had flown to Charlottesville a day earlier. Not thinking the pregame snack mandatory, Eric Renkey and Chris Cisar had been late for it and been reprimanded. Paterno talked about the preseason; his players dreamed. Donnie Bunch would be wearing jersey number 1, and Tony Sacca and John Gerak hadn't been redshirted after all. They wouldn't be going home until Thanksgiving. But that didn't matter. They were in the big time, though not yet a big part of it.

"We walked out onto the field after we got to the stadium," said Graham. "We were in suits and ties. I looked around and said to myself: 'Yeah. This is all right. This is college football.' "

Some first experiences:

Chris Cisar: "I don't remember running down on the first kickoff. The second time down, I got killed. Picked myself up off the turf, and my helmet was half off. Somebody had just clocked me."

Eric Renkey: "My first series, I got in the huddle and didn't remember the defense or anything. I just lined up, in the wrong place. But it was lots of fun."

Donnie Bunch: "I got in for a couple plays. But they were all runs. All I did was block. Guess Joe wanted me to get the feel of the game. Going off the ball. Things like that."

Gerak rushed six times for 15 yards, O. J. McDuffie caught two passes for 28 yards, and Tony Sacca completed the only pass he threw, for 15 yards. With about three minutes left in the game and Penn State coasting toward a 42–14 victory, Graham was summoned by Dickerson and trotted onto the field. "It seemed so weird," he said. "Everything was so spread out. They had a receiver who was supposed to be an All-American, and he was still in the game. Real tall guy. Lined up across from me. But everything turned out all right. Nothing was thrown my way."

The next week was the second first taste of everything—the home opener. On football Saturdays, Penn State is the magnetic hub that causes the faithful to arise around sunup so as not to be clogged too long on the limited number of access roads. Anticipation is always keen, what with Penn State winning about four games out of five during Paterno's era. Two weeks before the start of the 1978 season, some fans in a small town even held a practice tailgate party.

A stroll around the Beaver Stadium parking lot not too long

before kickoff includes such must-sees as the Happy Valley Express. This is an area about ten yards square that features dancing to polka music, tambourines being shaken, cowbells stuck on pogo sticks, blue hammers going tap-tap on white blocks. Nearby, the university choir meanders through what surely is the world's largest collection of RVs and other oversized campers and gives impromptu concerts. The Beavers, Sue and Bill, are likely to have their pet skunk on a leash.

The players at that time are about a half mile away, in the east locker area. Having spent the night before in a hotel, they also are dressing in a manner that suggests an away game. In front of each locker is a numbered garment bag that the player fills with his regular student clothes. The garment bags are collected and taken at halftime to the stadium. After the game the player slips out of his uniform and back into the clothes he took off a few hours earlier.

From the east locker area, the players board buses. To avoid campus roads jammed with fans, the buses travel a back route that winds past empty chicken houses, and within a few minutes they pop into an end-zone entrance to the stadium. Four buses carry the players; a fifth bus is marked: "Recruits."

In the stadium locker room, the players are segregated by offense and defense. Then Graham and the others gather in an open area for their unforgettable, entrance-of-the-gladiators parade onto the field. Instead of Paterno alone among 83,000-plus empty seats during those August scrimmages, the stadium is packed.

"The first home game was unreal," Graham said. "Every time you looked back in the stadium all you saw was heads. Really strange. And the initial entrance into the stadium. All the cameras. So many reporters. What a feeling. One weird feeling I had was while stretching before the Alabama game [in Birmingham's venerated Legion Field]. Watching Joe. Everywhere he went dozens of people were taking his picture. Picture after picture. When I was in high school, I was looking at scenes like that on television. Here I was, a year later, actually there. Among people of such quality."

There were entrances to Beaver Stadium, and then there were entrances. The grand one had Paterno out front among players in those blue and white suits and black shoes the rest of the world considered boring but Penn Staters thought inspiring. Graham, Cisar, Renkey, Sacca, and the other freshmen slated for part-time duty were part of that thrilling full-trot, fists-in-the-air parade.

The other entrance included all the inactive players and was scattered, almost unnoticed by the sellout crowd. Ivory Gethers would hop toward the bench on his crutches. Other redshirts, such as Rudy Glocker and Ron Fields, would be casually dressed and feeling slightly out of place. They might go into the locker room, where Sacca and the others were strapping on their pads, but only briefly. The room was surprisingly small, and they didn't want to get in the way.

Sometimes immediately before, sometimes immediately after the entrance, the inactive and the wounded would meander toward the sideline near the bench. They would stand and watch. Never were they to venture into the actual bench area, from one 35 yard line to the other. That no-mingle zone was for players and coaches.

That first home game, against Boston College, proved tougher than anticipated. None of the freshmen offensive players got a statistical mention, and the 23–20 victory came about through a blocked punt and 37-yard field goal in the final two minutes. Little did anyone suspect that the next week one of the Little Pit understudies would be thrust into the spotlight.

The quarterback order for the start of fall practice was junior Tom Bill, senior Lance Lonergan, sophomore Doug Sieg, and Sacca a redshirt probability. Then Sieg's uncooperative back went gimpy, and Paterno became uncommonly bold. Even before Lonergan suffered a thumb injury that would sideline him for much of the season, the coach had called Sacca into his office. The 6-foot 5-inch freshman with the rifle arm was being moved from no-play status to second team, behind Bill.

Never had the coach done such a thing. Still tucked in the mind of Sacca's mother, Peg, was Paterno saying less than a year earlier that he would never force anyone into action before he was ready. And with his general lack of maturity, inconsistency, and inattention to detail, Sacca seemed the freshman most in need of a redshirt season.

Even the freshmen closest to Sacca—Todd Rucci, Gerak, and some others—were not quite sure what to make of him. The talent was abundant. But he often was aloof and seemed not to get animated over much except during long, long-distance phone calls to Lisa James back in Delran. They would argue, neither realizing that Chris Cisar was sometimes outside, his ear pressed against the closed door, doing play-by-play of the spat.

Also, Sacca would try anything on the field—the toughest pass into the tightest coverage. But he was surprisingly mild in the huddle and away from football. In the dorm someone would suggest pizza, and Sacca would say: "Sounds good. You order." This is a leader? Sometime in the future, perhaps, but certainly not yet.

Still, everything worked decently well for two-plus games. Quarterback Tom Bill was sharp against Virginia and adequate against Boston College as a revamped running game without the injured Blair Thomas pounded out 423 yards. Sacca waited and learned. Near the end of the third quarter against Rutgers, however, with the Nittany Lions trailing by 21–10, Bill suffered a dislocated kneecap. Out for the season.

The number 19 trotting onto the field, the eighteen-year-old still unfamiliar with most of campus and not inclined to attend many of his classes, was suddenly in control of State's mighty machine. This was in no way Sacca's team, yet he was at its throttle. "I remember listening to the radio for the Rutgers game," Peg Sacca said. "Everybody else had gone to [younger brother] John's high-school game. And when Tom Bill went down and Tony was going in, my dad phoned and said: 'Well, is that your kid up there?'

"I said: 'Oh, God, yes!' "

This was the scene: Six plays into his true freshman season, Sacca in slightly more than a quarter was being asked to help rally a team from an eleven-point deficit. Quickly, almost miraculously, that started to happen. First, the Nittany Lions got within five points, on a 4-yard run by Gary Brown. Sacca's two-point conversion pass failed. Then came first and goal from the Rutgers 4 yard line with plenty of time left.

Storybook stuff was unfolding. Sacca was dramatic enough for some to link him with some other number 19s: John Unitas and Bernie Kosar. In front of a formerly forlorn crowd of 85,531, the kid from "little old Delran" with the recruiting envelopes still pasted to his room at home was being heroic.

However, the plays that came immediately before and the ones that immediately followed first and goal four yards from the winning touchdown were what offensive coordinator Fran Ganter called "the downfall of me physically." Later, in his office, Ganter smiled and reached for a bottle containing pills that the Rutgers experience had helped drive him to. "The doctor calls what I have the yips," he said. "Sweaty palms; my voice starts to quiver; I feel lightheaded and my knees get weak. It started there. In the Rutgers game."

The trip to the yips ended one play and two yards short of victory. On first down from the 4, a running play gained nothing; on second down, a running play gained 2 yards. Third and goal. A play called "21 Shoot." Sacca rolling right, with the option to run or pass.

"He makes a [run] fake and comes out to the corner," Ganter said. "It works exactly how you want it to. He comes out. He's on about the 5, there's a defender and Dave Jakob, our tight end. And nobody else. He's either going to put his head down and run past the guy or just bloop it. He blooped it. Jakob was backpedaling in the end zone, and the ball went off his fingers. I'll never forget that as long as I live. We tried something on fourth down and didn't make it.

"From there, it went downhill. For me and for everybody. Because Tony's the quarterback, Joe came in that Monday and just totally watered down the offense. It was like the bare minimum. No audibles. None of the checking off [at the line of scrimmage] the quarterback has to do a lot. What it amounted to was that after a quarter or a half the other teams started to gang up on us. We were running bad plays, plays we normally would have gotten out of." Before that happened, however, another Nittany Lion had a run-in with the law.

To Todd Burger, the downside of celebrity literally smacked him in the face around 1 A.M. after the Rutgers loss in a small restaurant near campus called CC Peppers. The strongest player on the team, his boyish countenance masked a quick temper. Rowdies hoping to make a reputation by fighting football players had been a frequent topic Paterno spoke about to the squad; in an instant, the coach's words were reality. "I was alone at a table and wearing black Nike shoes," Burger said. "There's six or eight guys nearby and one of 'em says: 'Hey, look at the big guy with the football shoes. What's he think, that he's on the football team?' I ignore it, like Joe says to do. Then somebody says: 'Ohhh, he's pretty big. Maybe he *is* on the football team.' I totally ignore that.

"Then I hear: 'The football team sucks this year. They can't even beat Rutgers.' I look up at them and say: 'Okay, that's strike two. You got something else to say, say it now.' They didn't say nothing. I'm eating. All of a sudden, I hear: 'One ... two ... three.' I look up and wads of paper are sailing at me. Tinfoil. I snapped.

"I jumped up over the table and between all of 'em, which meant my back was to three or four. Still, in my mind, I wasn't going to do anything. I was trying to psyche 'em. Make 'em believe I'm crazy, and they'll leave me alone. That didn't work."

Burger was pushed in the back, fell down and got up. "Then a kid yelled: 'What're you gonna do, tough guy? There's eight of us and one of you.' I say: 'Eight? One ... two ... three ... four ... five ... six ... seven ... eight. Bam.' I hit the eighth kid, right in the face. I did throw the first punch. That's why I got in trouble. The guy behind the counter helped me, and it soon ended up out in the street."

When the police arrived, Burger, who'd been drinking, began

to run. Across College Avenue and down the sidewalk to his
right. "The only thing going through my mind is: 'Joe, Joe.' I
tried to outsmart the cops by running the wrong way down College Avenue. There's a wall [next to the left side of the street].
I'm trying to jump it when five policemen grab me. Tackle me
off the wall. I get handcuffed. Jabbed in the ribs with billy
clubs."

Burger was processed and then released. At about 4 A.M., out
of breath, parts of his clothes torn, he burst into the dorm and
woke roommate Tony Matesic. (In retelling the incident, Burger
put the height of the wall the police had pulled him off at eight
feet. In fact, it was about three feet, or half his size. Had he not
been drinking, Burger could have hurdled it with ease.) Summoned also was the upperclassman with whom Burger had
roomed as a recruit, Dave Szott. Got to tell Paterno before he
finds out, Szott advised.

"I go to Franny Ganter [who had recruited him], and he says
to go to Joe's house," Burger said. "It's Sunday. About three in
the afternoon and we've got a squad meeting at five. I walk the
mile or so to Joe's house. I ring the bell, and no one answers. I
walk back, call on the phone, and Joe answers. Everything eventually gets resolved to fifteen hours of community service." Burger never inquired as to how those fifteen hours might be served,
and no one ever pressed him about them.

Against Temple the next game, and Cincinnati after that, the
no-frills offense worked. Sacca threw for two touchdowns each
game and was a combined 18 for 47. He also ran 12 times for
25 yards.

Then came two real teams—Syracuse at home and Alabama
at Legion Field in Birmingham—and two losses. Alabama was
an 8–3 struggle and featured a 68-yard Sacca completion for a
touchdown that was nullified by a holding penalty.

"You start to think too much," Sacca said of his four-plus
games. "Everybody starts to talk about it. That's when the pressure starts. I'd only run the second team before. I didn't know
any of the [first team] guys, didn't even know half of their

names. It's hard to lead in the huddle when you can't say what you want to say. I was excited coming in against Rutgers but not nervous. I relied on my instincts out there, did what I knew how to do. No pressure. It was the only game all year there wasn't pressure. It was fun."

One of the upperclassmen Sacca did not know was tackle Matt McCartin. "On television," McCartin said, "the huddle looks so serene. It isn't. Guys yelling back and forth: 'I thought you were suppose to get so-and-so.' Linemen are always talking to each other. Lots of times, you'll have confusion in the huddle if the quarterback doesn't get up and say: 'Shut up!' "

The injured Tom Bill was much admired by the players and coaches because he had all the intangible leadership virtues in abundance. Bill had a natural feel for people that Sacca lacked. Where Sacca arrived late to the locker room and left early, Bill mingled. Also, Bill had been around long enough to master the line-of-scrimmage audibles that State's offense demanded. Bill's mind in practice was focused; Tony's drifted. Bill's technique was excellent; Tony's was erratic. In terms of raw talent, however, Sacca was vastly superior. Sacca could get an old coach to dreaming about more big banners.

By being in the unique-for-Paterno position of actually starting several games at quarterback as a freshman, Sacca was the most gawked at among his classmates. He was unfazed, having been similarly celebrated in a much smaller pond. The vibes Sacca sent off to strangers were not especially endearing. He loved playing to big crowds; he avoided the limelight away from football.

"People thought you were the biggest jerk," blocker Greg Huntington told Sacca during a bull session three years later. "I thought so too, before I got to know you."

"It's like you don't care what people think," said Sacca's roommate for two years, easygoing lineman Todd Rucci.

Replied a smiling Sacca: "I don't."

Ganter noted, "I may be overreacting, but I never felt Tony realized how important the little things are. Like coming early to a meeting. Or maybe taking some film back to his room.

Everything is so easy for him. He is so great. You get excited at him on the field, and he'll say: 'Keep cool, dude.' Calling me dude on the field. I want to shake him and say: 'Do you know what you can do if you make up your mind to do it?' "

Sacca's role as starter ended after the eighth game, a 51–30 blowout by a West Virginia team that would have its legitimate hopes for an unbeaten season and national championship pricked by Notre Dame in the Fiesta Bowl. Healthy now, Lonergan started the final three games of the worst Penn State season (5–6) in half a century.

"Could Tony have handled more?" Ganter said of the restricted offense Paterno ordered. "I don't know, but we should have tried. Cause we put him in a no-win situation [during the Alabama game] against a good defensive team. They were dictating what was going to happen. We weren't."

"He was getting killed in the Alabama game," Peg Sacca said, "and then he comes home and watches the reruns. He runs each play over and over and tells me all the gory details: 'Well, now both my knees are bleeding.' He gets in there, through no fault of Joe Paterno. It was like: 'Who's the next to go down?' I like to see them win as much as anyone, but I got to the point where I could care less who won or lost. Just so he didn't get hurt."

"I was upset Tony wasn't redshirted," said his high-school coach, Jim Donoghue. "Everything Joe Paterno preached went out the window. The kid was not ready. He [Paterno] had a total disregard for the kid. His credibility with me went out the window."

Sacca was the most visible freshman, but Eric Renkey and Chris Cisar also played enough to letter. Particular moments were not vivid for Renkey, in part because the nose tackle position he manned as a backup involves so much clutter. "I do remember a couple of tackles in the backfield during the Pitt game," he said. "That was a big deal, because I know about half the Pitt team. I didn't play well the first half of the Notre Dame game but played really well the second half.

"I love to play football as a game, but I don't enjoy football as a business. And Division I is getting too much like a business for me sometimes. It gets blown out of proportion. A lot of some athletes' self-worth depends on how well they play football. I'll go to a party, see people I haven't seen for a year, and that's the first thing they'll ask. About football instead of how well school went."

Cisar became part of the defensive backfield when senior Eddie Johnson was injured. "I never thought that halfway through the season a freshman might start," he said. "But [secondary coach Ron] Dickerson had told me: 'We're not gonna baby you. We're not gonna baby you.' I felt comfortable from the first play."

Behind Sacca, Renkey, and Cisar were six freshmen who played just enough to be both excited and a bit frustrated: wide receivers O. J. McDuffie and Donnie Bunch, center Greg Huntington, fullback John Gerak, and cornerbacks Mark Graham and Leonard Humphries. McDuffie thought about that I-need-you letter from Paterno just seven months earlier, the one that swayed him toward Penn State, and wondered: "If Joe wanted me that much, why am I not playing more?"

The yo-yo feeling of sometimes playing, sometimes not, was best expressed by Bunch. During the Temple game he kept saying on the sideline: "Can I go in? Can I go in?" The reply: "Wait. Wait."

Huntington suffered a foot injury that took an extraordinarily long time to heal. He made every trip, even the one to his adopted state of several years, Alabama. But his playing time was limited to eleven plays the first three games, and he was given a medical redshirt, meaning he still had four years of eligibility. "The first scrimmage I was the third string center," he said, "so I was never on the foreign team until the last week of the season. And I was embarrassed by that. I thought some others"—he mentioned Todd Burger—"resented that. Going against classmates on the foreign team kinda separated me from them. The last week, before we played Notre Dame, when they said there was a chance for a medical redshirt and I knew I wouldn't be playing, I was on the foreign team. I thought that was great. At last I was paying my dues."

Many whose egos had suffered were, by season's end, happier than those who had played just enough to lose a year of eligibility but not enough to letter. One of them was Bobby Samuels, who had arrived at Penn State thinking he could step into the tailback position vacated by the injured Blair Thomas and had been disappointed.

"I expected to play, until I got there," Samuels said. "Then I realized it was a totally different game. Guys aren't out there just to play; they're out there to win. Make something of themselves. In high school, if they told you how to do something and you couldn't and you had the talent, they'd still play you. Up here, you have to have technique. Because talent won't carry you. You're not playing against kids anymore."

Bullfeathers, many at Penn State thought. Samuels could manage quite nicely on talent. "I never saw anyone run that fast," Rich Rosa said of the fellow who in high school had outsprinted the heralded Rocket, Raghib Ismail.

"We've never had anyone around here with more ability," said Paterno. "He could be Curt Warner. Maybe even better as a running back. Faster. Could also be a number one draft pick as a corner. Could be a number one pick as a wideout."

That was Samuels's limitless potential. What Samuels also showed was indifference that rubbed some of his new classmates the wrong way. Said another resident of Little Pit: "Bobby Samuels is a woman." Paterno was a bit more kind, saying: "He's lazy. A baby. Anything hurts, he doesn't want to practice." While Samuels was injured some as a freshman, he also would skip a turn if a drill seemed overly rugged. When he had to be tough, others noticed, he was. The operative word was enigmatic.

The irony of his freshman year was not lost on Rudy Glocker. One of the reasons he'd turned down an Ivy League education at Dartmouth the year before was not wanting to put in an equal number of football hours and playing on a 5–6 team. Here he was at Penn State, a non-playing redshirt on a 5–6 team.

However, from those who lettered to those who played to

those who served on the foreign team during practice and experienced the formerly foreign humility of not playing, even to
the still-limping Ivory Gethers, there was hope. What Mark Graham had called "the first taste of everything" was over. It had
to get better. Right?

6

Non-Football Gravity

It had to change, and those who had sought brief breaks in their football-dominated lives during the fall of their freshman year found time for larger ones once the season ended. Even though there were still weight lifting sessions three times a week and frequent conditioning drills, football could be moved to a side burner in the winter and early spring.

Mark Graham wanted some peace from big-time college and big-time college football, even from the frequent big-time parties. He found it with the Harpster family a few miles beyond campus. Their house is a small brick rancher, white with green shutters and a small figure of a horse and buggy on the storm door that opens to a side entrance off the driveway. A lawn about half a football field long that slopes toward the road features a tall evergreen and a flagpole. A two-car garage sits about twenty-five steps away; across the two-lane road is a farm where some horses occasionally could be seen.

This slice of almost-rural America is not where one would expect an African American from hustle-bustle New Jersey to gravitate. Graham's relationship with Joe and Mary Harpster started when he was introduced to their son, Brian, by an upperclass teammate. Brian was a student at Penn State but had no association with football, and that was fine by Graham. With Brian and with his folks in this setting, he found welcome calm from the risks that he sought both on and off the field.

Because freshmen were not allowed to have cars, Graham rode to the Harpsters with Brian. They would wash cars, frequently turning the hose on each other, cook steaks on the outdoor grill, lie around on the lawn, or watch the horses across the road. Horses always had been appealing to Graham, but not these rather plodding farm types. He grew up not far from the Meadowlands and in the fifth grade fell in love with thoroughbreds and the quick money they could bring.

About that time, Graham also decided he wanted a career in business. Daydreaming in grammar school, he saw a skyscraper and near the entrance in distinctive and tasteful lettering was: Graham Enterprises. He wrote that, Graham Enterprises, on all his notebooks.

"After practice in high school," he said, "we'd go to the track. I liked the atmosphere, hanging out with my friends. I didn't like to bet favorites. I liked the thrill of a long shot, being able to win a couple hundred dollars just"—he snapped his thumb and second finger—"like that." Five hundred dollars was the most he ever won on a single race.

As a young entrepreneur in high school, Graham sold expensive vacuum cleaners and also manned the most nerve-rattling position in football: cornerback. If a lineman blows an assignment, only his teammates usually realize it; when a cornerback gets beaten for a long touchdown, everybody in the stadium knows it. All kinds of risky business fascinated Graham early at Penn State, including the controversial junk bonds favored in corporate boardrooms during the late 1980s. He wanted to major in finance.

Of his relationship with Joe and Mary Harpster, Graham, who lived in his native Jamaica until he was nine, said: "I grew up in a kinda mixed neighborhood [in New Jersey]. I never had a problem getting along with people, black or white. Clifton High had 3,000-plus students, but only about a hundred or so were black. This is so rural, so warm. Shows that you can't ever generalize about the way people think."

Among the situations with which Graham had to cope was the breakup with his girl back home, Migdalia. "She ended it mostly," Graham said. "She'd say: 'I don't know what you're doing up there. All those women. I can't sit here and thing about it. It's driving me crazy.' I could understand that, but it still was hard to take."

Rudy Glocker during the winter and spring sometimes got to thinking about big-time football and why it appealed so to him. There was the glory, no doubt, and the chance to excel and to have several million people acknowledge his good work. Glocker most wanted to please one fan, his father, whose presence even at pre-high-school games had meant more than Rudy had ever told him.

But there was an attraction beyond fame and showing a father that he'd raised a take-no-quarter son. And by the end of spring practice, Glocker had figured it out, had learned one of the universal truths about college football: what he'd joined was a fraternity. The largest fraternity at Penn State, with famous chapters in South Bend, Indiana; Tuscaloosa, Alabama; Los Angeles, and dozens of other places. Why do a relatively small number of football players join even the most prestigious Greek fraternities? Because they're already part of a better one.

"Most freshmen don't know many people," Glocker said. "By the time classes started here, I had 120 friends. Not necessarily friends, but guys who when I walked around campus would say: 'Rudy, how ya doin'?' We all got initiated at various times; we all went through summer ball.

"The harder the initiation, it's said, the more loyal you are to the group. Summer football practice brought that home. We as a team, 120 guys, went through a very difficult time. And the only people we were around were ourselves. There's a bond between people on this team, even with the ones you don't especially like, that nobody else has. And nobody ever will, because of what we went through.

"We don't have a special handshake. We don't have a hat to wear. We don't have a house. But it's a fraternity. Some of my non-football friends in fraternities don't like all their brothers, but when they meet on the street they stop and talk. Same here. There's a bond, and it extends to anybody who plays football here for a year. They don't have to prove anything to me. Or if they played at Oklahoma, Nebraska, Virginia, Pitt. They don't have to prove anything to me. You go through a couple of bloody Tuesdays. We're all in this thing together."

Outside the fraternity, Glocker was also quite active. He attended the weekly Bible study session not far from the locker room and taxed the energy of moderator Tim McGill with such questions as: "If God is omnipotent, why do people go to Hell?" Glocker and a few friends he'd met in his Shakespeare class attended plays and films on campus, taking turns going early to the theater and buying tickets for everybody in advance.

In contrast, Bobby Samuels and O. J. McDuffie were not inclined to explore much beyond the imaginary football-influenced triangle bounded by the dining hall, the Nittany living quarters, one or two nearby dorms, the workout facilities, and the building that housed the coaches' offices.

"I never realized until the spring that things like the Black Cultural Center existed," Samuels said. "Everybody [in class] always talked about going to the cultural lounge in the HUB [Hetzel Union Building, the on-campus social magnet]. I'd wonder what they were talking about. Where is the HUB? I didn't even know where the Creamery was [the Creamery being the ice-cream shop where Peachy Paterno sold briskly]. Other than classes, I didn't get to that side of campus.

"I don't think freshmen should live with just football players. [His roommate that first year had been McDuffie; in the adjoining room were Rosa and Adam Shinnick. Most of the nearby rooms in Nittany Hall were occupied by football players.] Out of four guys in the room, somebody always had a bad day of practice. Somebody was complaining all the time, which kept everybody at a low level. One day, I had a real good practice. I came home happy, and O. J. was packing. Said he wanted out of here."

That love-hate feeling about football among all the players became more intense when spring practice began in early March. Among the most worried was tight end Derek Van Nort, whose analytical nature was ideally suited for the engineering degree he was pursuing but was unable to comprehend what was coming at him in football.

"They don't tell me anything," he said, "other than what's needed to happen right there. They don't give us a schedule [other than the one for that day's practice taped to the bulletin board in the middle of the locker room]. That's a little frustrating. You came here kinda confused anyway. You're nervous. I have a lot of questions, just don't know what's going on."

At 6 feet 4 inches and 215 pounds, Van Nort was a possibility at several positions, and he was switched a mind boggling seven times during the three-plus weeks that constitute spring practice. He opened at tight end and then got moved to all four linebacker spots: Fritz and Backer (the inside positions, where Sarra was his coach), Willie and Sam (the outside positions, where Tom Bradley was his coach).

"Then five tight ends got hurt," Van Nort said. "Five out of six. So they moved me and a couple of others to tight end. With very little preparation, I played tight end for the spring game and thought: 'This is dumb. I can't do anything.' I talked with Joe. He felt I didn't have a good spring at all, and he had a perfect right to feel that. He said I'll be at outside linebacker in the fall. That's what I'd like to try. I want to contribute as soon as possible."

Unfortunately, the very day Van Nort saw some hope, or at least some position-order to his life, defensive coordinator Jerry Sandusky was saying: "He has some athletic ability. But he's got to get tougher if he wants to play here. He's been told that."

At the other end of the confidence spectrum was fullback John Gerak, who during one of those marches-from-hell scrimmages in Beaver Stadium talked about his future as though it were already scripted. Still breathing hard, his every pore an open faucet, he said: "Start the next two years, then the last year improve my position for the [NFL] draft. That's everyone's dream. I'll be disappointed if I don't get that far."

For others, the spring game was a jump start. Bobby Samuels was sensational. As a running back he gained 53 yards on 11 carries and scored a touchdown. He also returned two kickoffs for 58 yards. Donnie Bunch ran a punt 61 zigzag yards for a touchdown. Rich Rosa played quite a lot in the secondary and made two solo tackles.

However, the spring took a heavy toll on bodies. Rudy Glocker suffered a serious finger injury that also hampered his note taking in class. And Tom Wade became the third freshman to tear his anterior cruciate ligament, when he got caught up in a tangle of bodies and all of them seemed to roll against the knee. All ACLs are bad, but this was an ugly ACL.

"I'm lying in the dressing room, naked," Wade said. "My knee is hanging all over. Every which way. Todd Rucci is helping get my clothes." In his misery, Wade sensed another figure nearby, looked up, and saw an ashen-faced Paterno. "He told me he was sorry," said Wade. "That this was a terrible, terrible thing. Then he looked hard at me and said: 'Just stay on your grades.' As soon as he said that, he turned and walked off."

At this point, one season and one spring practice into their football lives at Penn State, the class soon would endure the third of the worst operations: reconstructive knee surgery, because Wade was headed for the hospital. Ivory Gethers was recovering nicely; he missed spring practice but was scheduled to return in the fall. The third player, 220-pound fullback Chad Cunningham, had missed his freshman season but returned for spring ball.

Cunningham's injury had occurred about ten months before he enrolled at Penn State, midway through his senior season at Divine Child High in Dearborn, Michigan. Like Gethers, no one had touched him. "I made a cut [running with the ball during a game]," he said, "and [the right knee] went out."

Recruiting changed dramatically after that. Michigan State canceled a visit; Michigan and Indiana stopped calling. Penn State was the only big-time school that kept its scholarship offer, although there was debate among the staff over whether to. Actually, there was a compromise. Cunningham paid his way the first semester; then what Paterno called "the scholarship clock" turned on.

Cunningham, Gethers, and much-publicized running back Blair Thomas were together often in the training room. Thomas had torn his anterior cruciate ligament during a no-contact, pre-Citrus Bowl drill in early December 1987, the very week Paterno was making home visits to Renkey and Cisar in western Pennsylvania.

Although he was the first of the trio to return to action, for spring practice his freshman year, Cunningham had not regained his previous form. And during a subsequent meeting with Paterno there was a blunt exchange, Cunningham asking if he would ever be more than a white-jersey practice player and the coach answering: Probably not.

The coach also suggested Cunningham might want to transfer. He emphasized that his scholarship was not being taken away. Cunningham was most welcome to stay, all expenses paid. If he wanted to play regularly, however, it might be best to go to a school that played a less demanding brand of football. Paterno offered to help find such a place; Cunningham said he'd stay.

Speed was the problem. No longer was Cunningham in the fast lane among runners, his time for 40 yards having dipped to a lineman-like five seconds. Cunningham thought the fifteen-pound increase in weight from the inactivity was his major problem and one that could possibly be overcome. Melt down; speed up. He'd be slim and faster by the fall. Swift enough to prove Paterno wrong.

"This year," he said during the summer before his sophomore season, "my goal is to make the travel team. The following year, it's to play more. I'll see what happens after that. I want to graduate on time and use the extra year to get a master's while they're still paying. I'm gonna prove, eventually, that I'm good enough to play here. I don't know when, but I will do that before I leave."

Cunningham and Gethers had time, during their rehab, to examine life without football. Each found it alluring. Cunningham participated in theater and found he enjoyed playing before crowds in other, though smaller, arenas. Gethers became the first football player in five years, and only the second since 1971, to pledge Omega Psi Phi. "I began looking at other things," he said. "I got to know people in my field [landscape contracting] and other students. It helped me get a wide view of why I'm here. You don't forget about football, but you realize it can go at any second to anyone."

Gethers would not be returning to full contact until the fall, and he was optimistic about his and his class's future. "We're the new breed," he said. "I think we'll be very good. I'm very confident about this class." He looked at the appropriate fingers of each hand and said: "I see one national championship ring here and another here."

For Eric Renkey, football went far better than school his first year. Renkey's grades were so lousy that Paterno excused him from spring practice. "Joe would write notes to me, about how he expects more of Eric," Marilyn Renkey said. "If anybody ever says he doesn't care about his players academically, I can give him a personal endorsement." Said Eric: "I expected the courses to be harder. I just didn't do anything about it. I made sure I got ten hours of sleep [to be fresh for football]. I had my priorities mixed up."

In truth, Renkey's grades were not the worst of his problems. With no football, he'd gotten a 2.44 his spring term and boosted his cumulative average to 1.80. The serious trouble was getting suspended from school, for the summer term, for a fight during a street hockey game in late January. "Kid hits me with his stick after I checked him," Renkey said. "I punched him. He swung his stick and missed. I punched him again."

Renkey almost got another suspension, for the fall term, which would have made him ineligible for his sophomore season. That was for his allegedly being part of a massive waterbattle in an area near his dorm. Mel Renkey got involved, and nothing came of it. "Every time I turned around," Marilyn Renkey said, "I was getting a registered letter."

Paterno's opinion of Renkey had changed drastically in the eighteen months since the recruitment process. "Talk about how you can misjudge a kid," he said. "I thought he would be right down the middle, straitlaced, probably a captain prospect. Fortunately, I've been around long enough to know kids like that grow up a little bit. Basically, he's a good kid, still has tremendous potential for leadership. I'm still feeling my way about how to get it out of him. He's not afraid of me yet. Somewhere down the line, I gotta scare the hell out of him. I'm trying to pick my spot."

In relation to his class academically, Renkey with his 2.44 was almost exactly in the middle. Eight players had two-semester averages above 2.5; seven had two-semester averages below the 2.0 C. Bobby Samuels and Ron Fields were among those under a 2.0. Along with Rick Sayles, Donnie Bunch, Adam Shinnick, Todd Rucci, and Ivory Gethers, they had taken some remedial courses.

"I think not playing has some affect on Bobby's grades," Robert Samuels said of that 1.93 first year performance. "If he'd been more at peace with himself, I think he'd have studied more. When he was in high school, his grades were better during the season than the off season."

Bobby's girlfriend, Laurie Mosely, who had attended a Penn State branch as a freshman, would be on the main campus the coming fall, and Patricia Samuels said: "He won't have the problem of missing her. Football will take care of itself, so all he has to do is study."

As spring melted into summer, none of the soon-to-be sophomores was on shakier ground than Donnie Bunch, and none was more wildly optimistic about the rest of the year than Rudy Glocker.

Two semesters and twenty-three official football plays into Penn State, Donnie Bunch in late June sat in an empty meeting room and called most of his collegiate experience a waste. "All I did about the whole time was worry. About problems back home. What my mom was thinking. What my dad was thinking. I thought I had to get home, had to get home. Then when I got home I thought, 'God, this is what I was trying to get away from.' Here, I pulled away. Did a lot of wrong things: going out drinking, hanging with the wrong crowd. I was around people who found themselves the same way. Sometimes I would get up at two o'clock in the morning and just walk. My roommate [John Gerak] thought I'd be doing something wrong, but a lot of times I'd just walk to this park not far away. Sit there. Try and find myself."

Bunch and Gerak were half of room 105 in Nittany Hall. The others, partially separated by a wall but sharing a sink, were Ivory Gethers and Derek Van Nort. Of all the freshmen, Bunch was the most outgoing, the most entertaining, the one most in need of attention, the one Paterno bent his rules for the most, and the one who seemed most out of place at Penn State.

"Culture shock," Van Nort called Bunch's transition from Camden to State College. "Not that he didn't belong here, but he was out of his society. His room was just an occasional place to sleep. There were times when the four of us, or two of us, or even one-on-one we'd seem to have a close relationship with him. Seemed like we'd be able to touch through to the real Donnie."

That was the responsible Donnie that his coach at Woodrow Wilson High, Greg Singleton, had seen. The Donnie who helped raise his five younger brothers and sisters for his troubled mother after a divorce his freshman year. The Donnie who made the honor roll and excelled in football. There was more than a modest amount of drinking in room 105. There was more than a modest amount of drinking among all the football players. "But I don't think there was more drinking among the football team than there was among the student body," Van Nort said. To get the notice he craved, Bunch sometimes felt he had to talk the loudest, growl the longest, and drink the most.

"Everybody's fighting like crazy to make sure he doesn't fail," said Paterno. "He comes from such a tough situation. Know what he does with his Pell Grant money [the government-sponsored grants for needy students beyond their scholarship aid]? He sends it home."

In a speech class that morning, Bunch had startled the other students. "We had to bring something to describe ourselves," he said. "I stood up and said, 'I see everybody coming up here with things. I knew about this yesterday and thought I wouldn't bring anything.' Everybody looked funny. I said, 'I wouldn't bring nothing because I'm on the verge of finding myself.' I told 'em about last year being a waste, but that I was planning on making a change. All my life I've wanted to get up in front of a big crowd and talk. Speak out to people and have them listen. And be respected by a lot of people. Cause I want to give something back to my community. Right now, my community is falling apart. Drug wars. Lots of families falling apart. It's hell back home. There's no way I'm going to waste three more years. Life is too short."

Bunch insisted that he had changed. Part of it, he said, was coming to terms with his father during a visit after the second semester. Another part was good counsel from academic advisor Don Ferrell. "DF was the one person here I could show my true side to," he said. "He told me to cut the BS. I thought maybe it was time to open up to him. As I was crying, I got the sense this wasn't the first time he'd experienced something like this. He didn't say anything, just came over and handed me a box of Kleenex. Then he hugged me. When I left his office, I had some doubts about his sincerity. I didn't realize how much he cared until I walked into his office a couple of days later. It was like I hadn't seen him in years. 'Where you been?' Then he hugged me again."

"These kids you reach out to because you want them to make it," Ferrell said. "You give a little special effort. There could be

several right directions for Donnie. I don't want to say any particular direction is wrong for him. But he will know when it's
not right. And if he backs off that and tries another, that's when
I've got him. I've seen signs of that.

"Just one helluva street-smart kid. Never been challenged academically [although Bunch's 2.07 average after one year was as
good as or better than eleven of his scholarship teammates].
When he's challenged too much, he doesn't like what he has to
do to perform the challenge. So he'll sulk and back off. Will
come up with excuses not to do it. Will make up his mind he's
not going to class. Just drop out of sight for two or three weeks.
Then he'll come back and be apologetic, shed real tears, and say
he's going to make it up. He'll be all right for a couple of weeks
and then—bingo!—he's right back into it."

Rudy Glocker was outrageously bold as he and his parents sat
on the back porch of their colonial-style home in late June. An
older sister, Regina, was swimming in the nearby pond. His injured finger had come around nicely; his 3.00 grade point average, considering the difficulty of his classes, was admirable. He
planned to graduate ahead of schedule, in three and a half years.

The rooming experience with Sayles had been difficult but
also enlightening. Glocker once noticed a paper that Sayles was
preparing. It was on the controversial Proposition 48, and how,
in Sayles's mind, it was unfair. Glocker always had taken the
opposite view, that if an athlete could not muster one of the
minimum standards of the rule, 700 on the SAT, he had no
business being in college.

They later talked, though in no great depth, and Glocker came
away thinking that the SAT might, as many insisted, be racially
biased. "Now I understand why sometimes the black students
get together and say they're being discriminated against. It was
good for me to see how he thought. Joe did a very good thing
when he put me and Ricky together."

In Glocker's mind, he, Ricky, and all the others soon would
be flying. "I've got to make my goals so high I'll almost never
reach 'em," Rudy said. "If I don't make All-American next year,

I'll want to be the first tight end in Penn State history to be an All-American three straight years." He paused and smiled: "There may have been one, so I'll be the first three-time All-American from Bucktown."

"We're gonna be 12–0 this season," he suddenly declared. "We're gonna go to the Fiesta Bowl or the Orange Bowl and win the national championship, cut and dried. If I don't think that, and if everybody on my team doesn't think that, it's not gonna happen. We'll be in every game, and sometimes the ball takes funny bounces. I see nothing that can stop us. We're gonna win, and I'm gonna be part of it. Next year and the next year and the next and the next. Every year, we're gonna be 12–0. We're gonna win forty-eight games in a row."

PART THREE

TO HAVE AND
TO HAVE NOT

7

Wake Up the Echoes
—In Happy Valley

Halfway through their five-year allotted time at Penn State, the class had not achieved Glocker's beyond-grandiose expectations. The Nittany Lions were not unbeaten for the second straight season, as he'd dreamed; they had won fifteen of twenty-one games, however, or very close to the success rate that had gotten Paterno a place among college football's immortal coaches. And as the buses pulled into a Holiday Inn near South Bend, Indiana, about 9 P.M. on November 16, 1990, the chances for still more glory loomed ahead. Late the next afternoon was a chance to knock off the top-rated team in the country, Notre Dame.

At the meeting after the team had checked into the hotel and completed its snack, Paterno was as animated as anyone had ever seen him. That was a slight surprise, because the coach seemed to crackle most before games that didn't mean nearly so much.

This is why: Players stoke all the necessary competitive fires themselves for the genuinely important games. It's for the teams that are better than his players *think* they are that Paterno hauls out his motivational tools. So he was more likely to be on edge before, say, Boston College than a nationally televised showdown with Southern Cal.

But Notre Dame was special for Penn State. Off even the big-game charts and into the stratospheric mist where rivalries get very personal. If there was one football program Penn State in the early 1990s felt even slightly inferior to, it would be Notre Dame's. In their drive under Paterno, the Nittany Lions left cleat marks on every independent in the country except Notre Dame. Before it started playing in the Big Ten in 1993, Penn State had a schedule that included every geographical area. It frequently played to a national television audience, but Notre Dame had its own *network*, NBC.

One of Penn State's important athletic officials once watched an early season Notre Dame-Michigan game on television in the Beaver Stadium press box. All logic insisted that Notre Dame beating the top-ranked Wolverines would help the Nittany Lions' chances of winning the national championship. The official realized that—and then consulted his heart. Finally, he turned to a half-dozen others and said: "Sorry. There is no way I can root for Notre Dame."

Also, many of the players to whom Paterno spoke in the large Holiday Inn ballroom, quarterback Tony Sacca among them, had said no to Notre Dame and its top salesman, coach Lou Holtz. Knowing the depth of feeling in this room and among nearly all Penn State's fans, Paterno sensed a close-to-unique situation. His players just might be too anxious. Emotional to the point of being tight. Possibly intimidated about performing in one of football's shrines. So the coach tackled some Notre Dame lore, saying, "Knute Rockne won't be out there to put a spell on you." That broke the tension. Everyone enjoyed it when the old coach got passionate. He went on, "The Four Horsemen aren't going to be around. Nobody's gonna put a curse on you. I don't believe in ghosts, so you shouldn't believe in ghosts. The best eleven will win."

"I was in the back of the room," said Todd Burger, "and I thought about that. Incredible. A speech I'll remember for a long time. Everyone laughed. I sat in my room later and told some guys that was the best specch ever."

Unfortunately, many of the guys who had started at Penn State with Burger were not with him in the large meeting room to hear Paterno at his spellbinding best and to anticipate one of the biggest of big game. Four more had dropped out—boom, boom, boom, boom—some thirteen-plus months earlier, before the opening game of their second season.

First to leave was the cutup Adam Shinnick, a 190-pound defensive back whose enduring memory was the time his mountain bike flipped and tossed him, pancakelike, over the handlebars and onto the parking lot outside Nittany Hall. His brief career at Penn State seemed a continuum of injuries: two hamstring pulls and two ankle operations. His father, Don Shinnick, had been a linebacker with the Baltimore Colts and an assistant coach with the Raiders and Patriots, so Adam had been closer to high-pressure football than any of his classmates.

During much of May and early June 1989, Shinnick's mind had been in stay-or-go flux. Less than three weeks before quitting Penn State, he had been enthusiastic about coming back, saying: "I'm going to put everything in the past. Make like it never happened. Start all over."

The start of Shinnick's physical decline took place less than a month before freshman camp at Penn State. While doing a 40-yard sprint near his home in suburban Boston, he felt a twinge in his right hamstring. Then, during his first workout at Penn State, about the time Ivory Gethers was going down with the knee injury that would sideline him for a year, Shinnick pulled up short in a no-contact drill and grabbed that hamstring.

"I took about a week off," he said, meaning a week without hitting, but not a week away from football-related activity. At Penn State the walking wounded do not take part in full-contact drills but are involved in some sort of exercise each practice. Like everyone else, they come in full-pads uniforms. However, each injured player wears a jersey with a cross on it. A red cross means no practice; a green cross indicates practice with care. Almost everyone rides one of the several stationary bikes set up at one end of the field.

When Shinnick returned to all-out contact, he said, "I just really ripped the crud out of that hamstring. Took a month and a half off and practiced the rest of the season. Never 100 percent, though I rehabbed over the winter. But I went into spring ball not 100 percent. A mistake on my part; a mistake on their part for even letting me participate in spring ball. But I wouldn't say that to you the day we started spring ball."

Shinnick's reflections came nine months later, at Cal-Berkeley, where he transferred, in part, to be close to brothers Josh and Joel, who lived in northern California. It was his first day off crutches from the second of two ankle operations.

"Now that I have a chance to look back," he said, "I can say I never should have gone out for spring ball [with the hamstring not completely mended]. Second day, I broke my ankle. I came up and made a tackle and there it went. Just got caught up on the artificial turf the wrong way. The feeling of sitting on the sideline with an ice bag on my ankle the second day of spring ball was one of the lowest feelings I've had in my life. I was in the hospital three nights."

Shinnick said he fooled lots of people, including himself, by firmly telling Ron Fields and other close friends he would return for his sophomore season and then informing defensive coordinator Jerry Sandusky shortly thereafter of his decision to transfer. About one point, however, he was certain.

"I do blame Penn State for part of this. I blame them for my hamstring. For forcing me back into practice. Not really forcing me but suggesting I should be out there. Not coming up to me and saying: 'You're not going to go today.' But coming up to me and saying: 'How do you feel? Why don't you go out and try some things on it?'

"You can't say that to a freshman. Maybe a fifth-year guy or a fourth-year guy who's gone through the system. But you can't go up to someone like me, because of course I'm going to say: 'I'll give it a shot.' They'd even say: 'When you feel something, stop.' Then it's too late. It's too late with a pulled hamstring. Maybe I'm the only case where a hamstring has taken so long with them. But that's not the point. I had a meeting with Paterno and he said: 'We like what you did at 80 percent.' So even he knew. If he knows I'm 80 percent, then why in the heck am I out there? It just didn't make sense to me."

"Adam had ability," Paterno reflected. "I know he was really not a hypochondriac, but one of those kids everything had to be right for him to do it. George Young [the general manager of the NFL Giants and a former aide in Baltimore with the Colts] told me his father was the same way. Came out with so much protective equipment you couldn't see his eyes. Had tape all over him. There were no hard feelings about him wanting to see another trainer. [Adam had consulted the Patriots trainer.] They're young. Some haven't been hurt much. I think you've got to baby 'em a little bit. Not too long, but you baby 'em some."

"When Adam came here," said academic advisor Don Ferrell, "he had a lot of mouth, a lot of opinion, and knew nothing. He just wanted to be heard, to talk. Adam Shinnick is one person I grabbed by the Adam's apple in the dining hall one day and said: 'You open your mouth out of context one more time, and I'm sending your ass home.' He looked at me, didn't know whether to say something back, decided not to, and Adam and I have been best friends ever since. He's the only kid who before he left brought his parents by to meet DF, telling them: 'I want you to meet the guy I had trouble with.' "

Next to leave, although that was farthest from his mind when Shinnick said his good-byes, was Derek Van Nort. He had gone to summer school at Penn State, had worked out with other football players also getting ahead academically, and had been optimistic during the early days of fall camp.

"I had felt I was over the reason I did poorly in the spring, over my initial shock of being in a defensive position," he said, meaning outside linebacker. "Spring gave me a lot of stress. I wasn't ready for it. I should have been, but I wasn't. After the [early August] drills in shorts and helmets, I felt very positive. And some of the coaches at first were very happy, seemed pleased with my progress.

"Then it seemed to get progressively more negative. At first,

I was in [second team] red. Two to four practices in red and then to [third team] maroon. Nobody gave me a reason. I just figured I wasn't playing so well, some technique I hadn't gotten a grasp of. Like taking the tight end on one-on-one. Instead of explaining how to do this, they just yelled. They'd yell at you once, telling you what to do. Next time, if you didn't get it right, they said: 'Let the other people do it. Get out of there.'

"Having *big* fullbacks and *big* tight ends coming at me unnerved me. So I wasn't confident enough to be tougher. I got frustrated. Started getting in the frame of mind I was in in the spring. Very uncomfortable. My stomach started turning. I was on the edge of getting sick right before every practice. I just realized I could probably make it through the season, and improve, make special teams, and possibly play. But I looked ahead and saw spring again. And I knew I'd never be able to go through spring again. It was useless."

Van Nort shared this insight with his roommate, Ivory Gethers, whose reconstructed knee had healed and strengthened to the point where his being able to play in the fall seemed certain, and with several other classmates whose rooms were nearby: Tony Sacca, John Gerak, Todd Rucci, Chad Cunningham, and a walk-on with whom he'd become close, Bill Spoor. He also spoke with his parents, who supported his decision. All that remained was to tell Paterno. Van Nort set up a 9:30 A.M. meeting in the coach's office. Except that when 9:30 arrived, Van Nort was in the football building, but Paterno was not. Van Nort went across the street to the east locker area, where the coaches also have a locker room. Paterno was not there either.

"The thing that unnerves you about that," he said, "is that he yells at people a lot for missing appointments. If you miss an appointment with the team doctor, he'll make you get up in the morning and run. [Those sessions, for relatively minor offenses, were called the Breakfast Club.] You missed a meeting *he* called, and he'd probably hang you out to dry." Van Nort got Paterno's home number from defensive coordinator Sandusky and called. "He seemed impatient," Van Nort said. "Okay, I'll meet you in the locker room right before practice." Practice was at 2:00. He said he'd meet me at 1:30.

Paterno was cordial, Van Nort felt, but preoccupied. "We talked for about ten minutes, and it wasn't about anything. It was me trying to get hold of myself more than anything. I would have liked to have been comfortable talking with him a longer time, so he understood why I was leaving and maybe so he could explain some of what they'd done.

"I'm sure a lot of what they did was on purpose, put me in high-pressure situations to test me. So many head games. I was going up against a tight end once, and Joe says: 'Van Nort, we're not going to waste our time with you.' That's all a test, to see if you rise to the occasion. A lot of what you see on the practice field is negative, to see if you'll get mad and get better. Some people respond to that. I didn't. I took it as: 'If they didn't feel this way, they wouldn't be telling me this.' I would like to have been able to talk to him about that." But there wasn't time.

The coach and his latest former player shook hands. Even more awkward was Van Nort then having to walk through a locker room filled with players, many of them close friends, preparing for practice. Some of those to whom Van Nort had confided spoke briefly to him as he moved toward the exit door near the training room and then walked out and away from football.

Van Nort left Penn State football but not Penn State. "That first day without football was a relief, big relief. Not having to go to practice. Not having to think about leaving or staying. A very big weight off my chest. No doubts about having made the right decision. When I was in football, there had even been inner stress when I was away from it. During summer vacations, I'd keep thinking: 'Should I be lifting? Should I be running? Should I be resting?'

"A couple of weeks after I left the team, I realized what kind of [financial] pressure I'd put on my parents. I felt some guilt. They still were supportive [as well as able to pay for his education without it being too much of a stretch]. That made me feel better. I got over that.

"When the season began, there was a freshman [Reggie Givens] at the outside linebacker position I'd been playing. He's very good, but I realized I would have had a chance at playing. But every time I think like that I remind myself of the reasons I left. I go back to the thoughts I was having before I left, and I assure myself I made the right decision.

"I have a lot more direction in my life. I've added five credits, so I have eighteen now. Plus I've been into karate since the summer. I'm not into Engineering Science yet, but that shouldn't be a problem. [Not with a grade point average of 3.30.] Before, I felt like I'd put my life on hold, so I could have the experience of playing big-time college football. My father had said you could always go back to school, but that you could never go back and play college football again. That's a once-in-a-lifetime experience."

Late in the fall Van Nort admitted a part of him still had not gotten over football. "Maybe if I'd gone somewhere else, there might not have been so much pressure," he said. "North Carolina State, or Northwestern. I don't know if it would have been better, but I'd like to have given it a try. I play racquetball once a week with Chad Cunningham. To get the energy out. And it offers me a form of competition I enjoy. The thrill of winning and the agony of defeat that everyone enjoys so much."

Van Nort's racquetball partner, Chad Cunningham, had been running faster on his mended leg during preseason. But the practices kept becoming more and more nerve-racking. Also, Paterno was especially biting; at one point during a workout inside Holuba he said to Cunningham, "Maybe you ought to take up music." Another time, when another running back hit the wrong hole, Paterno yelled: "You've been watching Cunningham too much."

Even so, Cunningham had been promoted to second team green at fullback when he, too, decided to quit. "I was thinking: 'I don't see how I'm going to do this for four years. My heart's not into it.' I said this would be my last year, but a couple of days later there was no way I could do it anymore. I started hating the game. I think it was just my time. It's like an NFL player who can't do it anymore. He retires. That's what I did. I retired at twenty. It was nothing Joe did. He got on me, but that was a test. He said they needed me to be the third fullback."

As Van Nort had done, Cunningham consulted his parents. They also could afford to pay his college expenses and supported his decision to quit. Unlike Van Nort, Cunningham had the good fortune to walk into a vacant locker room after his meeting with Paterno. But that didn't make leaving any easier. He had hoped to beat the 1-in-12,000 odds and make it in big-time college football. He had hoped that awful ACL tear would not take away the tenths of a second so vital to a running back at this level.

Cunningham was not a quitter, yet he'd just quit what not so long ago excited him as nothing else. He walked into the empty locker room and headed toward what soon would be his former football residence in Little Pit. He grabbed his knee brace and a pair of tennis shoes. He considered taking the nameplate over his locker as a souvenir, but didn't. It stayed atop an empty cubicle for several weeks. As he was leaving, the head equipment man, Tim Shope, called his name and said to take care. Tears in his eyes, Cunningham pushed open the door to his next life.

Several weeks later, and slightly heavier because of less vigorous activity, Cunningham said: "They allow me and Derek to use the weight room, but I make sure to go by when everyone is out at practice. The knee changed my whole life. If it hadn't gotten hurt, I wouldn't have been here. I'd probably have gone to Michigan." But Michigan backed off after that serious ligament injury, same as everyone did except Penn State. "Seems like I fit here," he said. "Being away from home helped me grow up."

When Paterno spoke about Cunningham, his voice was far softer than when he'd yelled at him. The coach had humiliated an earnest, enthusiastic, hard-working youngster, and now, in his office, he was explaining why. Sitting on the sofa near his desk, Paterno leaned forward, as he sometimes does when trying to be gently persuasive.

"Another good kid," he said. "I kinda felt bad about getting on him. But there's an old saying: 'I hope I don't lose your friendship because I tell you the truth.' I just felt he had to make up his mind, one way or another. I hate to see them waste their time. Van Nort was another one. I challenged him about how tough he was. I told him: 'I don't know if you're tough enough.'

"But that doesn't mean he lacks courage. It's a different thing. People don't understand that football-tough isn't a question of courage. It's a question of whether you want to do those things over and over. You've heard this spiel before, but I've got very serious doubts whether big-time football is worth it. It was a lot better when we didn't have weight rooms, and the other stuff, when the Mike Reids would walk away when the season was over and you might not see 'em for weeks. Now we've got winter workouts, and you've got to do it to compete."

The fourth player gone well before the class's second season, 1989, began was the one everyone felt sorriest for: Donnie Bunch. He'd been kicked out of school because of his fifth drinking violation. Also, although this was not related to his dismissal, Bunch had tested positive for marijuana during one of the team's random drug tests. The concern for Bunch was that, unlike Shinnick, Van Nort, and Cunningham, all he might have to fall back on were the sad streets of Camden. Or worse, for when I met Bunch on September 6, three days before the 1989 season opener, he was in Centre County Prison. He'd admitted stealing $11 from the bedroom of a woman disabled with cerebral palsy.

"Who told you I was in jail?" he said. His voice was soft, his clothes the same lavender-and-black-striped shirt, jeans, and sneakers that he had worn when he had entered the lockup eight days earlier.

"Don Ferrell."

"I thought so."

The academic advisor had been as close as anyone at Penn State to Bunch, and earlier that day he had said of the player who had worn number 1 for the Nittany Lions the season before: "We know what environment we're pulling kids out of. We know what their backgrounds are. When we bring them here, we're saying we can change that." Bunch and Penn State were not close to the Paterno-tailored fit Bunch's high-school coach, Greg Singleton, had so desperately wanted. "He felt like a fish out of water," Singleton said. "He was out of his element."

Bunch was a city kid suddenly placed in a laid-back environment. Even in a crowd, he sometimes felt alone. Out of place. His meager wardrobe seemed out of fashion, although roommate Gerak said Bunch rarely washed the few clothes he had. Bunch craved attention among new teammates equally gifted at football and equally glib at parties. He got it by being louder than loud, wilder than wild.

Now and then during that first year, Bunch would be summoned to Paterno's office and charged with being too much the party boy at such-and-such a fraternity. Bunch would deny all, the coach would shoot back with some details, and the player, guilty as charged, would hang his head and say: "Right." Soon Bunch would go back to the same behavior.

"We've got to be careful we don't oversell what we can do for these kids," Paterno said a few months after Bunch was gone. "We should do a better job than, say, Maryland, because we're in the country. I should know more about what's going on. They can't hide in as many places. Most of the time, I know pretty quickly. But that doesn't mean you can solve all the problems."

Bunch admitted the $11 theft, recorded in Common Pleas Centre County Criminal Division as case no. 1989–1007. Jessie McKinney's room in the Nittany Apartments had been near one where Bunch had gone for hot dogs and beer. According to court records, teammate Sean Love, who earlier had borrowed a match from an aide to McKinney, testified: "Donnie Bunch went into Jessie's apartment and stole the money." The theft occurred on June 30, five days before Bunch's nineteenth birthday.

Bunch was sentenced to costs and restitution, plus one hundred hours of community service, in addition to the eight days he'd served in a jail whose bars were painted the same shade of dark blue found everywhere else near Penn State.

"I just ran out of money," Bunch said. "I know all I had to do was ask [for that kind of pocket change]. I just got tired of asking."

"It's a sad, sad situation," Singleton said. "I sent Donnie money a couple of times. I don't know if he sent his [government-funded] Pell Grant money to his mother, but I suspect it very strongly. Donnie's mother has very serious problems that dig deeply into the family's economic situation and togetherness. Donnie loves her dearly. She loves Donnie. But she's almost helpless. She needs more than what Donnie could give her."

"If he'd been a non-athlete," said Paterno, "I could have said: 'Here's a couple hundred bucks.' I couldn't help that kid [because of strict NCAA rules against loans]. Nothing I could do for him. Talk about being a victim of the system."

Players in Bunch's financial squeeze had been topics of considerable debate within the NCAA for years. Those pushing for some sort of stipend, usually $150 or so a month, do not undervalue the current wage scale: a free education. Still, they argue, a system that generates tens of millions of dollars ought to at least provide walking-around money to those who help generate it.

After Bunch was released, I drove him back to State College. During the eleven-mile drive he said: "I don't mean any harm. How will people perceive me? How will people look at me? My dad said he would come get me, but then called and said he was working on the truck. The truck can't handle the hills [that must be negotiated to get to Penn State]. I understood where he was coming from."

Near the apartment where he was staying, Bunch got out of the car. He accepted $20 and said he would continue working at the paving company job that someone in the football office had arranged for the summer. The next day, Ferrell was fuming. He had spoken with Bunch that morning and said: "I've trusted you seven times, and you've let me down seven times. You've got to show me."

Bunch's dismissal from school came too late for his picture and bio to be pulled from the 1989 Penn State football guide.

Still listed as number 1, his smiling face was near the upper-left corner of page twenty-two. After noting that he had returned four punts for 98 yards, including a 61-yarder for a touchdown, in the spring game, the out-of-date blurb said: "Bunch is expected to be more of a factor in the air game this fall."

Nearly a year later, in his grandmother's apartment in Camden, Bunch said: "Joe lectured me. Lectured me. Lectured me. Lectured me. And lectured. He'd call me in there every two weeks. Toward the end of the year, it was two times a week. He gave me a lot of chances. He liked me a helluva lot when it came to football. He wanted me to get my act together. I'm spoiled as hell. My dad would give me anything. My grandmom, too. Spoiled from day one. Still am. Joe wanted to make me a man. I really respect Joe. I have no resents. Just regrets."

Bunch and his girlfriend, Audrey, had met me at a convenience store. We walked about a half-mile, past weeded areas with broken-down cars and brick buildings with boarded windows to his grandmother's well-kept ground-floor apartment. She was away. Bunch had gained about twenty pounds since he'd danced into the end zone during the 1989 spring game and looked slightly puffy in a red tank top. He and I sat at the kitchen table; Audrey stayed in the living room. Now and then a relative would drop in and quickly leave.

"When I came [to Penn State]," Bunch said, "people would look at me and say, 'Camden thug.' I'd say the place wasn't that bad, but everybody expected me to be a hood. I think I portrayed it. I'm a people pleaser. If I didn't get attention, I wasn't satisfied. I love attention." Even bad attention.

It was also in his grandmother's apartment, many years earlier, that Bunch had become enamored of Penn State football when he watched its weekly highlight shows on television. Now he was catching his former teammates on TV. Just the other day he'd caught a glimpse of Rich Rosa in a game. Also Tony Sacca, the emerging quarterback from nearby Delran. Sacca triggered Bunch's recollection of his official visit to Penn State as a senior in high school. The official visit was a time for families to share a new experience. Owing to the trouble within his family, Bunch for his official visit had caught a ride with the Saccas.

"I think about O. J. [McDuffie] a lot," said Bunch, about 150 miles from where the Nittany Lions would be practicing later that Thursday. "I was able to open up to O. J. He related to me a lot, tried to keep me straight. And Ivory [Gethers]. He stayed on my butt: 'Not gonna tell you what to do; you're your own person; you know what you gotta do. Just do it.' Like that. Ivory's a great guy."

Bunch had a job stocking shelves in a store. Temple had made inquiries about him transferring, but nothing came of it. Bunch said he was thinking about enrolling at Glassboro State next year. Its coach, former Philadelphia Eagles linebacker John Bunting, had contacted him. "I hate to see him home," coach Singleton said, "because I know that every time that boy turns on a television [and sees Penn State play], it hurts him. Because he knows he could be playing. He knows that. He has that ability."

Bunch recounted a vivid memory from high school: "Playoff game. Cold. So cold that day. Seemed like I was running [as the option quarterback] in slow motion. My hands were cold. I couldn't cry. And I'd wanted to cry so bad after that [loss]. I scored the first touchdown for us. At halftime, we went in this room and got cursed out from A to Z. I was sitting there like: 'So? It's cold.' Know what I mean? You can call me any name in the book; I can't move. One time, I ran the option and saw this big gap there. But I couldn't turn like I wanted. I turned, and as I turned, the hole closed. Just like that."

8

Tony's Time

Just like that, or so it seemed, Donnie Bunch and the six others who either had left the team or left the team and Penn State had become memories largely blurred by the fog of time. Fresh and clearly in focus the crisp morning of November 17, 1990, were specific assignments for top-ranked Notre Dame in a few hours. Especially for Tony Sacca. By now, late in their third season, the class for football purposes had boiled down to this: Sacca and everybody else. Although Leonard Humphries also was a starter, at cornerback, Sacca had become the central player. During the class's thirty-three-game experience, Sacca had drawn the most attention and had played the most minutes. He also had endured the most humiliating put-downs by Paterno.

Sacca had almost transferred more than a year earlier, before his sophomore season, when Paterno on the eve of preseason drills in 1989 announced which players would be wearing which colored jerseys for the first practice. When Sacca was set for second team green, he was furious. He had replaced the injured Tom Bill three games into the 1988 season and figured: "I beat him out."

Paterno disagreed. True, sophomore Sacca had more ability, but redshirt junior Bill was the more complete quarterback. Sacca could throw; Bill could lead. Sacca drifted in practice; Bill learned. Sacca would don green for the fall; Bill would be in blue. "Tony doesn't understand what it takes to be a leader," Paterno said before camp started. "He's a likable kid, a bright kid. But very, very immature. Somebody asked him in the spring if he'd be here for summer school [when quarterbacks and receivers frequently work on patterns and timing]. He said: 'You're kidding?' And he thinks he should be playing.

"The best thing that could happen would be for Tommy Bill to be very good and for Tony to be willing to sit out a year. Then he'd have three great years. We would not be a great football team with Tony at quarterback this year, unless he changes his whole attitude. Pays attention to details. For instance, so many things happen at the line of scrimmage, and if you've got a quarterback comfortable there, you don't have to block everybody. Tony doesn't know what the hell is going on."

In one respect, however, this slightly immature nineteen-year-old knew exactly what was going on. Of all the players in his class, Sacca was the one with the most leverage. He could actually make demands on Paterno. And he knew it.

"During the first week," he said, "I wasn't allowed to run the first team at all. So on Sunday, after the first scrimmage I went to Jim Caldwell [the soft-spoken quarterback coach] and said if I'm not gonna get the shot to win the job, I'm leaving. I hadn't told my dad yet. But I had told my high-school coach. Three days later, I was splitting time with Tommy with the first team [and both were wearing blue]. He'd run the first half of practice; I'd run the second."

Was Sacca serious about leaving?

"Definitely."

Sacca's high-school coach, Jim Donoghue, was willing to help Tony. But before discussing the option of transferring to another school with Sacca, Donoghue asked a friend on the New York Giants coaching staff whether Tony should leave Penn State.

The pro coach said Tony should stay put. "He said playing was such a big thing," Donoghue recalled. "The pressure of games. He said the pros would teach him whatever was necessary. He said 99 percent of all college quarterbacks are not prepared for the pro game anyway."

Sacca stayed and tough-talked his way into what he wanted. His position coach, Caldwell, thought that cockiness was a facade, observing, "He has a lot of defense mechanisms. When you're young and inexperienced, you try and hide those fears. Try and act as if you're not afraid, not scared. In the situation he was playing in last year, as a true freshman, in front of 85,000 fans, I know he was shaking in his boots a bit."

"They said I'd play against Virginia [in the season opener]," Sacca said. "Hopefully, a couple games into the season I'll be starting. I knew they weren't going to start me in front of Tommy. But I figure I should see a lot of time. Everything's like a big secret around here. They don't tell you anything."

As Sacca expected, Bill started the 1989 season opener, at home against Virginia. Only a few insiders at Penn State expected anything but a Nittany Lion victory. The year before, at Charlottesville, the Cavaliers had lost to Penn State by twenty-eight points; the week before, in the Kickoff Classic on national television, Virginia had lost to Notre Dame by twenty-three points.

One of those closest to Penn State football, however, remarked, "Both [Virginia coach] George Welsh and Joe kill their guys in preseason. The players don't have their legs for the first game. But they do for the second." With those fresh legs, Virginia scored a 14–6 upset in what turned out to be a national coming-out party for itself and one of its players. Within a year the Cavaliers would shoot to the top of the wire-service polls. And the wide receiver who scored both touchdowns, 6-foot 5-inch Herman Moore, would be the tenth player chosen in the 1991 NFL draft.

Sacca replaced Bill briefly in the first half and misfired on both of his passes; Bill played the entire second half and was diplomatic about the time-sharing policy at quarterback. Sacca was blunt, saying to reporters, "It affects him and it affects me. If you're not in there for a majority of the plays, it's tough to get into a groove . . . There were should-have-beens everywhere. The first half we weren't ourselves. We choked."

As the lead bus pulled into the side entrance to Beaver Stadium for game three against Boston College, Sacca once more was in the seat across from Paterno that the starting quarterback occupies. Three months earlier, the coach had said Penn State would not be a great team with Sacca at quarterback. Now he had no other choice than to turn the offense over to Sacca. After being falling-down drunk and arrested a week earlier, Tom Bill had been suspended from the team and enrolled in rehab.

It was a day shy of one year since Sacca as a freshman had leaped into emergency action for the injured Bill. This time, he had several days instead of several seconds to prepare. And the game plan for Boston College was similar to the one that had worked under Bill in a 42–3 victory over Temple the week before: run, run, run, and then run a little bit more.

The entire game was played in wind and rain, with the temperature under 50 degrees. And Penn State's defense was splendid, limiting the visitors to 121 yards and one field goal in the first half. Under normal circumstances, this would have allowed the Nittany Lions to gain a substantial lead; this day, the Penn State offense actually had two fewer yards and three fewer points than Boston College at halftime.

"I couldn't throw a wet football," Sacca said, "and [All-American senior] Blair Thomas couldn't get going," And an offense that could score no points in the first half actually deteriorated during the third quarter and the first series of the fourth.

Toweling his hands, blowing on them, nothing was working for Sacca. And anger was beginning to surface among Penn State fans with a sense of déjà vu. With just under eight minutes left in the game, the Nittany Lions were on their 33 yard line and still behind by 3–0. Was this near-anniversary for Sacca also going to be a repeat loss to an underdog? Was Boston College about to become this season's Rutgers?

Sacca had thrown fourteen passes and completed just three. On first and 10, however, he hit one for 33 yards. Then Thomas gained 16 yards on a draw play. But on first down at the Boston College 17, State lost the ball on a fumble. Doom was piling on gloom.

With 3:49 remaining, Penn State got the ball back one more time and advanced it to the crunch-time dilemma of fourth and eight from the Boston College 21. Paterno called time. He considered a tying field goal, then changed his mind, saying later: "I said to Fran [Ganter], 'Aw, nuts. Let's go for it. We're never going to be any good if we're going to start hoping they're going to make a mistake.' We just decided to suck it up and go for it."

The go-for-it decision was what Paterno called "kind of a gimmick play," a fake screen pass to Thomas and a pass to the tight end over the middle. Sacca took the ball from center, dropped back, and faked a short pass to Thomas. Turning, Sacca was surprised to find a defender all but blanketed over his intended receiver, senior tight end Dave Jakob.

Trailing an inferior team, down very likely to his last play, and with the teammate to whom he was supposed to throw this rally-extending pass on fourth and a bunch not close to open, the situation seemed hopeless. Instinctively, Sacca pulled the ball back toward his body and started running. Slipping in the muddy grass, dodging a couple of tacklers, he kept the drive alive. Needing 8 yards for a first down, Sacca scrambled for 13.

"So the place is going wild," Sacca later recalled, "because it's the first time we've done anything all day." Panting, exhilarated as he returned to the huddle and accepted slaps on the back from his muddy teammates, Sacca had shown the improvisational skills that made him so highly coveted. All he'd done, however, was extend the drama.

Now first-and-victory from the Boston College 8, Thomas got half the yardage necessary on the first play. He then bulled for two more yards and, on third down, for another. On fourth down, the Nittany Lions still were a yard shy of the end zone. Surely, Thomas would carry one more time. He would not.

Paterno figured he had the Eagles set up for a slight variation of "21 Shoot." That was the play-action rollout that almost exactly a year earlier had failed in the final moments against Rutgers, Sacca's pass just bouncing off Jakob's fingertips in the end zone.

This time, Sacca set the ball in Thomas's belly and then took it away. Boston College fell for the fake. This time, Sacca didn't have to throw. This time, he ran into the end zone and quickly was mobbed. The clearing block for the winning touchdown came from guard Greg Huntington, whose effort could be seen in the picture that the school paper ran of the pivotal play. Forty-four seconds remained for Boston College to rally, but a long pass on third down was intercepted. Although Sacca had provided the crucial play and the winning touchdown, his teammates decided the publicly humiliated Bill needed the bigger boost and presented him with the game ball.

As the season moved along, the Nittany Lions kept winning *with* Sacca, though not necessarily *because* of Sacca. But the coach's attitude had changed in an encouraging way. The previous year, when he was starting as a freshman, Sacca would be called to Paterno's office once a week because the coach was so concerned about his young quarterback's preparation for games. This year, Sacca had been there once, the week after Tom Bill was suspended. The chat was a this-is-your-team confidence builder. The key point: Take charge.

This was eight weeks into the 1989 season. With a 19–9 victory over West Virginia, the Nittany Lions were now 6–2. They could have been unbeaten with Sacca at the helm had the snap from center on Penn State's last play against Alabama not been high. That led to a blocked field goal from the Alabama 8 yard line and a 17–16 loss.

Sacca never threw more than twenty-one times in any of his six games; he completed half his passes just once, in a 17–0 shutout of Rutgers. Sacca's main role was taking the ball from center, handing it to someone else, usually Thomas, and then getting out of the way. Penn State ran 51 times against Rutgers, 62 times against Syracuse, 53 times against Alabama, and 52 times against West Virginia. It was no wonder that McDuffie, now a starter at wideout, felt so lonely out there on the flank, waiting for passes that mostly did not come.

In his sixth start, against West Virginia on Homecoming, Sacca threw a 31-yard touchdown pass to tight end Jakob. But he could manage only one other completion in thirteen tries. He also had one huge worry: Tom Bill had returned from rehab and was in Paterno's good graces once more.

The next game was against Maryland in Baltimore, and it started splendidly. The Nittany Lions quickly forced a punt, and an eager McDuffie returned it 20 yards. From Maryland's 38, Sacca completed two short passes, and Thomas ran six times. Then came fourth and goal at the 1 yard line, and with it "21 Shoot" and the damnedest bit of bad luck anyone at Penn State could ever remember.

Sacca's brief career so far had been tied to the "21 Shoot" play that had him fake a handoff inside and then roll out, either keeping the ball or passing it to the tight end in the end zone. The play had failed a year earlier, and Penn State lost to Rutgers. The play had worked six weeks earlier, and Penn State beat Boston College. Here, as Sacca completed the fake and turned to his right against Maryland, it seemed as though "21 Shoot" was going to be successful once more. Nothing except green grass was between him and the goal line a few yards away. The sixty-two-year-old former quarterback on the sideline, Paterno, could have scored. Sacca didn't. He slipped, and Maryland took over on its own 4 yard line.

Normally, this sort of madness struck the Terrapins. They had lost twenty-four straight times to Penn State, often under similarly strange circumstances. This was an early indication that their luck today would be different. The Nittany Lions could have grabbed a 7–0 lead and deflated Maryland sooner than usual had Sacca kept his balance. They didn't; the Nittany Lions could have gotten a 3–0 lead early in the second quarter, but missed a field goal from the 27 yard line.

So it went. Although Sacca accumulated decent enough stats (6 for 12 for 45 yards), he was shackled to the sideline three minutes before halftime. Bill was 8 for 16 for 119 yards and ran 8 times for 42 yards the rest of the way. The offense produced thirteen points, but the defense yielded thirteen points, and Maryland celebrated the tie as though it were a victory in some minor bowl game.

That was the first of three games in which Sacca was yanked in favor of Bill. Penn State emerged with one victory, one loss, and one tie. The loss was to a Notre Dame team that ran a staggering 71 times for 448 yards in Beaver Stadium; the victory was against Pitt in the regular season finale as Bill mustered the drive that led to the winning 20-yard field goal with seventeen seconds left. Sacca's hopes were sinking.

Sacca reflected on his two-year career: "You take a beating mentally. It's tough to come in and play right away. Pressure. The media gets on you because your stats aren't that great [his two-year percentage, on 283 passes, was a less than mediocre 38.9]. You're in awe of everything. Joe lots of times thinks I don't care. That's not right. Talk to anybody. The pressure'll get to you, even though you don't show it. It's always there and you always have to worry about it."

Sacca had received about a half-dozen letters a week from Penn State fans. Most were supportive. One of the few he saved was unsigned and read: "You're a bum. Tom Bill's back, and you're gonna be riding the bench the rest of the year." Sacca was standing by his locker when he produced the letter. "Pretty funny," he said, knowing it was anything but.

The writer of that cruel letter did hit on a point that, after his second season, increasingly bothered Sacca: Bill still had another year of eligibility. How would that affect him, halfway though his college career? If Bill was going to get equal treatment in the spring, Sacca was going to transfer. He thought he'd earned the number-one spot. A meeting the day of the annual early

December football dinner between Sacca and his parents and Paterno was arranged at a restaurant, Elby's, along one of the main roads into town.

"Joe picked me up that morning in front of the football office," Sacca said. "On the way out he got lost, didn't know where Elby's was. I guess he was a little nervous. He kept calling me John [Sacca's younger brother was named John, and Penn State was recruiting him]. He asked me directions, and I had no clue. But we ended up there."

During the meeting Paterno told the Saccas that he'd wanted to give Bill a shot, because he might not be around much longer. "That basically made sense," Sacca said. "Tommy had problems, and Joe wanted to give him some direction in life." The end result as a consequence of this meeting was that in the Holiday Bowl, a tight game during which he was luckier than good, Sacca played every second.

For the class, their first bowl game brought both fun and another unwelcome reality. The squad arrived in San Diego a week before the December 29 game in an upbeat mood. Practices were less stressful than usual, and there was enough time to enjoy one of the country's loveliest areas.

Still, youngsters who had had to adjust to life away from home a year earlier when they first arrived at Penn State were hit with having to spend Christmas in a hotel. "I missed my family, not having Christmas dinner," said Rich Rosa. "I was eating Chinese food on Christmas. But being together made things easier. Me and O. J. having pillow fights. Dumb stuff."

Fullback Bob Daman, whose back troubles were serious enough for this to be the final game of his career, mentioned the Christmas sadness and that he and several players had pizza on Christmas to a reporter from his hometown paper, Ron Christ of the Harrisburg, Pennsylvania, *Patriots-News*. Christ printed it.

Paterno was livid and berated Daman in front of the squad. "That's hell," Daman said. "Getting your name brought up in front of everybody. I swear, every time I go to a squad meeting, I'm scared that he's going to call me."

Truth be known, there had been a worse scolding a few

months earlier. Paterno in his autobiography, *Paterno by the Book* (1989), made references to "a few arrogant young jackasses in study hall who had alienated a lot of other athletes from other teams because they go in there and kind of shove people around and take over the computer and do anything they want to do, including play games on them when other people want to use them for study. Because they're football players, they're big shots. I'm mostly talking about some of the freshmen." One of those he'd fingered in front of the team was Daman.

Even though the absences from home and the quality of food on Christmas had been more than a slight irritant to many, it was not hard to get excited about the game. On the field against Brigham Young, the Nittany Lions offered a show the likes of which their fans had never seen. This was Sacca's game, and he completed half of his 20 passes for 206 yards and 2 touchdowns. One of those touchdown passes, the 52-yarder, was an acrobatic, juggling reception in the end zone by senior David Daniels that would remain vivid in everyone's mind for years. Sacca was halfway home. Two seasons down, two more to go.

Over breakfast in early December 1989 Paterno had all but given Sacca the quarterback job. During the spring of the class's third season, he applied all the pressure he could muster to make sure the junior quarterback was up to keeping it. The coach would prod; the quarterback would resist. Finally, during a lackluster practice on the hot afternoon of April 17, 1990, Paterno erupted. Alone among 40,000 empty seats halfway up the west side of Beaver Stadium, Paterno noticed more nonchalance and yelled: "Sacca, you're the biggest quarterback flop in Penn State history!"

Say what? There had been other verbal volcanoes, but none that had spewed down from Paterno and over the players quite so heavily. Nearly all the starters at some point in their careers had been told by Paterno, loudly and in front of their peers, that they couldn't possibly play for Penn State. They had played, of course, and played well. Two of Paterno's coaching foundations were: Fear me more than any opponent; rarely will your games be more pressure-packed than your practices.

Still, even by Paterno's lofty sarcastic standards this outburst was wicked, and it got repeated by the players. Among themselves and to Tony, and always in as close to Paterno's high-pitched voice as possible, they would say, "Sacca, you're the biggest flop in Penn State history!"

In truth, Paterno had been even harsher in private with Sacca. "I'm about fed up with him," Paterno said a day later. "He's gonna drive me up the wall. I had a real tough meeting with him yesterday. He's one of the toughest kids I've ever had to coach at that position. Very immature. Silly. I got my message across, that he's not doing anywhere near well enough."

Paterno was livid with Sacca's career-long completion rate, an embarrassing 39 percent. He'd told Sacca during that meeting, "I got you off the hook [with the press] by saying it was because of the [long, low-percentage] passes we throw. But John Shaffer, who had a lousy reputation [and who also was the quarterback on Penn State's last national championship team], threw 200-some passes and had a 55 percent completion rate. I've never had a guy who didn't throw 50-some percent. You're a 39 percent quarterback because that's what you are. Inconsistent. You're lousy. We can't win with you."

As he later talked out of earshot from Sacca, Paterno calmed some: "He should be coming off a redshirt freshman year. I think he did as well last year as we had a right to expect. I felt sorry for him. I was trying to protect him, and he believed some of that crap. He's got to get better each day. Better touch. He can't be bouncing those short passes. And he's got to read [defenses] a little better. The honeymoon's over for him. He's gonna get better or be an awfully unhappy kid. I think he'll respond. If he doesn't, he'll just be another of those big high-school flops." By a stroke of supreme coincidence, Paterno's scolding had come on Sacca's twentieth birthday. Next morning the quarterback was outwardly low key, as usual, but did admit: "When he says some of that stuff during practice, I'd like to grab him by the throat. But you have to let it go in one ear and out the other."

Because of injuries, Sacca played quarterback for both teams in the annual Blue-White spring game. The night before, he walked into the room shared by cornerbacks Mark Graham and Leonard Humphries and cheerily announced: "Interceptions for sale." That was Tony, still refusing to treat football as more than a game.

However, late in the summer of 1990, a couple of weeks before preseason camp, Sacca surprised his teammates and Paterno by driving up from Jersey and joining afternoon workouts. Maybe some of what Joe had said was finally sinking in. Or maybe Sacca realized, before his next-to-last season, that time was running out on him.

The opening-game test for Sacca in 1990 was at home against Texas, and he was buoyant and optimistic. Hosting Texas and playing Southern Cal, Alabama, and Notre Dame on the road was the most ambitious schedule in Penn State's history. Even better for Sacca, some of his pals had caught up with him on the field.

"Last year," he admitted, "it was me and Tommy, and the team was sorta divided. This is my team now. This year, most of the guys out there are my good friends. It's different. It's like back in high school again. A lot more comfortable."

As he had been for most of 1989, Greg Huntington was one of Sacca's key blockers. And O. J. McDuffie caught Sacca's first completion of 1990 for fifteen yards. Nothing unusual about that. However, it was a surprise—and a most pleasant one—that Sacca's second completion of 1990 was to Rick Sayles. After being bounced from outside linebacker to tight end to outside linebacker and back to tight end, the first member of his class to wear a blue jersey was making a contribution. At long last. Three years later. And still at a pencil-thin 215 pounds.

"Joe always thought I would choke under pressure," Sayles said. "He always thought I thought about the crowd, those 85,000 people. He'd dwell on that. But when I play, I can't even hear the crowd. It's just like me and a bunch of guys. I hear the pads, but I don't hear the crowd. The crowd has no effect on me whatsoever."

At first, Sayles, on his break-through play, had thought Sacca was going to run. "He threw it at the last moment," Sayles said, "and when he did, everything got solid. I saw the ball coming and said to myself: 'If I miss this, I'm going to the locker room.'"

With a Texas defender in his face, Sayles made the catch. Then he twisted loose, got two blocks and gained thirty-four yards in all, to the Texas 15, before being hit from behind and brought to earth. He and an upperclass teammate, fullback Sam Gash, exchanged high-fives. That was about as good as it got, however. The Nittany Lions missed a field goal on that drive and later kept coming just close enough to make the 17–13 defeat especially vexing. The hurry-up offense on Penn State's final drive was out of sync, and Sacca's last-ditch pass in the end zone had no chance.

Sacca was in a daze as he walked off the field. His eyes searched the stands but made contact with nothing familiar. Texas players, overjoyed with the upset victory, came by and tapped his shoulder pads.

For the game, Sacca's father had arranged for nearly six dozen tickets for family and friends. That meant that Tony had to be more polite after a bitter defeat than he might have wanted. When he emerged from the dressing room, he was gracious to everyone from back home. Several youngsters wore blue and white jerseys that on the back read: "SACCA 19." He signed autographs and posed for pictures. He was not discouraged, he said, but did let his guard down for a moment. When someone shook his hand and said things would get better, he said: "You think so?"

During game two, Sacca got the better of the quarterback with whom he'd been compared his senior year in high school, Todd Marinovich. But Marinovich's team, Southern Cal, scored a 19–14 victory in the Los Angeles Coliseum.

"Tony has gotten a lot better as far as detail goes," said offensive coordinator Fran Ganter. "We constantly quiz him on the field during practice. We'll say: '40 pitch. What formation do we run that from?' This year, at least he guesses. He's right maybe 80 percent of the time, which for him is good."

This was damning with faint praise, and Ganter knew it. He said: "So far, we've probably run ten plays [in two games] from formations that are incorrect. Tommy Bill has outperformed Tony in practice. But we're looking for the future."

The future included five straight victories, and an appearance by Tommy Bill during the final one, against Alabama in Tuscaloosa. On Wednesday of that week, Penn State's new president, Dr. Joab Thomas, dropped by. Thomas had been under football-related pressure when he resigned as president of Alabama in 1988, and most of the Nittany Lions knew it. So they recognized the special significance of Thomas's unusually crude parting words: "I hope you kick some butt." Only Rudy Glocker noticed that Thomas seemed a dead ringer for the new associate justice of the Supreme Court, David Souter.

Saturday, October 27, 1990, was cloudless and warm in Tuscaloosa as Penn State prepared for the critical late afternoon match with Alabama. Despite their early season losses, the Nittany Lions still had a chance at a major bowl and a Top 10 finish in the polls. Thomas could not have scripted a better beginning, because Penn State used an interception on the third play of the game and took a 3–0 lead on a 34-yard field goal by freshman Craig Fayak.

However, Sacca was just 3 for 9 the first half and twice missed very open receivers. Early in the third quarter, Bill began to warm up. When Sacca was intercepted on the third offensive possession after halftime, he was benched. Sacca had been yanked in the ninth game last season and then in the tenth and again in the eleventh. This season, the hook was coming earlier.

Bill wasn't a whole lot more effective, with four completions in nine tries. But the up-and-coming Fayak was, kicking field goals of 50 and 34 yards. On the last play of the game, Leonard Humphries intercepted a Bama pass, returned it 34 yards, and Penn State won 9–0.

"Not a bad move, going to Tommy," Sacca admitted. "But it wasn't really my fault. We weren't prepared for their scheme.

Their front people were good, and we knew that going in. What they did was bring in seven defensive backs and mix up the coverage. They would bring everybody on a blitz. Or they would back everybody off. Really caught us off guard, I think."

Ganter had admitted that Sacca was not the best at thinking at the line of scrimmage. And the offensive line was young and not overly talented. Still, Sacca admitted: "It bothered me more than last year. Because I'm a junior now." Here was Sacca, near the end of his next-to-last season, seemingly going backwards.

That rare lack of self-esteem had a carryover effect on Sacca the next week. During a 31–19 victory over West Virginia in Morgantown, Bill came in with nearly seven minutes still left in the first half. "I had no plans to go with Tommy at all," Paterno told reporters.

Privately, Sacca suggested otherwise. "Joe brought me in Tuesday [after the Alabama game]," he said. "He told me there was no quarterback controversy. This and that. He says I'm start-ing to get a little careless with things. Stupid things. I'm sitting there thinking: 'Here we go again. This guy's starting to put the pinches on me again.' He said I'd be starting, but he was sorta telling me I'd better watch out. I went completely off the shelf. Totally bugged myself right out.

"I went out [against West Virginia] and didn't even play. Just so mad at everything I couldn't get involved in the game. [Sacca threw incompletes on three of the four passes he tried.] Tommy came in and played well [completing 7 of 12 passes for 99 yards, throwing for one touchdown and one interception, and running 5 yards for another touchdown]."

Next came Maryland at home, and another meeting for Sacca with Paterno early in the week. "He said being pulled had noth-ing to do with the incompletions, that I looked like I wasn't into the game. Which was right. I told him I wasn't happy about what happened the week before, that I was concerned that what hap-pened last year would happen again. He was pretty good about that. Said I was still starting and that helped me out a lot more. I relaxed and said to myself: 'Let's go out and play ball.' "

Well, the first half against Maryland was statistically horrible for Sacca: 1 for 5 for 11 yards. Penn State had a 10–10 tie, thanks to a 74-yard interception return by Leonard Humphries for a touchdown. (In addition, Humphries for the game made three tackles, one for lost yardage, and defended four passes.)

At halftime nearly everyone in Beaver Stadium figured either Bill would open the third period at quarterback or that Paterno would leave Sacca in but limit him to nothing but handoffs. Surprisingly, Sacca said he didn't think at halftime he'd be benched, but in no way was he prepared for the strategy that Paterno used.

The previous week Sacca had gone 1 for 4 and been yanked about halfway through the second quarter. Sacca this week was 1 for 5 the first half. So what did Paterno call immediately after the kickoff? A pass. And a long one. Sacca completed it, to David Daniels for 46 yards. Paterno soon drifted even farther out of character. On fourth and 21 from the Maryland 30, the suddenly reckless coach called for another pass, and Sacca drilled the ball to Daniels for a touchdown!

"He's weird like that," Sacca said of his coach. "The whole third quarter, we threw. Sometimes he gets so stubborn, doesn't want to throw. Sometimes he says, 'Keep throwing.' You never know what the heck he's gonna call. So erratic." Also unusual for Paterno was the postgame flattery he heaped on Sacca. Only Paterno appreciated how far Sacca had come and how much he had gone through, privately and publicly, and he said: "He makes the kind of plays that very few people can make. The ball is downfield like a shot. He's got a shot to be really great. With all of his problems in the last two games, he came through in the third quarter. I think that shows he's got something in him that we haven't seen before."

And then, a week later, his confidence surging, Sacca found himself in the third quarter against Notre Dame shaking his arm in pain. Mild panic broke out on the Penn State sideline. Bill moved to start warming up. "Joe on the sideline is like: 'Get him out of there,' " Sacca said. "I see Tommy warming up, and I say to myself: 'What a time to go! I'm having a good game, and I can't even hold the football.' "

The suddenly shaken Sacca had completed a thirteen-yard pass for a first down at midfield when his right thumb got jammed against a defensive lineman's helmet. Having experienced an almost identical rush of pain in high school, Sacca immediately thought: "It's broken."

For an instant, he was angry and dumbfounded. Here for the plucking was the top-rated team in the country, but with more leaks in its pass coverage than a Congressional subcommittee. Sacca had the Nittany Lions, still trailing by 21–7, on the move, and his damn thumb might be busted.

But Sacca stayed in the game and immediately gained 12 yards on a quarterback draw. After a penalty he threw terribly toward Sayles and then brilliantly to the other tight end, upperclassman Al Golden, for 14 yards and a first down on the Irish 26. Maybe the thumb wasn't broken after all. But the drive was, ending with Fayak missing a 39-yard field goal. Penn State still trailed, 21–7.

As Notre Dame moved the ball, Sacca on the sideline was asked by concerned medics and coaches about the injury. Thinking he was lying, he said: "Just jammed it. I'm all right." And when the defense intercepted a pass and returned it to the Irish 11 yard line, Sacca was back on the field.

Very soon fabled Notre Dame Stadium became for Sacca and Sayles a field of dreams. In his two seasons prior to this one Sayles had been on the field exactly twice; Sacca less than five minutes earlier thought that he'd suffered a season-ending injury. On third and 10 from the 11, however, Sacca and Sayles hooked up for a touchdown.

It wasn't as easy as it seemed. "The defender just missed getting the ball," Sayles said. "It hit my hands and bounced up. I knew I was in the back corner of the end zone, nearly out of bounds. I wanted to keep my feet where they were, as I was bobbling the ball. Finally, I got it. I looked down, and I was in there. I could do nothing but rejoice." Notre Dame 21, Penn State 14.

Midway through the fourth quarter, a short Sacca pass was turned into a 24-yard gain by redshirt senior Terry Smith, and

Penn State had a first down on the Notre Dame 34. A screen pass fetched another 20 yards. Sacca then rolled right and threw back left, to a wide-open Golden at about the 3. Golden dragged a tackler into the end zone. Tie game.

From the Notre Dame 7 yard line with slightly more than two minutes to play, Todd Burger nearly dropped Fighting Irish quarterback Rick Mirer for a safety on first down. Later, on third and 8, Mirer overthrew his receiver, and senior Darren Perry intercepted the ball and returned it 20 yards to the Notre Dame 19.

Paterno decided he'd rest his fate with a field-goal team that, all season and all game, had been anything but stellar. A running play on first down and a Sacca sneak on second down set up what would be a 34-yard field goal with eight seconds left. This was as tense as sport gets. And the moment, quiet literally, was in the hands of a storybook character. Trotting onto the field, about to launch the ball from his center position for one of the more important kicks in Penn State history, was the fellow who had been the team manager two games into the season: Bob Ceh.

Ceh was in this unique position because the regular snapper, senior Mark Lawn, had been involved in a fight at a State College eatery the night after the season-opening loss to Texas. "Disorderly conduct," Lawn said the police report read. "Nothing more than if I'd played music too loud in my room. I did not throw a punch, but there was a disturbance and we were thrown out. Then the cops arrived. No one was convicted of anything."

The incident made the papers, and Paterno reacted. Lawn normally would have been suspended from the team immediately, but there was a problem: Penn State's two back-up snappers were injured. So Paterno the following week said to Lawn: "We aren't going to lose a game because you made a mistake." Lawn snapped against Southern Cal, and Penn State lost anyway. And although Lawn remained on the team, he never snapped again.

Until the Lawn incident, Ceh had been perfectly content, at 6 feet 4 inches and 230 pounds, to be among the largest managers in college football. He'd been the regular snapper for his high-school team but had done nothing more than fill in at practice for Penn State. Now he was about to become vital at an important, albeit overlooked, position.

Ceh had been flawless in his seven-game performance and had been featured in most of the country's major newspapers and many of the major television sports shows. But this was a situation that staggered the imagination. He recalled, "I kept telling myself: 'This is too big to screw up. You've come too far. You've done too much.' I looked at the defensive players as they came off the field [after Perry's interception] and I thought: 'You're coming off with a victory.' "

Up in the press box, State's sports publicity chief, Budd Thalman, put the proper tingly touch on the situation about to develop: "We've got a shot at beating the number one team in the country. On national television. And our destiny hinges on a guy who started the season as a manager [Ceh] snapping the ball to a walk-on [Bill Spoor], who is holding it for a freshman [Fayak]."

Snap . . . hold . . . kick.

Good!

In the postgame delirium, Todd Burger's line rose above all others: "Best high I ever had." Back at Penn State, about 1,200 fans headed to dark and empty Beaver Stadium and tore down the goalpost at the south end of the field. This treasure was part of an impromptu parade that wound its way about campus, with a brief stop at Paterno's home.

9

Inside Joe's Head

One of those in the hysteria after the Notre Dame upset, but not part of it, was Penn State's biggest dreamer, Rudy Glocker. He had dared imagine even grander scenes and wanted more than a small share of whatever attention they attracted. When the Nittany Lions were jumping and hugging in the dressing room twenty or so minutes after the team's biggest victory since winning the national championship five years earlier, Glocker was several hundred miles away, stuck in traffic back in State College. His latest lousy luck was the dreaded torn anterior cruciate ligament suffered during a no-contact drill on, yes, the artificial turf in Holuba Hall.

"I wanted to be there, especially since the tight ends [Sayles and Golden] did real well," he said. "Especially since I hate Notre Dame. But I just try not to think about those things. Too depressing. I'm glad we won; I just wish I'd been part of it. That's the way the cookie crumbles."

Glocker's experience at Penn State late in his class's third football season had been the most complete. He was one of the few players who was exploring parts of student life that did not include sports. Plays. Speaking at public schools, working with the Special Olympics. He had spent nearly all of a Christmas vacation bumping around New Hampshire with a friend doing research on David Souter, associate justice of the Supreme Court, for a political science class.

Like a great many in the recruiting class, Glocker also learned early on that there was something worse than being yelled at by Paterno. That was not being yelled at by Paterno. Overlooked, if not quite ignored. Never able to upgrade from the backup-colored practice jerseys that meant playing time in games would be limited to a few special-teams runs for some and to all but being stitched to the bench for others.

Only a few months after airing his ambitions ("I want to be the first tight end in Penn State history to be an All-American three straight years") on the family's back porch, Glocker near the end of the 1989 season had been agonizing about playing time.

Glocker thought he'd at least be a starter by then; instead, he had been all but groveling for playing time. And that playing time itself could be measured in seconds. A game might last up to three hours, but a play, from snap to tackle, takes no more than fifteen or so seconds. An entire series—first down, second down, third down, and punt—might consume no more than one minute of meaningful action.

The following spring Glocker had said to walk-on John Hamm, a non-scholarship player beaten around in practice: "This is kinda silly, this college football. Think about it. You practice, do all this stuff. Let's say you play four years, and I mean really play. I'm talking about lettering all four years. You might spend a whole hour of your life out there actually doing something. We've already spent twenty-five hours this week getting ready for it. If you studied that much for a test, you'd be a straight-A student. I played a little over fifty plays last year. I spent a good 2,000 hours preparing for those fifty plays. Those fifty plays lasted a time-space of what? Fifteen seconds a play, or about 750 seconds. Twelve-plus minutes. Anything else we'd do and spend that amount of time on it someone would call us nuts." Glocker smiled. After listening to that irreverent look at college football, the walk-on soon quit.

His fifty plays, those precious few seconds of action in his sophomore season in 1989, had been no laughing matter for Glocker. "I'm not getting a whole lot of satisfaction now, tell you the truth," he had said. "Lots of times it doesn't seem like it's going anywhere. Seems like I'm going backwards. Against Temple, I was the second tight end. I'd go in on double tight end situations. Next week, I just wasn't."

There had been a battle for playing time involving himself and upperclassman Al Golden on the kickoff team before the Alabama game that assistant coach Bill Kenney had resolved in favor of Golden. Later, Glocker said that Kenney told him: "You know, I didn't think it meant that much to you."

Glocker was incensed. "Didn't mean much!" he thought to himself. "I gave up a lot of things to come here. An Ivy League education. Maybe West Point. I came here mostly for football. And you didn't think getting in a game on national television, even for a few seconds, didn't mean anything!"

Glocker was faced with what seemed a major contradiction. As a student, he would have no qualms at all about going to a professor and getting to the heart of a problem. As a football player, he was loathe to approach assistant coach Kenney with his frustration.

"I think it's that you always want the coaches to see you as being sorta like a rock," Glocker said. "Something like: 'I got two strikes against me. So what?' I think you're always trying to make 'em think you're someone they just can't beat down. Trying to be tough. It's sort of a mind-set. I think you want things explained, but you don't want anybody to know that. Maybe it has to do with the macho image."

But Glocker was still dedicated to his football career. "I try not to complain, because that makes it worse. Some fault is with the coaches; some fault is with the players. If a coach asked if you're all right, you could say: 'Life really sucks right now.' And he'd say: 'Oh, work on it.' Because I don't think they really want to know. But yet they also really want to help you if they can.

It's a Catch-22 thing. I think a lot of things should be explained more. I've always felt better if I knew where I stood."

In their second winter at Penn State, Glocker and some of the others had been beginning to find themselves in a former life. Walking around campus, bunking in the dorms and hanging out at parties were high-school seniors on their officials visits. Recruits, potential pledges to the fraternity of football. This time, Glocker and his buddies were the wise old sophomore hosts.

The last two years Glocker had shepherded two offensive linemen, Bucky Greeley and Tom Prawdzik, whose homes were relatively close to his. Each trip around campus reminded Glocker of his own official visit, and that one of his lasting memories of Paterno had been meeting him while hung over.

"It was at breakfast," Glocker said. "Randy Cuthbert, who ended up going to Duke, was on my left. Rich Rosa was across the table. I'd been up till three-thirty or four-thirty the night before. Gotten very drunk. I'm drinking orange juice. Water. Joe pulls up a chair between Randy and me. I turn, and all I can remember is that Joe's glasses were so thick it looked like his eyes were in the backside of his head."

Also while squiring his bright-eyed recruits, Glocker found himself not being very candid about Paterno and about his football experience.

"The part I remember about Bucky is him asking me questions," Glocker said. "I sat there and gave him the same thing people had given me." He recalled some of the innocent Greeley's questions, how he responded to them and what he actually thought:

How bad is practice?

Not that bad. ("I'm sitting there thinking: 'Practice is drudgery. It really is.' ")

How long is practice?

Two hours. ("I used Joe's math. Joe's math is that practice starts at stretch. Before that, we have early work, get a little warmed up. Then we do punt returns, kickoff returns, a couple of drills. And then comes stretch. I gave him the old two hours, which is true from stretch. But a lot of times we practice twenty-five minutes before that.")

What about getting up for breakfast?

Not all that bad. Kinda makes you feel good about yourself. ("I mean, I'm saying all this. And Bucky's a high-school kid. Impressionable. He doesn't know a thing. He probably had some kind of faith in me. I'd been here for two years.")

Does Joe ever yell?

Not all that much. ("I answer that kinda differently from most players. In high school, I got yelled at all the time. Constantly. So I don't think Joe yells all that much. I really don't. I remember [upperclassman] Sean Love telling me as soon as Joe crosses that line and steps onto the practice field he's a different man. He runs around for two hours and then comes back down to being a good guy.")

What are my chances of playing as a freshman?

Good. ("I felt like I was a coach. Sure, you can play as a freshman, if you have a really good fall. Which is true. Of course, your chances of that happening are slim. I'm saying just what people told me.")

As snow jobs go, this wasn't exactly a blizzard. But Glocker took pride in being an upfront, stand-up guy. "I kinda felt sorry for Bucky," he said. "I looked at everything through rose-colored glasses. Bucky asked me some good questions, and I gave him the old no-answer. Before I was a freshman, Joe sat in my living room, on a Wednesday night. I don't remember the date, but he said: 'You know. I think you can play for us next year.' Looked me right in the eye. I'm not saying he lied. I could have, if I'd had a really great fall. And he said I could be a heckuva first-round pick for somebody some day. I gave Bucky the same line."

Glocker had been redshirted as a freshman and had suffered a serious finger injury during the next spring practice. In the fall of his sophomore year, he had been on the field fewer than fifty times and had been livid when an assistant coach denied him what would only have been a couple of additional plays on the kickoff return team.

All this Glocker failed to mention to recruits, because his loyalty to the fraternity/team had become stronger than he'd imagined. Greeley and Prawdzik came to Penn State, and Glocker was glad.

There was this ironic topper: At about the time new recruits were making their final decisions, Glocker during a tag drill in Holuba Hall tore the anterior cruciate ligament in his left knee. He would not even suit up for the entire 1990 season.

There were few advantages to Glocker's season without football in 1990. He hadn't played as a freshman, either, so his football bottom line after 1990 would be this: three years at Penn State, about fifty plays, maybe eleven minutes of action in for-real games. What that inactivity did allow Glocker, however, was a unique look at Paterno.

Glocker and Bob Daman, whose career had ended a year earlier because of back problems, served as undergraduate assistants during the 1990 season. It was routine for players out for the season with injuries to earn their scholarship keep in some football-related way. One might work in the weight room, another with academic advisor Don Ferrell, and so on.

By assisting the assistant coaches, Glocker and Daman could remain close to the team and also get an occasional glimpse into how decisions were made. Part of their duties were "running the cords" on game day, following assistant coaches around on the sideline and making sure phone communication with other assistant coaches in the press box stayed constant. That offered entree to seat-of-the-pants strategy by Paterno and his aides.

"So interesting," Glocker said. "You know why we do things. As a player, you're so far removed. It opened my eyes. I can see why coaches are so nit-picky. Because little mistakes really do make a difference." Glocker recalled a play during the Southern Cal game and said: "If Rick Sayles had put a little more effort into the block, [the Nittany Lion back would have scored instead of being downed nine years short of the end zone]. The tackler came all the way across the field to make the play."

What had Glocker gleaned about Paterno?

"Before, I was under the impression Joe was a good coach and a great recruiter. He has talent stockpiled. I used to think he didn't use it very well. Now, my view is: He takes a great deal of talent and utilizes it to the fullest. And that's hard, because he's so picky. He's got to find people who can do the job the way he wants it done. Like we're doing a punt drill. I never fully grasped before how deadly important those plays are. You can indirectly blame the kicking game for both our losses. Texas blocked a field goal and partially blocked a punt. And we missed a field goal [from chip-shot distance]. Lost by 17–13. If we hadn't missed that early field goal against Southern Cal, we'd have been down just two near the end and could have played for a field goal at the end instead of having to go for it all.

"As a player, you know this is important. But you're there with the coaches and you hear: 'What the hell's going on out there?' It really sinks in. I've learned a lot about Joe's philosophy: fewer penalties, fewer turnovers win. Texas and Southern Cal proved that. A field goal to him is like taking the other guy's rook. He's playing a game of chess. Take three here and three there and three more. Pretty soon, he's got nine points. The other guys get a touchdown, and they're still losing. One of the things you hear about Penn State is: 'How did they score so many points?' They just build real slow."

What takes so long to build can crumble in an instant, and so Paterno after the glorious victory over Notre Dame in 1990 was worried about a letdown the next week against Pitt. His concern was justified, for midway through the fourth quarter the Nittany Lions trailed by a point. Sacca had been inconsistent, though spectacularly so, throwing two interceptions but also running six times for 115 yards.

After a 59-yard kickoff return with eight minutes left, Penn State ran three times and then Sacca threw 16 yards for the go-ahead touchdown. His pass for two points failed, and the defense twice had to protect a 22–17 lead. It did, the most dramatic play being an interception by Leonard Humphries at the Penn State 9 yard line.

After Penn State's ninth straight victory Paterno was reflective.

About Sacca, he said: "Everybody doesn't understand how complicated it is to play well at quarterback in this day and age, with all the different blitzes and blitz control and all the checkoffs at the line of scrimmage. It takes a while. Tony should be a redshirt sophomore now. It he were a redshirt sophomore, he'd be right where you want him."

The resurgence after those season opening losses to Texas and Southern Cal vaulted Penn State into the Top 10 nationally and into the inaugural Blockbuster Bowl, where the opponent would be another Top 10 team, Florida State.

For the first time under Paterno, however, it appeared as though a class would go through Penn State without at least a shot at the national championship. Still Paterno said: "If we beat Florida State, with 10 wins in a row, I think we can yell as loud as [anyone can]."

Before the bowl game, on December 6, there was a squad meeting to determine what each player should receive for Penn State winning the Lambert Trophy, symbolic of eastern football supremacy. The vote was for CD players, but the captains overruled the majority and decided on clocks.

Cracked one player: "It'll have Joe's picture on the face." Another, in his best high-pitched Paterno-voice: "Four o'clock. Time to lift." The year before, the players had received rings. On his, Eric Renkey's last name had been misspelled.

In the Blockbuster Bowl, anticipation of what Paterno had hoped would be as much yelling as anyone for the national championship started going sour when Florida State grabbed a 10–0 lead midway through the first quarter.

One of the early Penn State standouts in the game was Leonard Humphries, the quiet, pencil-thin cornerback whose season had been smashingly productive. Humphries had become the best cover man in a secondary ranked among the top ten in the country. He intercepted six passes in ten regular-season games. One of them was on the last play of the 9–0 victory over Alabama. Two more saved the Pitt game.

Humphries easily had made the transition from mostly kick coverage to starter. Having returned a blocked punt (all of two yards) for a touchdown against Texas as a sophomore, he returned an interception seventy-four yards for a touchdown against Maryland as a junior. His final game as a junior was both daring and destructive. He grabbed another interception against Florida State in the Blockbuster Bowl, his third in two games, then suffered a shoulder injury that required surgery.

Sacca threw a 56-yard touchdown pass but was intercepted twice. Tom Bill replaced him early in the fourth quarter and rallied the team from a 14-point deficit to 24–17 with a touchdown pass. However, the final effort of his career, on fourth down, was intercepted in the end zone and Florida State won.

"It was the only game it didn't bother me," Sacca said of being benched. "I felt good for Tommy. It was his last game. He deserved to get in."

Penn State finished 9–3 and was ranked eleventh in the country by the Associated Press. Sacca began an assault on the record books. His 1,866 yards was the fifth most productive season of any Penn State passer. It also was 351 yards more than he had passed for in his two previous seasons combined. Best of all his completion rate was almost 50 percent. Even a modest improvement the following season, his last, would make Sacca the school's most prolific career passer. All this less than eight months after Paterno had called him "the biggest quarterback flop in Penn State history."

10

Field of Reality

In three football seasons, Sacca had come the farthest in his class. However, his adventure at Penn State was by no means the most unusual. By the end of their third year, the class realized that all college football players fall into two categories: the haves and the have-nots. The difference often is small and subjective, but also right there for everybody to see and make judgments about.

During the week the haves wear starter-status blue jerseys or one of the other big deal colors, green on offense and red on defense; the have-nots wear white jerseys. The haves get their names in the papers and frequently make public appearances around town. The have-nots are anonymous.

The haves and have-nots dress alongside each other in the locker room. They get equal treatment from Paterno during practice; they trot onto the field before games and mingle near the benches. The best friend of a have may very well be a have-not.

During games, however, the haves cross the narrow sideline and play. They gather bruises and glory. They strut. The have-nots pace the sideline, careful not to get in the way of a frantic coach explaining something to a have. The have-nots wait. They gather rust.

Everybody starts as a have-not. The progression can be quick, as it had been for Tony Sacca, Eric Renkey, and Chris Cisar. Sacca was the starting quarterback four games into his first year. Renkey and Cisar also lettered as true freshmen.

The progression can be slow but steady, as it had been for Leonard Humphries, who mostly played on the kick teams his first and second seasons and became the starting left cornerback as a junior. The progression can go back and forth, depending on injuries, performance and, it sometimes seemed, a coach's whim. Worse, the progression might not ever take place at all. A fellow could start as a have-not and mostly stay that way his entire football life.

Much of the earlier part of this section was the second and third seasons as experienced by a have, Sacca. The remainder is the second and third seasons as experienced by players who either drifted between have and have-not territory, sometimes in an instant, or who stayed stuck in the lowest form of football existence.

When Ron Fields had walked toward the locker room his first few days at Penn State, he had the air of a young athlete headed toward immortality. He had glanced at the pictures of former Nittany Lions, All-Americans all, on the walls and vowed that someday his photo would be there. He'd chosen Lawrence Taylor's number, 56, and vowed: "I want to go pro and get that degree."

A year later, in mid-morning of August 31, 1989, Fields did not bother looking at the wall of heroes as he headed toward his locker. His pace was slow, his mind filled with doubt and disappointment. His job as a bouncer in a downtown bar during summer school had not provided enough hours and, therefore, not enough money; his status at the inside linebacker position called Fritz was so low that a freshman during preseason drills had moved ahead of him on the depth chart; his academic load, even with several remedial courses, was starting to get too heavy to bear.

Worse, when Fields opened the dark blue door and entered the locker room, he moved directly toward the far end. Not to the left or to the right, to a place among the esteemed. Or even several paces straight ahead, to one of the lockers that faced the door. Fields took his overworked body and overtaxed mind back to Little Pit, the repository for freshmen and upperclass outcasts. In a year, Ron Fields had not taken one step forward.

Lockers in the main room also were assigned alphabetically, although Paterno sometimes switched players to break up cliques, or for reasons no one but he fully understood. That's why Bobby Samuels, for instance, dressed between a couple of A-guys. As always, the fellow who had come up with Little Pit the year before, Rich Rosa, had a keen eye for these new digs.

"I've got names for every part," he said. "The ghetto is where I'm at [meaning close to a corner off the wide entrance to the equipment room]. So many ethnic groups." He and an upperclass defensive lineman were of Puerto Rican ancestry and mingled with several African Americans, including Rick Sayles. The whites in this melting pot all were from Rosa's class: Tony Sacca, Eric Renkey, Todd Rucci, and Matt Nardolillo.

"On Tuesday [known as Bloody Tuesday, because of the intensity of practice], everybody else is down in the dumps, and we're over here giggling and laughing," Rosa said. "Everybody else is all depressed. We've got the happiest corner of the locker room."

Directly across from the ghetto was what Rosa called "the pig's hole." That was the cluttered residence of John Gerak and some others affected by untidy habits. "They live out of their lockers," Rosa said. "Gerak must pile his laundry in his locker, he has to dig through so much stuff. He's got things in there he doesn't realize. All the messy guys are over there. Forget it.

"Along the side over to the left is the real serious section. Where Chris Cisar is." When it was mentioned that the volatile upperclass linebacker Mark D'Onofrio dressed in the think-tank area, Rosa said: "His locker's there, but he doesn't hang out there. He'll migrate to the other side."

Rosa called the other side "the sub-project area," and it

included Leonard Humphries and Mark Graham. D'Onofrio either gravitated there or farther down the line, to a row of lockers Rosa called "the condo area." Everybody at some point drifted there, to where Greg Huntington, Tony Matesic, and some others dressed, because it included two team captains and a water cooler.

"Everybody has his own section," Rosa said. "But we have the best seats in the house. Bobby Samuels is blocked [by another cooler, which usually contained red fruit punch]. We can see everything." Among the sad sights were Fields and the still-overweight Brian Dozier walking through the main room to the showers and then back to Little Pit. Dozier still was inclined toward earrings when Paterno and the assistants were out of sight. Unlike Fields, Dozier was progressing academically. His mother worked in the admissions office at Swarthmore College, and he said: "I don't live for football. If I don't play pro football, I'm definitely going to grad school. Joe said I should be competing for a second team spot, but I dug a hole for myself [by staying so out of shape]. I said I understood. I'm living with it."

Everyone in the class knew that 1989 would be a critical year, athletically and academically. Pro scouts take notice of someone who, as a sophomore, causes a positive ripple at an elite school, such as Penn State. Academically, this was weed-out time, the rule of thumb being that any student who lasts two years has a decent chance to graduate. Already, six of the twenty-seven other scholarship players who arrived with Fields a year earlier were gone, among them his good buddy Adam Shinnick.

A few days earlier, Chad Cunningham had dropped off the team, and Fields was among those who had gone to his room to find out about the experience. Had it been hard? What was Joe like? Fields at that moment also was trying to summon enough courage to quit. He knew that cornerback Humphries the previous spring had actually packed his bags, but had been persuaded to stay by Rosa, O. J. McDuffie, and most importantly Paterno. But Humphries was a featured player, having been one of the nine who had seen at least limited action as a true freshman; Fields was not.

Toward the end of a scrimmage once in near-empty Beaver Stadium, when back-up players were on the field, inside linebackers coach Joe Sarra had yelled: "Fields!" And Fields had snapped to attention and moved toward Sarra and the defensive unit forming about ten yards away. As last, he was going to be part of the late afternoon action. Almost as soon as Sarra yelled for Fields, however, he became preoccupied with someone else, and Fields, his helmet snapped in place, waited for several awkward seconds. When it became embarrassingly clear that Sarra had completely forgotten he'd called Fields, the linebacker turned and walked slowly back to his lonely place on the sideline. Two years earlier, throughout that mating dance called recruiting, it had been the other way around. If Fields had snapped his fingers in the Bronx, Sarra would have come running from Penn State.

Circumstances change. Sarra still cared for Fields, but his job was to put the best inside linebackers on the field each week, and the outgoing youngster he'd once romanced wasn't one of them.

"We have to sort out who we work with the most," Sarra explained. "The big thing is to let [Fields and the other back-ups] know they're not a disappointment to us. Lots of times there is pressure from people back home: 'Hey, you're not doing so good.' Maybe he's actually making big strides. Maybe he's playing behind someone who's better. With a lot of these kids, it's not where they are today but where they'll be next year."

Fields was so close to the action he craved that he could literally reach out from the sideline and touch it. Yet that chalk mark, even during scrimmages, was like a thick barrier infrequently hurdled. Fields also struggled in the classroom. His first semester, he took remedial English (C-plus), remedial reading (C-plus), and remedial math (B). His transcript did include one A, in P.E. 1351 ("football-varsity"). He failed his one college-level course, anthropology. In the spring and summer, the results were much the same. So if he couldn't raise his grades, Fields might not even be at Penn State a whole lot longer, much less become one of its storied linebackers.

"He's gotten Ds or Fs in all the main courses he's taken, except English," said academic advisor Ferrell. "He is progressing, but not at a very rapid rate. He's a good kid, tries hard, wants to attain something other than football. The smaller the load the better. If he could take nine credits each semester, he could get 2.5 [a C-plus]. With twelve credits [the necessary average the NCAA requires for normal progress], a straight-C is about right." Shortly after breakfast that morning of August 31, Fields had gone to see Sarra. The assistant most responsible for his being at Penn State told him to wait, that he didn't have enough time to give everyone equal repetitions in practice so close to the season opener. "Work hard. We'll be watching you," Sarra said. "Your chance will come."

Even so, Fields within the hour was on the phone with his mother in New York. He wanted out, he told her. Dolores Fields said he could do that, but there was a catch. If Fields dropped out of Penn State, she would make him join the service. Unlike Van Nort and Cunningham, he needed a scholarship to attend college. So it would be either Penn State's uniform or Uncle Sam's.

Fields stayed, saying that morning in Little Pit: "Service is a nice idea, but it's not for me." Over the phone, his mom had said: "Stick it out, baby. If you have to wear a white jersey, do it. Work your way through college. It'll get better."

That also is what Rich Rosa kept hearing, over and over, as the 1989 season opener approached: It'll get better. Academically, he was fine; football was another matter, and the situation took a dramatic twist before a special-teams workout in empty Beaver Stadium. As Rosa was helping another defensive back with a stretching exercise, Paterno walked over and interrupted. The coach had an idea. How would Rosa like to play wide receiver? The shocked Rosa's mind went blank for an instant; then his emotions started to curdle. Say what? If Paterno had slammed him with a sledgehammer, he could not have made Rosa feel smaller, more beaten down.

Wide receiver? Hell, Rosa was a defensive back. Since high school he'd been certain his future was somewhere in the secondary. He had chosen Penn State over Michigan mainly because there seemed a much better chance to crack the defensive backfield here, especially the strong safety position called Hero. All of a sudden, a year into his college career, while holding the leg of a teammate flat on his back, Rosa was being told, in so many words, that he had no chance at significant playing time where he felt most comfortable.

One of the difficult parts of football is being smacked—and hard—without actually being hit, those inside-the-head blows to confidence. Other than during games, the sport Americans seem most passionate about is not fun. Not even close. Practices are long, hard, and often brutal; the coaches frequently are abrasive on the field and distant off it.

Also, if football were like academics, with a credit given for every hour spent in class and in practice/labs during the week, it would qualify as about a twenty-five credit course in the fall and spring terms. The academic load for most terms is twelve credits. So a football player carries something like a thirty-seven credit burden.

Here was Paterno, with that soft-spoken question, suggesting that Rosa for quite some time might not be more than a practice player. Rosa could have said no to Paterno and most likely not gotten more than a shrug in response. He had seen the sort of subtle pressure Penn State puts on players to switch positions and knew that it could be resisted. The coaches for ever so long had been trying to convince the enormous Todd Rucci to move to the other side of the ball, from the defensive line to the offensive line, and had been spectacularly unsuccessful.

"There's just a vision of offensive linemen that I hate," the 6-foot-6 Rucci said. "Big and fat. I think of myself [at 265 pounds] as a little guy. I really try to be quick. I can never picture myself on the offensive line. Plus I love defense. You're not busting your butt for nothing on the D-line. You make a tackle, and your name is announced over the loud speaker. Blocks never get announced. The rewards on defense are quicker."

The rewards are quicker if Rucci ever gets to play. That was the catch. The blunt fact of football life under Paterno is that a player can choose his position, but the coach decides whether he in fact ever sees a second of game action there. Knowing this, Rosa sensed that staying at defensive back might also get him nailed to the bench, possibly for his remaining four years at Penn State.

What the fast-thinking Rosa immediately did was say to Paterno about a wideout position whose depth had suddenly been weakened by injuries: "Sure, I'll give it a shot." Uncertain, angry, experiencing the first stomach-churning pangs of failure, Rosa that night called his high-school coach. He talked about leaving but was very quickly talked out of it.

So the first member of his class to commit to Penn State would not be the seventh of twenty-eight to leave. Sent to the printer before the position change, the 1989 Penn State press guide said of Rosa: "A promising defensive prospect . . . appears ready to make a bid for considerable action in the secondary." Three days before the opener and less than two weeks after the switch, Rosa during practice on the grass field adjacent to Holuba Hall missed a tough catch in the end zone. He slapped his hands and, smiling, looked at recruiting coordinator John Bove and said: "You know where I should be."

For 1989 season opener fullback John Gerak was exactly where he hoped he would be—in the starting lineup. Because Sacca still was behind Tom Bill, Gerak became the first member of his class to open the season as a starter.

It's an axiom of football that a nasty break for one player is an immediate and positive break for someone else. And when junior Sam Gash suffered a leg injury less than a week before the Virginia game, Gerak was the beneficiary. Gerak had always seemed the most cocksure of his class, having less than a year earlier assumed he would, without interruption, ascend to starter status very quickly and eventually to the NFL. With his good looks, he had been attracting most of the girls, and now everything in football was super too.

Gerak learned of his promotion in a roundabout way. Shortly after Gash was hurt, Gerak asked offensive coordinator Fran

Ganter who would be moving to fullback. Even though he had split practice time with Gash during summer camp, Gerak was not certain he would be trusted with the position so soon. Smiling in a sly way, Ganter answered, "We've got a good fullback."

A second thrill followed in short order, when State's glittering offensive star, tailback Blair Thomas, turned to Gerak and said: "It's up to you and me now, big guy." Knowing about Gerak's fondness for female company, Thomas added: "I don't want to control your life, but after Wednesday I want you to stay home. And no girls over to your place."

Walking near the east locker area two days before the Virginia game, Gerak was wearing a baseball hat to hide a bad haircut. He joked that at Penn State a fullback is simply a guard who takes two steps backward a couple of seconds before the snap. Rarely does he do much more than block.

"Against Alabama last year," he said, "I gave up a sack. Joe had told me he didn't care if I blocked the wrong man as long as I blocked [All-American linebacker] Derrick Thomas. But Thomas went right around me anyway and sacked Tony. So Joe pulled me. One play I was in the whole game, and he pulled me out." Outwardly, Gerak's size and outgoing manner suggested supreme confidence. That was a mask. He admitted, "I'm really scared. Been throwing up every night after dinner. But I know what I have to do. I don't care if I get one yard, so long as Blair gets 200."

In high school, Gerak had been regarded as one of the premier tight-end prospects in the country. He'd asked to switch from fullback to outside linebacker after spring practice, but was told no. "The rumor was that they were going to move me to tight end [before Gash got hurt]," he said. "I'm waiting to wake up and be number 80 again."

Anticipation was bubbling as the Penn State players burst from the tunnel near the south side of the field for the 1989 opener against Virginia. This season, every able-bodied member of the class would be suiting up for home games. So even Fields and Dozier were part of the Entrance, dressed to play even though a rout by Penn State still might not give them that chance.

After the Entrance, of course, there were members of the class making the entrance. Three of them: Tom Wade, recovering from reconstructive knee surgery; Mark Graham, recovering from shoulder surgery; and Chris Cisar, recovering from wrist surgery. Wade's operation had been arranged as quickly as possible after he suffered the torn anterior cruciate ligament in the spring; Graham's injury also had happened in the spring, and the doctors were hopeful it would mend without being cut on.

"First practice [of the fall], I was okay," Graham said. "Second practice, light contact, and the shoulder came out all the way. I put it back myself and went numb. If it'd been operated on when I first got hurt, I would have been back by midseason. This puts me deeper in a hole. I'll miss the whole season, and we always have some great athletes coming in here every year. Joe screamed at the doctor: 'Why didn't he get operated on last spring?' "

Cisar's injury had not been close to as serious as Wade's, yet its impact was felt more by his teammates. Well into the final preseason scrimmage, Cisar's shrill screams from the south end zone suddenly filled near-empty Beaver Stadium. There was a pause, for the offense was huddled less than twenty yards away and headed where the medics were tending to his broken wrist.

The tailback moments before had made a cut to the left side of the field, and in the collision, he and strong safety Cisar had fallen back into a linebacker. "I tried to strip the ball," Cisar said, "and got my hand caught between his hand and the ball. Everybody landed on me. All of a sudden, my left forearm was perpendicular to the ground. All the weight had popped it out."

This was as harsh as football ever gets. Players already tired, aching, and angry see a buddy crying in agony. Most of the time, the injured either quickly limp or are carried away from the action. Cisar could not be moved. Seconds passed. Tension mounted. Finally, Paterno ordered everybody to turn 180 degrees and to walk fifty yards in the opposite direction. The next play then was run into the other vacated end zone. The hitting continued, and Cisar soon was on his way to the hospital.

"Chris got hurt and all they did was turn around and go the other way," Eric Renkey said that night. "I don't know if this is worth it all the time. I just want to stick it out. It's paying for my education. As [upperclass teammate Jorge Oquendo] always says, you want to make your money with your mind and not your body."

Cisar suffered some complications from his wrist surgery, mostly because the original cast had been wrapped too tight. Naturally, he was out for the year. Same as Graham and Wade. Fortunately for Cisar and Graham, they had played as freshmen and still had a redshirt year coming. Wade would be missing his second straight season.

Cisar in the weeks ahead often felt conflicting emotions. The injury drew him apart from his teammates. His rehab schedule meant that he often worked by himself, sometimes when everyone else was on the practice field; it also meant he ate at different times from the team, sometimes alone. A few days after the operation, his left arm in a sling, Cisar stood near a sideline and watched the sort of practice he always hated. "No matter how much it sucks," he admitted, "you feel uncomfortable not being out there."

Away from the action during the 1989 season opener, Cisar was delighted at how the game against Virginia was going early on. The first play of his class's second season was an inside handoff to Gerak, and it produced 5 tough yards. The combination of Gerak and Blair Thomas worked well until the sixth play, when Gerak fumbled. Although a teammate recovered the ball, for a small loss, the already jittery Gerak was shaken. And Sacca was 0 for 2 in a brief relief appearance during the first half.

Even though the Nittany Lions lost to Virginia, there were some positives. Back-up nose tackle Renkey had a tackle, as did reserve outside linemen Todd Burger and Tony Matesic. Back-up cornerback Leonard Humphries defensed a pass. O. J. Mc-Duffie caught a pass for 16 yards and ran once for 2 yards on a reverse. Bobby Samuels returned a kickoff 34 yards. The best news of all was Ivory Gethers, completely recovered from anterior cruciate ligament surgery, making three tackles on kick coverage.

"I don't like to waste a run downfield," he said. "Each run, I intend to make something happen. Hit somebody. Don't run down the field for nothing." The pain and uncertainty of rehab had been worth enduring. "Whenever I get tired of practicing or of hearing the coaches yell," Gethers said, "I ask myself: 'What would happen if I wasn't playing football? What would happen if I couldn't play anymore?' The answer is that I love it. I would feel left out if it was taken from me right now."

In game three against Boston College, the raw and rainy afternoon during which Sacca replaced Bill and led the team to a last minute comeback victory, Eric Renkey limped off the field after his second play at nose tackle. He had injured his right big toe, not so serious as to require surgery but enough to keep him sidelined the remainder of the season. Like Graham and Cisar, Renkey could take a redshirt season and still have three more seasons of eligibility.

However, there were some alarming facts. Three games into their second year, the class had watched six players leave and four more miss at least one season with an injury. Two of the three players who had lettered as freshmen, Cisar and Renkey, would be medical redshirts as sophomores. With Donnie Bunch kicked out of school and Graham out with a shoulder injury, four of the nine who played their first year would miss all but a handful of plays their second.

Very quickly, in game four, two players eager to join Sacca in the spotlight got their chance. Leonard Humphries actually won the Texas game—by being in the wrong place at the right time as the Longhorns were about to punt.

"I lined up properly," he said, "but at the last moment I thought I was wrong. So I went to the other side and was out of position. But when [senior Andre Collins] blocked it, the ball came to me. I scooped it up [and went all of two yards for the touchdown]. It wasn't that glorious. I just picked the ball up."

That good fortune put Penn State ahead by 16–12 with 6:52 left in the game at Austin. "I kept thinking," Humphries admitted, " 'Please, don't anyone score any more touchdowns and I'll be the hero of the game.' That doesn't happen too much. Two years down the road, if I don't play much, that might be the highlight of my career."

Everybody cooperated just enough. Sacca was 9 for 20 for the game, and in Penn State's next-to-last possession he was smart enough under pressure to throw the ball away rather than risk an interception. Twice down the stretch the offense ran three plays and punted; the defense held each time, partly because of the quickness and strength of reserve right tackle Todd Burger.

It was slightly more than a year since Burger had slunk all the way to the back porch of Paterno's doghouse, for being arrested after a fight in CC Peppers. Now, his life was on the upswing, and when the starter was hurt Burger got in for most of the fourth quarter. The play-by-play sheet said of one Texas five-yard loss: " . . . decked by Burger." And of another four-yard loss: "Burger eats him up."

Paterno over the years has mellowed about celebrations after big plays. At one point, he wouldn't tolerate so much as a gentle spike of the football after a critical touchdown. Lately, however, he allowed fist waving and the like after tackles, so long as the showboating was spontaneous. Well, with Bunch gone, Burger was the member of his class who most craved attention, the one most likely to be closest to Paterno when the team charged onto the field in pregame and, thus, almost certainly to be seen. So Burger's first bit of heroism for the Nittany Lions, in front of 80,000 mostly hostile fans, was not going to be taken casually.

"After one tackle," he said, "I'm jumping up and down, and Mark D'Onofrio comes over and tackles me. Jumps on me. We didn't realize it, but we were stepping on the hand and face mask of the guy I'd just tackled." On the flight home from Texas, Humphries surely was thinking what Burger said to everyone within earshot: "I contributed to Penn State football. Finally!"

As he skipped around a corner and up the steps that led to

the east locker area three days before the Syracuse game two weeks later, O. J. McDuffie had an uncommon bounce. "Looks pretty good for me," he said. "I'm going back on punts. We'll see what happens."

What happened, in the gushy prose of the Penn State publicity department, was that "Sophomore wideout O. J. McDuffie brought back visions of another O. J. of some football notoriety with a 203-yard all-purpose performance that took the air out of pumped-up Syracuse and a sold-out Carrier Dome."

McDuffie had two pass receptions for 40 yards, two runs from scrimmage for 48 yards, and five punt returns for 115 yards. The highlight of his performance was an 84-yard punt return for a touchdown in the third period that pushed Penn State's advantage to 27–6. McDuffie also was considered a major league prospect as a baseball outfielder, and he said of his flair for punt returns: "I'm nervous, being the only one back there and everybody's looking at you. But when the ball's in the air, it's like fielding a fly. Once you get it, you use everything you've got to break loose. It feels real natural back there. Catching the ball. Feeling free. Doing what I can do."

McDuffie's star began a sharp rise with that game; John Gerak's began a rapid fall. Gerak scored a touchdown against Syracuse, on a 7-yard run. But the fellow who opened the season as the starting fullback would carry the ball just three more times the remaining six games. "Just too long a strider to be a fullback," offensive coordinator Fran Ganter said. "No feet for the position. He can't make anybody miss."

So it went. Gerak began the season as a starter and ended it rarely playing. When upperclass regulars got hurt on the defensive line, Tony Matesic and Todd Burger filled in. O. J. McDuffie's punt-return average, 14.6 yards on 19 runs, was seventh best in the country. Ivory Gethers was a standout on special teams; Bobby Samuels had enough plays to letter but suffered a foot injury that required surgery. Sacca had the most plays, 516. Rich Rosa was in for just sixteen plays, Ron Fields for eight, Rick Sayles for two. Brian Dozier did not see a single second of action.

Their second season ended very positively, with the 50–39 victory over Brigham Young in the Holiday Bowl during which Sacca threw for 203 yards and two touchdowns. As usual, several classmates performed well in less obvious ways, and Eric Renkey was involved in mischief. Renkey's body during that redshirt year had gotten even more massive. From the 270 pounds he carried as freshman, Renkey had soared to 302 during the Holiday Bowl. That got him elected captain of a group of free spirits called the Yuk Squad. It also caused the assistant coach who had recruited him, Tom Bradley, to crack: "I've known Eric for 160 pounds."

Cracking 300 pounds had become a sort of Everest-like goal, Renkey said, adding: "I was so close that I figured I'd give it a shot in San Diego during the bowl. I made it. Gained thirteen pounds in two weeks. Tom Wade owes me $25."

One of the pivotal plays of the Holiday Bowl had been a pass by future Heisman Trophy winner Ty Detmer for two points after a BYU touchdown. It was intercepted by linebacker Andre Collins, who ran it 102 yards for two Penn State points. Collins's escorts were the standouts of the Texas game, Todd Burger and Leonard Humphries. "We both hit the last person who could have gotten Andre," Burger said. "I kind of clipped him."

Burger had a solo tackle on Detmer and assisted on another. A third time, Detmer broke free of Burger and completed a short pass. "I'm jumping up and down and screaming to the ref: 'In the grasp! In the grasp!' " Burger said. "The ref says: 'What the hell is the matter with you? There's no in-the-grasp [rule] in college, son.' "

Burger and everyone else in the class—those who stayed and those who walked away—could maneuver that in-the-grasp tidbit to suit their own circumstances. Just when something seemed certain, Gerak's status as a starter, for instance, it later vanished. Here one year, gone the next. A have early in the week, a have-not at the end. Healthy in the afternoon, in the hospital that night. That ref had no idea how profound he really was. There's no in-the-grasp in college, or in college football, son.

11

Free Falling

Sitting in a soft chair at the middle of the players' lounge near the locker room on the afternoon of July 11, 1990, Rick Sayles could hold back a piece of glorious news no longer. He blurted out, "I'm a father." That was not widely known among his teammates. Even Paterno was unaware that Raeleen, Sayles's girlfriend back home in McKeesport, had given birth to a girl on February 4. They had named the baby Ericka Rae.

At first, Sayles was against Raeleen having the baby. Spiteful. Saying that he was here, at Penn State, and he was not about to give up his college education. They talked and talked during the summer. She was adamantly against abortion.

"I was raised in poverty," Sayles said. "My father left when I was six and didn't make himself available as a parent until I was about twelve. And that was only a fly-by basis. He remarried, had his own little world; we had ours. My older brother went to live with my grandmother. I was sort of the man of our house. Me, my mother, and younger brother, Elrick.

"So I don't want to raise a child of mine in poverty. No way. But I couldn't turn away from her. That's what everybody else does. Everybody in the projects."

Sayles did not see his daughter until Easter, when she was nearly two months old. He recalled "I kinda melted. Fell in love. Everybody in both families loves her. Thank the Lord she had it."

To help support Ericka Rae, Sayles sent Raeleen $500 of the $700 that he received each semester from his government-funded Pell Grant. "I don't need much," he said. "I get fed here."

Fed and fed and then fed some more. As easy as it had been for the 6-foot-2-inch Renkey to hit 302 pounds, it had been as tough for the 6-foot-5-inch Sayles to hit 215. "I was on a stuff-your-face program last semester," he said. "Five meals a day. Every day, I sat at a table for over an hour. At first, it worked. I got to 216 [from 205]. All of a sudden, I got sick and couldn't eat. Everything I ate came straight out. I dropped to 210 before the spring game. I just can't keep weight on."

For the spring game, Sayles was switched from outside line-backer to tight end. And even though he started for the White team and caught one pass for five yards, he was not thrilled. He knew the change was in large part due to numerous injuries at tight end, among them the torn anterior cruciate ligament that Rudy Glocker suffered in that seemingly harmless tag drill during winter workouts. "Same as always," Sayles said, referring to his having worn a blue jersey as a freshman until an upperclass regular got healthy. "I'm saving a position for someone else."

Academically, Sayles had fallen in love with psychology. "All I ever thought about was what people thought," he said. "I grew up in a kinda bad neighborhood and wondered why people would do certain things when they knew down the line it would get 'em back. Like selling drugs, robbing people, dropping out of school. I wanted to major in psychology when I first came here but was talked out of it. Every advisor I spoke to wanted me to go into business. I told 'em I'm not very keen on math."

That summer, Sayles had taken an introductory psychology course and done so well that the professor wrote complimentary letters to Paterno and academic advisor Ferrell. "The prof wanted me to be a supplementary instructor," Sayles said. "But

I didn't have time. I don't have two hours to myself, let alone for someone else."

One of the class vowing after the spring term of 1990 to make an academic turnaround was Tony Matesic, who said: "I called a friend the other day and told him I've been on a two-year vacation. Seems like all I do is play football. That and sleep. My first year"—when being caught sleeping through class by Ferrell had led to Matesic tape recording the scolding that he got from Paterno—"if I had ten classes a week, I probably slept through five or six. This year was a joke. I would go two weeks without going to class. People would see me on campus and say: 'Tone, what's going on? Test today?' "

Even though his cumulative average after the spring semester still was slightly above a 2.0, it had fallen dramatically. His most recent semester had yielded a 1.25, and he admitted, "My father was really, really angry. I wanted to show him I can get it done. They say the older you get the more important classes become, and you'll start going. I see that happening already."

"Everyone has a semester like that," Todd Rucci said of Matesic's 1.25. "I went from 3.4, 3.3, 3.3, to a 1.0." Rich Rosa in the spring of 1989 had a 2.60; in the fall of 1990 he had a 0.85; in the spring of 1990 he had a 2.13.

Matesic had played quite a lot on the defensive line in the fall of 1989. His total of 205 plays was fourth among his classmates and almost a hundred more than his buddy, Burger's. "I was all screwed up during the spring," he said. "Injured. Not going to class. And watching freshmen moving ahead of me. Which I couldn't handle mentally. I'm playing during the season; comes the spring and I'm fighting for a job. Joe wasn't happy with me at all. One day I got into a fight on the field, and he chewed me out. Told me he didn't want to take me out because he enjoyed seeing me get my butt beat."

Early the next fall Matesic stopped me in the locker room and pointed to my tape recorder. "That thing on?" he said. It was. Moving closer, Matesic yelled, "I just want you to know that Tony Matesic hasn't missed a class in two weeks." He got a 2.51 that semester and a 2.47 the next.

By the end of spring in their third year most players were slipping into academic majors. Rudy Glocker chose political science, Todd Rucci exercise science, Rich Rosa liberal arts, Chris Cisar business logistics. With not a whole lot of thought other than football careers on their minds, Tony Sacca and O. J. McDuffie were in liberal arts. Greg Huntington, who picked economics, had a special incentive. If he did well academically for three years, his father would buy him an expensive car.

Eric Renkey still was interested in medicine, and a surge in his grade point average made it a more viable option. From that 1.31 the first semester of his freshman year, Renkey during the summer after his sophomore year had gotten a 3.42. "Now I actually study," he said.

Trouble is, Marilyn Renkey was getting more of those certified letters. The latest came after a beer-in-his-room incident that had Eric in danger of being kicked out of the dorm. In the family rec room in late July, she asked about the possibility of probation. From the kitchen, Eric took on one of those ah-mom tones of indifference and said: "There has never been a semester when I haven't been on probation."

The most uncertain academically were Burger, Fields, Humphries, Wade, and the two special admits, Gethers and Samuels. Although Wade had been admitted to agricultural business, his cumulative average after the spring semester of 1990 was the worst on the entire 118-member football team: 1.42. Gethers had qualified for landscape contracting, though barely. He also had undergone shoulder surgery—his second major operation in two years at Penn State—after the Holiday Bowl but figured to be completely healed by the fall.

Burger, Samuels, Fields, and Humphries were among those in a sort of limbo-major called Division of Undergraduate Studies (DUS). Students can stay in DUS only so long, but that foursome qualified for nothing else. Burger could do better, and he and Ferrell knew it. Ferrell was less certain about the others.

"Bobby Samuels is struggling for his life right now," Ferrell said. "He could be a vital link in this football program, because of his talent, but he's also a half-step away from not being here."

His girlfriend, Laurie Mosley, several times had phoned assistant Tom Bradley from campus and complained that Bobby was cutting class.

"Leonard Humphries is an enigma to me," Ferrell said. "Immature. Slated to play a lot in the fall, but had severe academic problems. Needs As and Bs [in summer school] to survive."

When Ferrell got to Fields, he smiled. With the help of some friends, Fields had gotten better. "Improved 200 percent," Ferrell said. "Stabilized his habits, his motivation. All his remedial work was done in the second semester of his freshman year. If Ron Fields doesn't make it back this fall, I'll give up my job."

About two weeks into spring practice, when football was going well after the shoulder surgery that forced him to miss the 1989 season had mended, Mark Graham received a letter saying he'd been admitted into the academic major of his choice: finance. "That made my spring," he said. No one in his class had become more comfortable at Penn State; no one had more of a sense of where he wanted to go after football. "This place seemed so enormous at first," Graham said. "Now it seems so small. Really small."

On his trips to the Harpsters as a sophomore, Graham no longer needed Brian to act as chauffeur. He was driving the 1984 BMW that his parents had bought him. He enjoyed the way the car handled the narrow roads as well as the heightened sense of independence that it offered.

Brett Wright had kept his pickup off campus as a freshman since cars were not allowed until the second year. And there was a ritual about them: Keys had to be turned in at the start of summer camp and were not returned until class began some three weeks later. That is mostly why Eric Renkey one August never bothered to fix the flat on his 1979 Olds for about a month. No compelling need to get the Blue Bomber out of the football parking lot; he couldn't drive it anyway.

A football program's parking area says a lot about it. At Penn State, the staff's courtesy cars tended to be understated and steady. In 1990 Paterno's was a red Buick sedan—and not a very flashy red, either. That year, the sportiest car was the white Camaro driven by one of the secretaries, Mike Franzetta.

In his BMW, Graham took Brian Harpster for the two-hour drive to Penn National, a racetrack, for a night of betting the horses. Graham's eagerness to make money also got them involved as business partners in a movie-rental venture.

With their huge satellite dish, the Harpsters could get channels from all over the world. Mark and Brian taped all sorts of programs and rented the videos to friends for $1 a day. The business netted no more than $50, however, because too many friends never returned the tapes on time and pressing them for the extra money could have created too much friction.

Also as sophomores, players could choose their own roommates. And when Graham and Leonard Humphries moved into room 106 of Nittany Hall, it meant that very good friends also would be competing for the same cornerback position. That competition never soured their relationship.

"Just a natural understanding," Graham said, "that we would compete, and compete hard, but it wouldn't affect us when we were together."

Both played as true freshmen, but when Graham missed his sophomore season, Humphries gained an advantage. It also meant that if Humphries stayed healthy and academically eligible he would be out of Penn State after four years and Graham would have the position to himself as a redshirt senior.

Graham was as anxious as anyone to play, and the possibility of the academically shaken Humphries not being available in the fall lifted his hopes in the spring. "I started being real aggressive," he said. "Not afraid of anybody getting behind me. I'm out there, and I'm not intimidated. Joe started telling me I was getting better and better. One day I was lifting in the weight room and Fran Ganter was there. He said Joe had told him that of all the defensive backs I played the position like a man."

More important to Graham, he was on the fast track academically. What he wanted most was to make money, and in a hurry. A fifth season, even one with the starting cornerback position to himself, had no appeal. "Right now," he said, "I'm on course with my studies. If I can graduate in four years, I'm outta here."

Also in the spring, as he'd expected, John Gerak was moved from fullback to tight end. That didn't go well, either. "He looks like an all-pro during practice," said offensive coordinator Fran Ganter. "In a scrimmage, he tightens up. Can't catch well under pressure."

Ganter was enjoying another position change, however, one he'd helped arrange. Not quite kicking and screaming, Todd Rucci had been moved from the defensive line to the offensive line. He and Ganter had differing stories about how the switch came about.

Ganter said that he and a couple of other offensive aides kept gently coaxing Rucci. One day, Ganter said, he went into the locker room, and Rucci assumed a pass-blocking stance; he was ready.

Not so, Rucci insisted. "One day during [winter] drills," he said, "Fran comes up to me. He says Joe talked to him and that he wanted to move me. I said if he wanted to move me, let him come to me. That day I ran with the defense, and Fran says: 'Get to offense.' I told him no, not a chance.

"Next day, same thing. Fran says: 'I'm serious. You're being moved to offense.' I really didn't want to. He said go and see Joe if I had any problems. I thought that was a shitty way to go about it. Joe himself never told me. I never had a one-on-one with Joe. I have yet to be in his office to talk about anything. I was pissed. But instead of making waves, I went over there."

At first, Rucci played the tackle position opposite the tight end. Then he was switched to center, which proved a disaster. "Either there was a good snap and I fell on my face," Rucci said, "or there was a bad snap and I got off the ball okay. True."

Still experimenting, Ganter also was convinced Rucci had a professional future at tackle. "He's gonna be a second-round draft pick. That's my prediction," Ganter said. "He has long arms, and that's great for pass protection. Get your arms out and

On the Trail: Joe Paterno visits with Eric Renkey and his mother, Marilyn, at the Renkey home (*top*) and puts his hand on Chris Cisar's shoulder during a visit to the Cisar home. Also in suit and tie at the Cisar home is assistant coach Tom Bradley, who developed a relationship with Renkey and Cisar that was important in their choosing Penn State. (COURTESY Eric Renkey, top, and Chris Cisar)

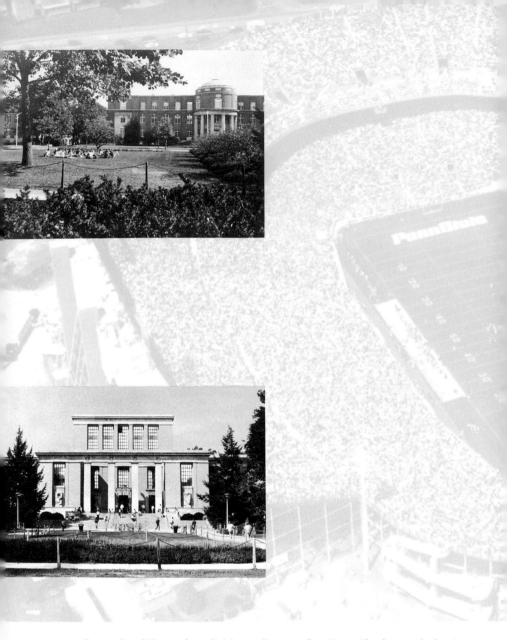

Dreamland/Sweatshop: Sold-out Beaver Stadium (*background photo*) is where every Penn State player hopes to excel. Empty Beaver Stadium during exhausting pre-season scrimmages in August is where the players earn their precious minutes in games. (COURTESY Penn State Sports Information)

New Home: Waiting for its incoming students are (*clockwise from upper left*) academic landmarks such as the earth and mineral sciences building, Old Main, the Nittany Lion shrine, and Pattee Library. (COURTESY Penn State Sports Information)

O. J., Oh My: Catches such as this didn't come as soon as O. J. McDuffie (24) had hoped. But he eventually became the most successful player of his class, a first-round draft choice of the Miami Dolphins, and one of the best players in Penn State history. (COURTESY Steve Manuel/*Blue White Illustrated*)

Sooner Doesn't Guarantee Later: Quarterback Tony Sacca (*top*) and defensive back Chris Cisar (*bottom*) both lettered as freshmen. Sacca kept playing, though not without clashes with Paterno, and left Penn State at the top of nearly every important statistical category. Frequently injured, Cisar (48) saw less action his last year than he did his first. (COURTESY Al Pisaneschi, Wilkes-Barre, Pa., *Sunday Independent*, top, and Steve Manuel/*Blue White Illustrated*)

Big Timers: Linebacker Brett Wright (*top*) was a captain in his final season. Todd Burger (67) lettered on both the offensive and defensive line, but was far less dedicated in the classroom. (Author Collection, top, and COURTESY Dave Shelly/ Penn State Athletics)

On the Field: Rudy Glocker had a mostly frustrating career. He rarely played until his third season but became a starter on the defensive line because of tackles such as this one against West Virginia. His chance for full athletic-academic glory ended when, for the second time, he suffered one of football's most severe injuries: a torn anterior cruciate ligament. (COURTESY *Blue White Illustrated*)

Off the Field: Glocker was the star of his class, graduating in three and a half years and earning a summer internship with Senator Arlen Specter, R-Pa. (*top*). During another summer experience, in Sweden, he was close to Mikhail Gorbachev. (COURTESY Rudy Glocker)

Young Love: Rick Sayles had higher highs and lower lows than anyone in his class. One of the highs was daughter Ericka Rae (*top*). On the day he was married to Carrie Ellen Mathiott, Derek Van Nort said, "If I'd stayed with football, I wouldn't have this." (COURTESY Rick Sayles, top, and Derek Van Nort)

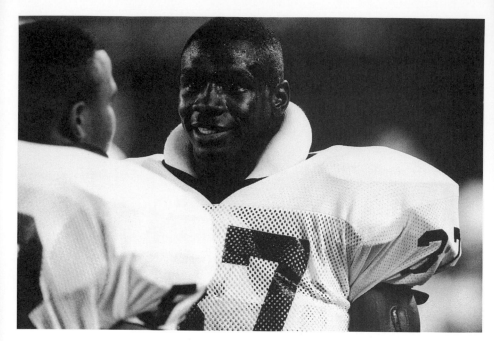

Not Quite: Ivory Gethers is smiling here, but his football career did not come close to what he'd hoped. Academic problems and injuries restricted his playing time. It took almost six years, but he did graduate. (Author Collection)

Told You So: Penn State did not recruit Greg Huntington heavily, but he quickly became a mainstay on the offensive line. (Author Collection)

Change of Heart: Todd Rucci (71) tried to avoid switching from the defensive line to the offensive line. After making the switch, he was judged the most improved offensive player during the 1990 spring practices and joined assistant Fran Ganter and the team mascot to receive the award (*top*). Even after returning this interception 12 yards for a touchdown against Rutgers, cornerback Mark Graham said he wouldn't come back for his final season of eligibility. He did. (COURTESY Dave Shelly/Penn State Athletics, top, and *Blue White Illustrated*)

Three for the Show: O. J. McDuffie (*top right*) was among the most highly recruited members of his class and lived up to every expectation. Mark Graham (*bottom right*) wanted a business—and got some practice at Penn State. Bob Ceh had no thought of being anything but a clean-up-for-everyone team manager, but he became a unique walk-on and the snapper for punts and placekicks. (Author Collection)

Tony Sacca as a Phoenix Cardinal quarterback. (COURTESY the
Phoenix Cardinals)

Todd Rucci (71) as a New England Patriot offensive tackle.
(COURTESY the New England Patriots)

Greg Huntington as a Washington Redskin center/guard.
(COURTESY the Washington Redskins)

Joe Paterno, whose magnetism attracted the class to Penn State, whose sarcasm infuriated every member at times, and whose dedication eventually impressed most. (COURTESY Penn State Sports Information)

a defender can't get hold of you. Plus he's tough and has an offensive lineman's demeanor: no ups and downs. Steady."

Also in the spring the seventh player in the class of twenty-eight, fullback Bob Daman, walked away from football. A back injury that he'd suffered and played with in the fall had worsened. Opinion about whether he should have surgery was divided. Daman opted against it, which meant that his career was over.

"He had enough ability to maybe play professionally," Paterno said. "He could have had an operation, but why get one if you don't need it [to stay healthy without football]. You ought to play football because you get some fun out of it. I hate to see a kid crippled." Recently Sue Paterno had undergone another back operation, her fourth. Also on Paterno's mind was the funeral for a former player, Joe Bellas, that he'd recently attended. Bellas was one of his mid-1960s defensive linemen, who seemingly had a hugely successful career with a Pittsburgh steel company but who had committed suicide. "So much trouble with his back," Paterno said. "Operations. He just couldn't handle the pain any longer."

Occasionally, Daman had second thoughts about giving up football. "When I came back from the doctors once," he said, "I walked around one of the dorm buildings. I had a partial view of practice. I just kinda stood there, leaning against a post. I stared up there—and then turned around and walked back inside."

Few games ever had gotten off to a more spectacular, positive start than Penn State's 1990 season opener against Texas in Beaver Stadium. A clear sky, temperature in the low 60s, and the Nittany Lions running the opening kickoff back 95 yards to the Longhorn 3 yard line. Trotting onto the field with quarterback Tony Sacca for the first series were three classmates: O. J. McDuffie at wideout, Greg Huntington at the line position called short guard, and Ericka Rae Sayles's father, Rick, at tight end.

Stepping in as a starter, after finishing seventh in the nation in punt returns the season before, McDuffie was no surprise.

Given their circumstances, Huntington and Sayles were. Huntington had been among the most lightly recruited members of his class, to the point of having to apply some I-might-go-elsewhere pressure just to get a scholarship.

Leonard Humphries had heard about the foot trouble that so frustrated Huntington most of his first two years. In the locker room once, he slid down the couple of yards that separated their lockers and asked exactly what the problem had been.

"My foot went like this," Huntington said. With that, he took an empty football shoe and lifted it, as a salesman in a store might. Then he put one hand over the toe area and pulled so violently that it bent over the laces and hit the back part of the shoe. Humphries recoiled. Some thin steel plates in the shape of the bottom of his foot helped, and Huntington's progress had been swift.

Offensive linemen are not quite so anonymous anymore. No longer can a scoundrel safely hide from the law by playing center or either of the two guard or tackle positions. Instant replay will finger them. Still, only family and friends notice much of what blockers do, and even their eyes often follow the running back past that huge .gap at the line of scrimmage instead of staying focused on the blocker, frequently with his face mashed into the grass, who caused it.

Because his recognition, after a play, after a game, sometimes even after a career, mostly is internal, there is a particular temperament for an offensive lineman. Like his defensive counterpart, a blocker must be aggressive. But he also must be passive at times, especially on passes, willing to give ground in order to keep the quarterback productive. Line play is much more intricate than most fans realize, so those who play there must be light on their feet and disciplined.

Huntington fit this emotional mold very well. Quiet. Studious. Among the first in the locker room before practice. After the spring of 1990, his average was close to a B. He could almost hear the fancy car his father had promised for long-term good grades purring. "Greg Huntington comes to see me twice a week, just to talk, to run things by me," said academic advisor Ferrell. "He's one of those kids you can't say enough good about. If you support Greg Huntington, he'll go the route for you."

When he was healthy earlier in his college career, Huntington had gotten experience at all the offensive line positions. Because he'd seen some action before getting a medical redshirt as a freshman, it was entirely possible that he would have the highly unusual distinction of playing some during all his five years.

How Huntington became a starter against Texas also was out of the ordinary, because it involved switching positions without as many repetitions as usual. He'd been a backup at tackle earlier in the week. But when one of the regulars got hurt, the shake-up included him switching to guard.

Huntington's one detriment was his size. There wasn't enough of it. "He's 253," said Ganter. "Ideally, he'd be 293. He came back at 263. Then he lost 10 pounds very quickly and hasn't been able to put it back on." Hunkering down, charging ahead, Huntington was one of the reasons the Nittany Lions took a 7–0 lead 90 seconds into the 1990 season opener on a running play up the middle.

After Texas countered with a field goal, Sacca completed a 15-yard pass to McDuffie and a 34-yarder to Sayles, whose twisting maneuver after the catch put the ball on the Texas 20. Moving from linebacker to tight end in the spring hadn't been the temporary injury plug that Sayles had imagined. He wasn't holding a position for someone else after all.

On defense, Brett Wright opened at inside linebacker, Todd Burger manned nose tackle, and Leonard Humphries started at cornerback. Humphries had survived academically, though barely, getting a B in twelve credits of Spanish, a B in a speech course, and an A in golf. That also lifted him into a major, criminal justice.

After the Sayles reception, however, the Nittany Lions failed to make the plays necessary to beat Texas and extend the nine-game winning streak that they brought into the game. For the second straight season, they had dug themselves a huge hole right away. "All I know is I'm sixty-three again," cracked a disappointed Paterno, who only a few months earlier had said he felt ten years younger.

The loss to Texas at home—the first game of their third year—seemed to be quite symbolic for many in the class. The team was nowhere close to what Paterno had hoped, and neither were they. The amorphous nature of any group close to two dozen was made even more tentative by an unseen but steadily ticking clock. Time was running out. By the end of this season, each football career would be at least 60 percent complete. And what would there be to show for it?

In two-plus years, more than half of the twenty-eight players had participated in fewer than fifty total plays, which meant that they had been involved in about four total minutes of big-time college football action. The oversized Brian Dozier hadn't even gotten on the field once. Yet he remained amiable and optimistic, saying: "This year, I should see some playing time." School was going better as his cumulative average rose to about a 2.5.

Dozier and some others could grab hope by watching Rick Sayles against Texas. Sayles had been at both ends of the practice jersey spectrum, from elite blue to worrisome white; he had moved from linebacker to tight end. In his first two seasons, Sayles had seen action for two plays. Against Texas at the start of his third season he had played often and had mostly played well.

Chris Cisar seemed to feel the most pressure. He had lettered as a freshman and suffered a broken wrist that sidelined him as a sophomore. As he walked toward his room after practice one evening during his third season, he stopped and said: "I don't know what to concentrate on. Studies or football. I've given all I can to football, and all I get is special teams."

Academically, Cisar was near the top of his class, with close to a B average. But he'd experienced such personal football satisfaction so early, all but walking into significant playing time in the defensive backfield at Penn State right from North Hills High.

Cisar was afraid his freshman season would be the highlight of his college career. Younger and faster players were coming on at his strong safety position. And the coaches had him confused. "They do things, I think, for the wrong reasons," he said. "They put you down on a lower string to motivate you. But you're not going to get better, because you're playing against worse people." In high school, Cisar had been a terrific pitcher, a lefthander timed at nearly 90 miles per hour. The Blue Jays and the Mets had been interested. Perhaps he'd give baseball at Penn State a serious fling in the spring.

By now, the notion was beginning to take form that elite college football for most players had more downs than ups. So much practice drudgery, so many injuries, so little playing time. And losing the first game of the season is especially difficult for a team that sets its sights each year on winning the national championship.

The players had expected football at Penn State to be tough. But they hadn't thought there would be so many hitches. Rudy Glocker, for instance, had suffered serious finger and knee injuries. Each had required surgery; neither had occurred during anything more meaningful than a routine practice. Just now, fate was knocking around two other players.

By the time the Texas game ended, O. J. McDuffie had a cumbersome brace strapped on his left knee. He had limped off the field and later returned to the sideline on crutches, having damaged ligaments while blocking downfield on a reverse to senior David Daniels. "The defender kinda set me up," McDuffie said. "He bounced around, like the play was over. Then he made a move on me, to make a play on Dave. I turned to get him, and Dave came down on my knee."

It was only a sprain, but a rising star had been suddenly stopped in its ascendancy. Several weeks later, when the injury was almost completely healed, McDuffie considered coming back. Then he decided that might be a waste, as his freshman season had been. Returning with half the season gone might bring just enough playing time to lose a valuable year of eligibility.

"Joe put it all in my hands, whether to redshirt or not,"

McDuffie said. "I decided to sit it out [and still have two seasons left]. Joe let me make the decision. That was kinda nice. Really, everything you do up here is up to you. He gives you lots of options, choices. But he puts the decision-making power on you."

There was not so much as a scratch on John Gerak at the end of the Texas game, yet he was more worried than either Sacca or McDuffie. In fact, Gerak was almost frightened by what he was facing. The most confident player in his class about making the pros as a freshman, the first in his class to open a season as a starter as a sophomore, Gerak as a junior was without a position he felt comfortable playing. Fullback hadn't worked last fall. Neither had tight end the next spring.

Gerak had been on Paterno's mind during the spring of 1990, though in a far more sympathetic way than Sacca. "He played fullback when we had to have a fullback," the coach said, alluding to the injury to Sam Gash just before the start of the 1989 season. "He has made a contribution, but we haven't gotten enough out of him yet. We don't have him in the groove yet."

Where that groove might be had Gerak deeply concerned. He arrived with so much potential, seemingly capable of playing fullback or tight end at the NFL level. He had done neither. Not even close. Could it be, he wondered, that he might never master anything?

More than the others in his class, Gerak felt pressure from hometown fans. "Kids and stuff," he said. "A five-year-old lives next to me [in a small town in eastern Ohio]. He knows when I'm coming home. He says: 'I'm watching for you [on television]. You playing? You playing?' He has my jersey on. The whole bit. I can't go out without somebody saying: 'Why aren't you starting? Why haven't you made a name for yourself yet.'"

Also, Gerak added weight easily, and this influenced the decision he'd reached before the start of the 1990 season. Ganter had called him a "blocking fullback." A year earlier, Gerak had joked that all a fullback was at Penn State was a guard who took two steps backward. So, why not take two steps forward from fullback? Why not try and master guard?

Gerak mentioned the idea to Paterno, that he wanted to switch to guard and that he wanted to take a redshirt year in 1990 to become familiar with the position. "That way, with a fifth season, I could get my diploma. I thought the diploma was the least I could do for myself. Maybe start grad school my last semester here." Paterno concurred. Relieved, Gerak started a very active season of inactivity.

On the sideline for the Texas game were four other players assessing what might remain of their college careers. Tommy Wade wore boots, a striped shirt, and cords. Eric Renkey had on a light blue pullover shirt and occasionally got close enough to listen in on defensive strategy. In street shoes, hands usually in his pockets, Bobby Samuels stood on the bench. In full dress uniform, Mark Graham paced and silently cursed his lousy luck. An ankle injury during the summer hadn't healed yet; his buddy Humphries had won their cornerback battle, partly by default.

Wade was moving along a one-way path. Unfortunately, it was a downward path that started after the terrible knee injury in the spring of 1989. When he recovered—a year and a half later, in the fall of 1990—he was academically ineligible. He was okayed to practice two days a week but could not suit up for games.

Samuels was in similar straits: ineligible for football. Only attention to detail and knowledge of Penn State's intricate and slow-moving academic system by academic advisor Ferrell kept Samuels in school at all—and then by the narrowest of margins.

Two weeks into fall practice, Samuels had been nowhere to be seen. On August 20, Ferrell sat in his office waiting for a phone call. "One individual had Bobby and Ivory Gethers in the same class," he said. "When I spoke to him two days ago, he said they'd each gotten a B. Now, it says each of them got a D. He said both kids passed the final. If this call is positive, Bobby will be back in school. But he won't be eligible to play. And Ivory, who's still in school, will be able to play. As things stand right now, Ivory won't be eligible to play."

A day later, after a morning practice on the fields near an area of several hundred yards filled with blooming flowers, Samuels and his father walked through the crowded locker room. Samuels was back in school. And Gethers, who'd been practicing all along, was okayed to play. Teammates were shedding sweat soaked jerseys and pads as Samuels strode by wearing a white baseball cap and a blue sweatshirt with lavender and gray trim.

Three years into college football, Samuels seemed to be starting all over again. Even his locker was in Little Pit. Paterno had gone to bat for Samuels to get him admitted to Penn State. He wasn't sure this second chance would prove worthwhile, but he granted it.

One of Samuels's concerns for more than a year was fatherhood. On October 26, 1989, Laurie Mosley had given birth, three months prematurely, to a daughter that she and Bobby had named Ashley. "She weighed 2 pounds, 9 ounces," Samuels said. "Most babies born that early don't make it. What finally hit me was that the whole world wasn't against me or she wouldn't have made it."

This year Samuels would be devoted to pulling himself out of the deep academic hole into which he'd dug himself. Unfortunately, as Eric Renkey was learning, a fellow can crawl out of a hole, take a few positive and hopeful steps, and then fall back into it.

After making a tackle during a scrimmage on August 27 of his third year, Renkey had suddenly felt a sharp pain in his neck. At the same time, his thumb and first two fingers went numb, as did a good deal of his left arm. It was another burner, similar to what he'd experienced in high school. Except this burner was worse. Much worse. "Instead of lasting ten or twenty seconds," he said, "this one lasted fifteen to twenty minutes." During fall practice, Renkey had found himself both in and out of Paterno's large and frequently crowded doghouse. On the one hand, he had reported two pounds under the required weight, at 273 pounds. From a whopping 302 at the start of the year that left stretch marks on his belly, Renkey in seven months had melted admirably. "I went up in twenty-pound increments," he said. "Maybe I'll go down in twenty-pound increments."

Even better, Renkey had pulled off a 3.42 grade-point average during summer school. "Twelve credits of A," he beamed. However, nothing in two-plus years at Penn State ever seemed to go totally right for him. There had been a problem, and a major one: He was caught with beer in his room during the spring. That was why his practice jersey was an unfamiliar color: orange.

Blue was first team defense; red was second team defense; maroon was third team defense. Chuckling, Renkey said: "They've invented something new for me." Pointing to the jersey that signified fourth string, he quickly added: "This is something I can work my way out of."

And he had. In the weight room Renkey was awful. Todd Burger could bench 225 pounds more than twenty times, but Renkey might not hoist it more than four. Yet Renkey was blessed with functional strength. Simply put, he was better on the field than Burger, and Burger was quite good. "Eric could be a big-time player," defensive coordinator Jerry Sandusky said.

Gradually, Renkey moved up from fourth string during the mid-August torture that is fall practice. "The day I was hurt," he said, "I was running first team." Renkey did not practice for a week, then tried again. "I could hardly move my neck afterward," he said. Penn State's doctors sent him for examinations in Williamsport, and then to a nationally acclaimed specialist in Philadelphia. The bottom line: no permanent damage. Let it heal and see what happens. The forecast: out for the season. That meant football for him was about to spiral even more dramatically downward. Renkey had lettered as a freshman, participating in more than a hundred plays. As a sophomore, he'd stepped on the field just sixty-four times before injuring his toe severely enough to miss the remainder of the season. Now this, his junior year, would be a full season without any action.

The timing could not have been more ironic, for Renkey had been starting to show the combination of athletic and academic discipline that had made him one of the nation's most coveted high-school players. With 1370 on his college boards, he had the potential to be the best in his class in every meaningful way.

Football had gone splendidly early, then slipped because of that toe injury. His grades had gone terribly at first, then risen sharply during the summer between his sophomore and junior years. As Renkey seemed about to excel in both areas, at last, the neck injury postponed football for at least a year.

There had been a pleasant ending to the beer incident. He hadn't been kicked out, but one more violation would make that happen. So Renkey got to live off campus, something he'd wanted to do all along. "For once," he said, "my bad behavior paid off."

The place he shared about four blocks from campus was large and on the inside recaptured the ambiance of the movie *Animal House*. Posters covered the living room; two stereos were on the mantle. Occasionally, tossed beer cans landed in the large waste-basket. Renkey's roommate, Mark, was slender as an exclamation point and came to about Eric's shoulders.

Intellectually, they were a matched set: bright and free-spirited. Mark coached a kids' soccer team, and one evening in mid-October he came home from the final game of the season, a loss, in a down mood. "Know the attitude of our team?" he said to Renkey. "They hate us coaches."

Renkey could identify with that. But he tried to be upbeat, saying: "Your guys are as well-coached as anybody you played."

"They don't look at me as an authority figure," Mark said. Suddenly, he grinned. "One kid came to me and said: 'I like you, cause I can look you in the eye. And I'm only twelve.' "

Renkey's looks and manner had changed. Instead of contacts, he was wearing glasses. That gave him a more studious appearance, more in keeping with the 3.42 that he'd earned the most recent semester and the 3.49 that he would get for the fall, failing to scale his academic Everest, the dean's list, by the tiniest step possible.

"Everything's come together this semester, " he said. "I've missed some classes, but I consider myself a class goer now. If I miss one, I feel bad about it. I'll make an effort to go to the next one. Before, if I missed one, I'd go: 'Oh, well, forget the rest of the week.' "

Renkey's work load included anthropology, physics, a high level psychology course, and an industrial psychology course that he took with Rich Rosa, John Gerak, Matt Nardolillo, and O. J. McDuffie. "Teacher's not exactly Mr. Excitement," Renkey said, "so you tend to drift off. O. J. takes real good notes."

Talk late into the night drifted to his neck. Might the last two frighteningly long burners be an omen? Is football still a risk worth taking? Hadn't the since-departed Jorge Oquendo, long ago, said it was far better to earn a living with your mind? Why not simply walk away? Now.

"Because I think I was given the talent to play football," Renkey said. "I want to do well at it. I feel a responsibility. I don't know to whom. Maybe it's to God. Maybe it's to myself to do well. Or as well as I can. Sometimes, I really don't like how much time you have to put in. Gets ridiculous. I don't like the time involved and how seriously people take it. I don't make any secret about that. But I also want to play. I've learned to live with the parts I don't like. Before, I thought I should like everything."

And Paterno?

"We had a heart-to-heart [during the summer]. I didn't like it at the time, but I needed it at the time. I hate to admit it,'cause when he's right it really bothers me. But he was right. That helped me. I'm doing a lot of the things I didn't do before. Discipline. Being consistent. I hadn't been at workouts consistently; I'd missed some classes. I wasn't consistent is what he was angry about. He really let me have it, set all these guidelines, told me I'd be off the team if I didn't meet 'em."

Almost a year earlier Paterno had been bluntly frank about Renkey, saying: "He's been in trouble since he got here . . . He's not afraid of me yet. Somewhere down the line, I've got to scare the hell out of him. I'm trying to pick the spot." Paterno had picked his spot, and the threats were working. Sadly, at almost the exact time Renkey was getting himself together in the classroom and on the field he was hurt too badly to play.

Maybe next season.

Maybe not.

Still, something about Paterno bothered Renkey. The coach was right about discipline and consistency, Renkey admitted, but he took his role too far. He intruded too much on what ought to be private. And he stifled individuality. "As far as your drinking habits, your social habits, how you wear your hair, whether you shave or not is your business," Renkey argued. "That's your lifestyle, your choice. Imagine if your calculus teacher said: 'Hey, you can't wear an earring in here. And go cut your hair.' Like I said, there are parts I don't agree with, but I can still live with it."

The Nittany Lions also lost their second game of the 1990 season, against Southern Cal in the Los Angeles Coliseum, and with it any chance at the national championship. But more members of the class were becoming important in their third year. Brett Wright once again started at inside linebacker ahead of upperclassman Mark D'Onofrio, and in the fourth quarter he made a play that for him meant that two-plus years of work in near obscurity was paying off. He sacked Todd Marinovich for an 11-yard loss.

"Like a dream come true," Wright said. "Getting a Heisman candidate on national television. In the Coliseum. The whole package. On the second or third play of the game, I broke free and made a solo tackle on the tailback in the backfield. Got my name on the loudspeaker. I thought: 'Yeah! Yeah! This is it.' "

A couple of backups, Mark Graham and Ivory Gethers, received even greater recognition. In addition to loudspeaker treatment each got a call from Keith Jackson on the ABC telecast. "Outstanding play by Mark Graham," Jackson gushed after a seemingly certain reception got swatted away. Of Gethers, the number 37 who seemed to be around the ball quite a lot, Jackson said: "I wouldn't be surprised if he gets some more playing time."

Up from gathering uniforms, polishing helmets, and the like as a manager a few weeks earlier, Bob Ceh made his debut as the snapper on punts and place kicks the next game, at home against Rutgers. Everything went so well that he even had an assisted tackle on a punt.

"I thought the 85,000 people would faze me, that I'd be real nervous," Ceh said. "You go out there, and it really is like practice. I was surprised. You don't notice the people at all." He realized who he was and where he'd come from about a month later, against Boston College on the road. "It was a quarter change, we're about to kick a field goal and it hit me: 'You're in the middle of all this! What are you doing? Get outta here.' "

For evidence about the strange twists college football players experience, consider this as Exhibit A: In this third year at Penn State, the highly touted, highly recruited Bobby Samuels, the running back who had Joe Paterno, Lou Holtz, and Johnny Majors at his feet at the same time, was back in Little Pit. And the high schooler with no ambitions beyond managing at Penn State, Bob Ceh, was in the exclusive part of the locker room, next to Tony Sacca.

In the team's fourth game—against Temple on homecoming, October 6, 1990—Penn State was comfortably ahead soon enough for Rich Rosa to get some playing time at wideout. Early in the fourth quarter, on third and four from midfield, he caught an over-the-middle pass from back-up Tom Bill for thirty yards. He and the quietly effective Greg Huntington slapped hands. One play and one penalty later, from the Temple 21 yard line, Rosa was wider than wide open in the end zone, but Bill overthrew him.

On the roller coaster ride that is the regular season for players not dominant at their positions, Todd Burger and Brett Wright by the seventh game, on the road against Alabama, had moved from starters to back-up positions. Rick Sayles, Mark Graham, Tony Matesic, and Chris Cisar were scrambling for action. Also, Keith Jackson had been wrong five games earlier: Ivory Gethers was not getting more playing time.

Few had endured as much as Gethers during his nearly three years at Penn State. He had suffered through two major operations, to his knee and shoulder. And his body was betraying him in other ways. It was not heavy enough for the inside linebacker position that he thought he would inherit when Andre Collins graduated; and the strong safety position for which his size and speed seemed ideally suited was being manned by a future pro, Darren Perry. The topper was that Gethers's grades were shaky enough to make his eligibility for each season in doubt.

Nevertheless, Gethers had immense ability and a passion for football. Some lesser-skilled teammates and rivals from high school were advancing farther in other college programs, which caused Gethers, after a particularly low day, to say: "I don't think it's always the case here where the best man wins a position. They include a lot of things outside football. Grades. Being late for meetings. Disciplinary problems. Lots of things outside of football determine whether you play or not."

Paterno in the first meeting with the class, in August 1988, had said that would happen; Gethers was in no mood to think about it just now. "Joe tells us: 'If you've got problems with a girl, or family, or your books, there's nothing you can do about it on the practice field.' Well, I think that if they have a problem with us off the field—with alcohol, drugs, grades, or whatever—they should deal with it off the field also. Abilitywise, you should be able to play like you're supposed to play, and if the best man wins a position, he plays."

Gethers was sitting in the empty team room, up front, a few paces from where Paterno always conducts meetings. He went on: "But what can you do? That's the question in every player's mind at Penn State. Sometimes, it's like mind games. They'll give it to you and take it away from you. Take it away from you and then give it to you. Turn me loose and let me play. I'm gonna go to the ball. I'm not gonna sit back and relax. The more they play me, the more I'm gonna make big plays."

That was the feeling among other classmates, that Gethers was the one not getting a fair deal from the coaches. Said Renkey: "I just wish they'd find a place for Ivory and turn him loose."

Mood swings were common. During midseason, when he was not getting much playing time, Sayles said: "I thought about quitting. I thought for hours and hours. Then I realized there was nowhere else I wanted to be. I couldn't think of a place to go. The guy playing ahead of me should be. But if he's hurt, how do I do well if I don't get the proper number of reps in practice? And they tell you to have fun. How can you have fun if you mess up one time and get demoted?"

Sayles also knew those demotions weren't as arbitrary as he'd said. Charts on nearly everything are kept at practices—catches, completions, field goals made. Each practice is taped; each tape is reviewed. Mellowing some, Sayles added: "Whatever is gonna happen is gonna happen. I'm more flexible now. More pleasant. More willing to roll with the punches. [Assistant] Bill Kenney stopped me one day and said I should have become a father two years ago."

And then, a few weeks after being so low, Sayles caught the turnaround pass in hallowed Notre Dame Stadium that helped Penn State upset the top-ranked Fighting Irish. In an instant, it seemed, life had gone from misery to not possibly getting any better. It was that way for the team, going from losing the opening two games to winning the next nine; it was that way for cornerback Leonard Humphries, who went from committing a costly pass interference penalty during the Southern Cal loss to making seven interceptions.

In 1990, their third straight year of significant playing time, Tony Sacca had much more written about him; Humphries had the superior season. He was consistent and had a flair for game-turning plays. He intercepted a pass against Maryland on the opening possession and returned it 74 yards for a touchdown. The second of his two interceptions saved the Pitt game.

Humphries had dramatic mood swings. He could be bubbly. In the locker room once he handed me a note from the great and cautious coaching minds across the street. The note read: "You have been selected to participate in an NCAA mandated Drug Testing procedure [tomorrow morning] at 7 A.M. Please report to the locker room on time. You will be expedited in order to make breakfast and any 8 A.M. class you may have."

The idea of Humphries on, say, steroids was ludicrous. At less than 170 pounds, he was the second most-slender player on the entire team. Rick Sayles, at 6-feet-5-inches, was skinnier. Humphries laughed and reported as ordered.

Humphries had nearly doubled over in laughter when the massively overweight Eric Renkey said to him after a mid-August practice in pads: "I have just experienced a freak of metabolism. Yesterday morning, I had a muffin and a small glass of juice before we worked out. For lunch, I had two chicken sandwiches. I had nothing for dinner, and I *gained* two pounds."

Much of the time, Humphries was serious. He had worried that the father he barely knew, who had gone to prison in Arizona, would somehow transfer to him his capacity for big-time trouble. Early at Penn State, Humphries had suffered four concussions in a three-week period, mostly from his helmeted head colliding with the knee of fullback John Gerak during scrimmages. Against Syracuse his freshman season he had been in a pileup so congested that he couldn't swallow.

Those injuries and his mother having a difficult time at home led to Humphries packing his bags before the spring game his freshman year and preparing to quit football. Rich Rosa and O. J. McDuffie were the first to find out and pleaded with him to stay. His position coach, Ron Dickerson, came running to his dorm room in Nittany Hall. So did most of the other defensive backs, who wanted him to stay even though his departure would create more playing time for them.

Word soon reached Paterno, and he and Humphries met in the equipment area off the main locker room. "He understood," Humphries said. "He told me I was a decent player and definitely had a future here. He told me to take a week or so off. Then he hugged me."

Later, during his sophomore season, his mood darkened. The situation at home had not improved; money had become even tighter. With roommate Graham gone, Humphries early one morning took several steps toward suicide. "I tied something around my neck and attached it to the shower curtain rod," he said. "A piece of clothing, I believe it was. Then I started to think about it. If I'd slipped, no telling what would have hap-

pened. But God told me not to go through with it, that I had to
be stronger than that."

(The ground rule for this book was that nothing the players
told me would get back to Paterno until their football careers at
Penn State had ended. I would have broken that rule for something as serious as suicide, but Humphries did not tell me about
his attempt until the spring after his final season, and I immediately mentioned it to Paterno.)

Humphries said religion had helped. "I didn't worry about
money," he said. "God would provide. He did it in very weird
ways. My mom had gotten fired from her job. I had no income
at all. But money came from relatives. On trips home, relatives
would slip me some. Say to take a little something for back at
school. I learned to appreciate things more, what God has given
me."

He also had cleared his biggest academic hurdles. Humphries
was barely eligible before his junior season, but by going to summer school he was set to graduate on time. Humphries had an
interception early in the Blockbuster Bowl against Florida State,
his third in two games. However, he also suffered a shoulder
injury and soon underwent surgery.

On the field for the class this third year, there was progress
and decline. Sacca had 666 plays. That was just four more than
Humphries and twenty-four more than Greg Huntington. Todd
Burger's plays increased from 125 to 327; Tony Matesic's plays
decreased, from 205 to 71. Sayles went from 2 plays to 147, Brett
Wright from 15 to 279, Ivory Gethers from 138 to 204. In two
seasons at wideout, Rich Rosa caught two passes. Ron Fields
more than doubled his playing time, but all that amounted to
was going from eight plays in 1989 to seventeen. Brian Dozier
finally stepped onto the field—for six plays.

Matt Nardolillo also expected to be playing. He was a good
quarterback about whom Paterno in June 1989 said: "I like Matt.
If Sacca weren't around, I'd think he was one helluva prospect.
Doesn't have Tony's arm, but it's good enough. He runs well. I
think he's a player."

Lots of other had schools felt similarly. And the 6-foot-1-inch

Nardolillo, once he determined Sacca would be favored over him, could have transferred. He chose to stay. With Sacca going into his final season and Bill graduated, Nardolillo could see some playing time light ahead. Mop up behind Tony for one more season; assume command of the team as the number-one quarterback in his fifth year.

"The way I look at it," he said, "there's always a reason for why I came here. Someone above told me to come here. That's how I feel." On his mind was his second choice, South Carolina, the school he turned down: "I came here and a year later the coach [of South Carolina] died. And then came a whole bunch of drug problems down there.

"If I was gonna transfer, it should have been in preseason of my freshman year when they said Tony would start in front of me. Soon as I came in, I was told Tony would be ahead of me. If you don't go early, forget it. If you stay, you get friends, you get used to the place. The longer you stay, the harder it is to leave.

"But I'll be angry if I don't come out of here with something. A couple of people on the team have asked if I'll be back for a fifth year. I looked at 'em like they have three heads. Of course I'm staying. Think I'm wasting my time? If I don't start my fifth year, I'll lose my mind or something. I'll rip this place down."

12

Spring Back, Spring Ahead

As Tony Matesic walked toward practice the afternoon of April 10, 1991, his life seemed mostly on the upswing. No longer was he sleepwalking academically. This new discipline produced back-to-back semesters in the 2.5 range and caused his cumulative average to rise well above a C.

Matesic that day was wearing a different color jersey from any he'd ever slipped over massive shoulder pads during his previous three-plus years at Penn State: green. His playing time on the defensive line had diminished, from 205 plays as a sophomore to 71 last season; progress by a couple of underclassmen was such that Matesic might well play even less in 1991.

So he volunteered to switch to the offensive line during spring ball and had advanced to second team green at guard. His best buddy, Todd Burger, also was on the offensive line, having been convinced by Paterno that he had a brighter future professionally as a blocking tackle than as a tackling tackle. By this time John Gerak was becoming familiar with his latest switch, from tight end to guard, during a redshirt fall. These three players were joining the classmate who had resisted the move from defense the most, Todd Rucci. So comfortable had Rucci become at long tackle, after moving there about a year earlier, that he would be judged the most improved player on the entire offensive unit at the end of spring drills.

"I didn't know I had been that bad," Rucci joked.

If all went well during the spring and preseason practices, the delightful possibility was this: Penn State might open the 1991 season with Burger and Rucci at the tackles, with Gerak at strong guard and with Greg Huntington at center. The class could hold four of the five starting offensive line positions, and Matesic might well be the backup to an upperclass regular at short guard, Paul Siever.

That was how it seemed before the offense during practice that day ran a play called 40 Pitch. Matesic pulled to his right and took aim on the outside linebacker. As he was about to deliver the block, the tackler's thumb slipped through his face bars and caused Matesic to hit the ground as though poleaxed. Pain soon gave way to panic, for when Matesic tried to open his eyes he couldn't.

"And when I did force 'em open," he said, "I couldn't see anything out of the left eye at all." The next morning, at the medical center that Penn State operates in Hershey, Matesic underwent two hours of surgery. He stayed in the hospital two nights and his vision improved enough for him to start light exercise two weeks later. Almost immediately, however, complications developed that another procedure at Hershey could not correct.

It was here that Paterno's bad eyesight became useful. The coach had been seeing a specialist at Johns Hopkins in Baltimore routinely the last few years. That man referred Matesic to a colleague in New York, who operated June 7. Matesic thought the worst, that he might be legally blind in his left eye for the rest of his life.

"I was scared to the point where I was crying," he admitted. "I stayed at home for about a month, without doing anything. I didn't want to let people know how I felt. I didn't go out of the house till July fourth. And when I did go out, I'd have problems with the sun. I refused to go out during the day because the sun bothered me so much."

More than anyone at Penn State, Paterno knew what Matesic was going through. "He was the one who pushed me to get additional opinions," Matesic said. "He told me to do what I had to do, to get the best care. That was a side of Joe I'd never seen before." Paterno had screamed at Matesic during spring scrimmage the year before, and Matesic had said: "Joe doesn't know the pain, so he doesn't feel like it's hurting." Joe knows eyes. The insurance policy his father had for the family covered most of the expenses, Matesic said. Penn State paid for everything else.

Gradually throughout late July and August, the eye improved. From barely being able to distinguish body shapes with his left eye, Matesic could see a finger wagging. And so on, until a test in late August yielded 20/60. Light exercise went well. Then came the best news of all. His vision still would be limited, but he might actually be able to resume football sometime during the fall. A plastic shield on his helmet would give the eye as much protection as possible. "I know there's a risk of detaching everything again," he said. "But I'd regret it if I didn't give it one more chance."

Injuries are an unavoidable hazard in the game of football. And as Leonard Humphries was recovering from shoulder surgery early in 1991, it seemed time to determine just how dangerous a game the class had taken on. Sacca and Humphries had completed their third season; everybody else had two more years of eligibility. So all careers were at least halfway complete.

Penn State's director of clinical services, Dr. Jay Cox, said nobody had done any injury studies on any classes but gave me an arbitrary measuring stick. Very likely, he said, at least half the class some time over five years would be injured seriously enough to require surgery. That seemed an ungodly high body count, until I started looking at the roster: Mark Graham (shoulder); Adam Shinnick (ankle); Rich Rosa (ankle); Tommy Wade (knee); Chris Cisar (wrist); Bobby Samuels (ankle); Leonard Humphries (shoulder); Ivory Gethers (knee and shoulder); Rudy Glocker (finger and knee); Chad Cunningham (knee). Bob Daman never had surgery, but his career ended because of back misery. Eric Renkey never had surgery but missed all of one season with neck trouble and nearly all of another with a toe injury. O. J. McDuffie never had surgery but missed a season with a knee injury.

The spring before, O. J. McDuffie had played on Penn State's baseball team and had excelled. As the starting center fielder, he batted .336, scored 23 runs and had 17 rbi. He set a school record by stealing 20 bases (in 21 tries) and tied one by hitting in 18 straight games. McDuffie opted for his first love, football, this spring and was flabbergasted at what happened when the hitting ceased. Paterno actually suggested that he might be a good enough wide receiver to turn pro a year sooner than expected.

"I never thought of myself at that level so soon," McDuffie said. "I thought it would take at least two more years to get to that point. But Joe should know. He called me in and said I could have a big year. He said if I have that big year that I might look at being drafted early."

McDuffie had grown to trust and admire Paterno, but he also felt the coach might have an unspoken agenda. "I don't know if it's a motivational type thing, but I do have more incentive now to work hard. Try to make spectacular plays. Hustle around. I'm pretty sure he's sincere."

A quick read of the numbers McDuffie had accumulated suggested Paterno's judgment was premature. In three seasons, McDuffie had caught just 16 passes. But those passes had yielded 221 yards. Besides, as a sophomore McDuffie had finished seventh in the nation in returning punts. He had been redshirted last season after suffering that knee injury during the season opener against Texas.

Paterno knew exactly how good McDuffie was, that his skills far outweighed his stats. It was to him that the unbending, proud old coach had written one of his gushiest recruiting letters. Nearly four years later, Paterno told reporters: "O. J. can be a Rocket Ismail-type player."

Few other than McDuffie knew about his meeting with Paterno. Even McDuffie didn't know that Paterno was planning to create situations that just might make those public Ismail-type predictions come true. In the fall the Nittany Lions were going to be wide open on offense, pass happy as no one in Happy Valley had ever seen.

Paterno kept that a secret, because Penn State would be opening the season in the big-deal Kickoff Classic in Giants Stadium on August 28. So as not to alert anyone from the opposition, Georgia Tech, the Nittany Lions had run nothing even remotely fancy the entire spring.

That Penn State was playing in the Kickoff Classic had surprised Paterno. He and the coaches had been inclined to turn down the invitation because the game was so early and the schedule was already tough enough without adding a team that had been voted national champion in 1990 by one poll. Almost as an afterthought, Paterno had put the matter before the players during a January meeting and discovered they were eager to play.

Sentiment was not unanimous, however. One of those who argued against the Kickoff Classic in a players-only meeting was Tony Sacca. "I'm always playing devil's advocate," he said. "Everyone wanted to play it, so I had to say: 'Why? We don't need this game to win a national championship.' Actually, it didn't bother me either way."

It did bother Sacca that he had not progressed more rapidly as a quarterback. With three years of a four-year career complete, he still was a very mediocre passer. The pros would take a chance on him, of course, because of his size and exceptionally strong arm. No NFL team had him rated as more than a middle-to low-round prospect.

Still, there was nothing Sacca could do to alter the past, so why get overly concerned. This attitude could be seen as both charming and frustrating. On the one hand, a part of him had resisted making corporate football all-consuming. He loved the games, loved taking chances, loved putting his ability on the line at the most critical times with millions of people watching. He tolerated practice and loathed watching film. Nothing outside football remotely excited him. Studies were a way to stay eligible; his real major was hanging out; he rarely dated.

Also nagging at Sacca was a great desire to excel at a higher level of football, and he knew that his lousy work habits might make that impossible. He recognized this enormous contradiction, the pulls between total fun and becoming an adult. He had turned twenty-one in April.

Sacca recently had spoken with his quarterback rival, Tom Bill, who had gotten a tryout with the Buffalo Bills. "He had a screwy way of gripping the football and would never change here," Sacca said. "For the Bills, he changed. Maybe that'll happen with me when I go away. All of a sudden I'll become this very studious football player. But it hasn't hit me yet."

Like McDuffie, Sacca did not realize the offensive innovations that Paterno was planning for the fall. Little did Sacca know that his dream of leading a pass-oriented offense was becoming a reality in the mind of the coach who a year earlier had called him the biggest quarterback flop in Penn State history. Sacca did recognize and appreciate Paterno speaking more positively about him during press conferences.

"I can't say I don't like him," Sacca said. "I even had problems in high school with Donoghue. Him always hollering at me. You never really like the guy who's coaching you at the time. After I got out of high school, he helped me out so much." If Sacca could have the sort of stunningly brilliant turnaround senior season under Paterno at Penn State that he'd had in high school under Donoghue, his stock once more would be soaring.

PART FOUR

"THIS IS MY HOME"

13

Fleeting Fame

$$\mathrm{T}$$he Fiesta Bowl long had been the setting for football magic by Penn State. In four previous appearances, the Nittany Lions had been out-gained and out-passed, had punted more often, had fewer first downs and more penalties—and also had won all four times. Over Arizona State and Ohio State,. Southern Cal with Heisman Trophy winner Marcus Allen, and Miami with Vinny Testaverde and Michael Irvin, when five interceptions helped grab that second national championship after the 1986 season.

Ah, but all of that seemed amateur sleight-of-hand compared to the Houdini-like wizardry taking place around nightfall on the first day of 1992. Penn State's offense was in the process of mustering 215 fewer yards and 13 fewer first downs than Tennessee's; Penn State's defense was yielding an astonishing five yards per play. Quarterback Tony Sacca was enroute to one of the lousiest statistical performances of his life, and yet Penn State was ahead by 25 points.

Rudy Glocker looked at the scoreboard as though what he'd been watching from the sideline the last several minutes needed verification. It read: Penn State 42, Tennessee 17. "A little while ago," he said, "I thought we'd be on the other end of something like this."

So did the 71,133 customers in Sun Devil Stadium and the millions watching on national television. From a 0–7 deficit, Tennessee had scampered to a 17–7 lead, shortly after halftime. However, starting with a 39-yard punt return by O. J. McDuffie with about five minutes left in the third quarter, the Nittany Lions made that scoreboard flicker like a pinball machine out of whack.

Sacca kept the McDuffie-ignited momentum going with a three-yard touchdown pass. After the defense recovered a fumble nineteen seconds later, Sacca immediately threw for another touchdown, from thirteen yards. When the defense set up a short touchdown run with an interception and then scored itself on a fumble recovery, the Nittany Lions had mustered four touchdowns in a second less than four minutes.

It was an appropriate way to end a bizarre season. The team had been demoralized at midseason but was about to vault to third in the country in the final polls. For the class, in its fourth—and for Sacca and Leonard Humphries, final—year, there had been many peaks and valleys and odd dances with fate, on and off the field. And nobody had flown higher as quickly or plummeted with quite so sad a thud as the tall young man wearing tan slacks and a windbreaker while his buddies were piling up the points a few steps away, Rudy Glocker.

The season began those many months ago with a terrifyingly loud bleep from the VW horn inside the dark blue box that the managers toted from room to room. The wake-up call had come even earlier than usual in 1991. Practice began at 6:30 A.M. on August 7, because it still was reasonably cool then.

Paterno was in an upbeat mood as the still-sleepy players stepped off three dark blue buses that brought them to a spacious area several hundred yards from Beaver Stadium. Nearby, a herd of Holstein cows was grazing in a large pasture.

Two of the players, Eric Renkey and Bobby Samuels, caught the coach's eye. That they both were here was a mild and pleasant surprise. Renkey was close to the Paterno-mandated weight of 275 pounds, and he had been given clearance to test his neck in full-contact drills. Samuels had regained his eligibility with a 2.9 average in summer school and was being tried at a new position, cornerback.

"They look ready," Paterno said, "but I've seen that before." Later that morning, the sun had burned off the last patches of fog from a campus starting to come alive when a bit of reality hit Rich Rosa. Inside the lounge near the locker room, on a dark blue leather couch, he was wrestling with the many implications of the short sentence that had just tumbled over his lips. What he'd said was: "I'm a senior now."

Rosa had the most expressive face of anyone in his class. When he was upbeat, hopeful, full of mirth, most of the space around him seemed to glow. His had been a grand accomplishment in many ways, Rosa realized in the early fall of 1991. He'd gotten through suffocating August preseason camps. He'd gotten through an operation on his left ankle. He'd gotten to the point in labor and industrial relations, with about a C-plus average, where graduation in May was all but assured. He'd gotten mellow at the ripe old age of twenty-one. That made him happy.

"I sit back sometimes and say: 'Boy, am I a bore.' It's something that happens to you. Freshman year, you run a little wild. That freedom. Sophomore year, you still have that in you, cause you can't go in the bars yet. Junior year, when everybody turns twenty-one, it starts all over again.

"Matt Nardolillo and I were talking about that the other night. How we'd hung out and sung by ourselves once at a frat when we were freshmen. Friday nights, we'd go out in twenty-man packs. We talked about how we're twenty-one now and have got to get things in perspective. Hit the books tonight. Get our résumés together."

As freshmen, Rosa and nearly everyone else could hardly wait to get back home. Tony Sacca and John Gerak even rubbed small pieces of tape to a pole near their lockers in Little Pit to mark off days until their first escape from Happy Valley. As seniors, when it was starting to become time to leave permanently, they didn't want to.

"I tell people this is my home," said O. J. McDuffie. "My home is where I go for vacation. And I'm the guy who packed his bags three years ago, wanting to get the hell out of this place. When I go home now, I don't pack my bags. I can't sleep in my bed, it's so uncomfortable. I like being here. The people. The atmosphere. Hanging out around here."

Also on Rosa's mind as the staff parking lot outside began to fill was being one of several in his class at a football crossroads this senior academic year. All had been redshirted, so they had two seasons of eligibility remaining. If they played sparingly this season, however, another year might be out of the question. Too embarrassing. Fifth-year players still stuck to the sideline on game days have diminished respect. After four years, one almost always either gets on the field or gets on with his life.

That mostly was why Rosa had arranged a meeting with Paterno the day before. He wanted to present his case for more playing time, and he prepared for it as though it were a critical exam. Actually, it was more important than that. Rosa had come to Penn State to make his mark in football; to date, very little of significance had happened to him. He'd been redshirted as a freshman, played sixteen snaps as a sophomore and forty-eight as a junior. He'd caught one pass his first season and one pass his second. That angered him, caused him to often be abrupt after games. "They've done it again," he would snap to his father, and both would stomp away. It was time to hash out his future with Paterno.

Rosa had not figured out his coach in the way Rudy Glocker had. Glocker realized that if you catch Paterno off guard, pop into his office unannounced or confront him in a casual situation before or after practice, you are very likely to get your way. Paterno's first instinct is to be accommodating. However, if the meeting or, more importantly, the agenda already has been established, if Paterno has time to think about what's on your mind and to consider the consequences, the likelihood of success is lessened.

Through the coach's administrative aide, Cheryl Norman, Rosa arranged to see Paterno after squad meeting at 4 P.M. Speaking into a mirror in his room the night before, he rehearsed his presentation: "I've paid my dues. I'm at the top of my game. I'm not looking for any limelight or headlines but I deserve more playing time." Rosa did not sleep well that night.

"I thought he was gonna blast me," Rosa said. "Jump all over me, but he didn't. You don't demand anything. You state your case, and he'll listen. I told him I didn't think I was getting anywhere, and he told me he thought I'd jumped a bunch of steps. Now I needed to stay there and rise gradually. He said to work hard and that things would pan out."

Rosa was playing behind his best buddy, McDuffie, but did not mind. McDuffie was exceptional, his superior by far. McDuffie also had confided that he might leave for the pros after this season, which might create more playing time for Rosa, although a couple of underclassmen were quite promising. Paterno's major problem with Rosa was inconsistency during practice. Too many mental errors. Too many dropped passes.

Even though Paterno made no firm promises, Rosa was confident and said: "He's a player's coach. He's very honest with you. You can't ask any more than that."

Also critical this year was the matter Rosa had touched on earlier: resumes. He and most of the others in the class not likely to be given a chance in professional football soon would be interviewing for real world jobs. They were concerned that their only outside activity would be football. Of the class, only Rudy Glocker and Mark Graham had gotten seriously involved in life beyond football and beyond the classroom.

This energy and time management, plus going to summer school, had Glocker on schedule to graduate in January. At a time when the graduation rate for football players throughout the country was less than 50 percent, when many barely got their degrees in five years, he was getting his in three and a half.

Glocker made time to maintain a grade-point average close to a B-plus 3.5. He had the only cumulative average above a 3.0 for the class at the start of its senior academic year. He'd made dean's list that summer, had been tapped for an honor society the previous spring, and recently had been elected president of the twenty-eight-sport student athlete advisory board. Where most others at the time had one-line resumes, Glocker's filled two pages.

Mark Graham, meanwhile, also was getting more practical experience in the line of work toward which he was gravitating: finance. He had tried video rentals with his good friend Brian Harpster his sophomore year. As a junior, he and another pal had sold T-shirts with cartoon characters ironed on them. They made enough to finance a week's trip to the Bahamas during spring break.

"I'm out of here in the spring," said Graham, who was carrying a 2.8 average into his senior year and was set to graduate in May. "I want Wall Street. Or Chicago. Or L.A. I want to be where the action is."

Rosa was worried about his future. He didn't figure to see much action on the football field in his fourth fall at Penn State. He wondered about the interview process, his scanty resume, and said: "Am I ready for that? Has this place prepared me for that?"

He thought it had. "You learn what Joe wants within a week of your freshman year. But I don't think you really know what it means for another couple of years. You learn to be prompt. Ten minutes early is Joe time. Guys who arrive five minutes early to squad meeting get yelled at.

"You learn how to present yourself in public, and that how you dress is important. You learn about discipline. Rules. That everything doesn't always work out the way you want." About the time that he realized an NFL career was unlikely Rosa had begun an academic surge. His last three semesters, he'd averaged close to a B. "Right now," he said, "you live in such a structured life. Football's hard. This program's hard. But you didn't come for anything easy. Life isn't going to be any easier."

For fall practice Tony Sacca had walked off the cover of a few preseason magazines. On *The Sporting News*, he had been rolling to his right, his arm cocked as if ready to deliver a hard spiral to the reader. The large headline near his left thigh pad read: "Pride of the Lions." Smaller type just under his right elbow said: "With quarterback Tony Sacca at the helm, Penn State's offense should roar." Paterno had been praising Sacca, saying during media day: "I think he'll have a fine season. . . . He's very critical to our success, until the offensive line gets good and the running game becomes established."

Privately, Sacca was saying: "We still have our differences and will have our differences till the day we die. But we've learned to accept each other a little bit more. We kid a bit more now." Indeed, Paterno was deflecting questions about him and Sacca by saying: "Hey, we're both Italian."

Both coach and quarterback knew that the uncertain phase of the offense was going to be the blockers. They mostly were new to their positions and would be untested as a unit in game situations before meeting Georgia Tech. For Sacca, the neat part was that almost all of his protectors would be his buddies: Todd Rucci and Todd Burger at the tackles, John Gerak at one guard, and Greg Huntington at center.

Most of the "Copa" gang from room 105 in Nittany Hall— Sacca, Rucci, ·and Gerak—had rented a house downtown. A fourth roommate was a smart but sloppy upperclass guard, Mac Gallagher, who was relegated to the basement, where from his bed he would turn the television off by grabbing the head of a golf club and poking the other end against the knob.

All about Sacca's room were reminders of past glory: his jersey from Delran High and his jersey from the Holiday Bowl. A framed story about him hung from one wall; a cartoon, titled "The Sack," of an enormous defensive lineman about to pounce on a tiny quarterback loomed above his bed. "He's retired all his jerseys," Rucci joked. "No one else will."

"Document how neat my room is," Gerak shouted, "because my mom cried my sophomore year when Tony said I was a slob."

Sacca was excited about the presumed emphasis on passing.

He and McDuffie were striving to reach the highest levels of football—the pros. Chris Cisar, Brett Wright, and Bobby Samuels on defense and Rich Rosa on offense were trying to position themselves for significant playing time. Each wore a jersey indicating second team. Paterno said to the press the day before that he hoped Rosa "comes through so we have some depth."

Everyone else in the class was less certain about any action at all during their next to last season of eligibility. Ivory Gethers, Mark Graham, Rudy Glocker, and Ron Fields were third team on defense. For Fields, that low status frustration was nothing compared to what took place about two weeks later. At about 4 P.M. on the tenth day of classes, Fields was blissfully walking around campus, unaware that he was about an hour from being kicked out of school.

Fields had come to what academic advisor Don Ferrell called "max time for his whole education." He had to get out of the Division of Undergraduate Studies and be in a major ten days after the start of school. During the summer Fields had gotten the three Bs necessary to nudge his cumulative average above 2.0 and to qualify for a major in broadcasting. Trouble is, he had forgotten to finalize everything with the proper officials. Simple paperwork stuff, but critical.

"I checked the records that tenth day on the computer, as I always do," Ferrell said. "At three o'clock, Ron wasn't in a major. So I found out where his class was about that time and ended up walking up to him on campus. I asked him how his major was going. He said fine. I told him no, that he had about an hour and ten minutes to get everything in order or pack his bags and go home."

At 4:52, eight minutes before the bureaucracy packed up and the day officially ended, Ferrell checked his computer once more. He smiled and sat back in his chair. Fields was safe.

During the final scrimmage before the season opener, Sacca was a split second behind on his decisions and his passes. This was serious stuff: first team offense vs. first team defense; second team offense vs. second team defense. Sacca, McDuffie,

Huntington, Gerak, and, mostly because of injuries, tight end Rick Sayles, were first team on offense. In second team green were Rosa, Burger, and Matt Nardolillo at quarterback. Rucci was hurt but still figured to start against Georgia Tech.

Leonard Humphries also was injured, though not seriously, which meant that Mark Graham opened at cornerback with the first team defense. On the second team, Renkey was at nose tackle, Cisar at Hero, and Wright at inside linebacker; Ivory Gethers and Rudy Glocker were in third team maroon. Bobby Samuels, who earlier had been injured and missed practice most of the week, never left the bench.

Sacca was not impressive; Nardolillo was. Sacca was intercepted on each of the first three offensive drives, the second time by Graham near the goal line. Nardolillo produced touchdowns the first two times that the second-team offense collided with the second team defense. For a few scary moments, Renkey was in extreme pain, his right shoulder limp as he left the field. Had the neck worsened? No. He soon was back on the field.

Near the end, Paterno could tolerate Sacca's dismal lack of results no longer. Sacca's parents and younger brother, Ralph, were among those in near-empty Beaver Stadium; that didn't matter. The coach tore into Sacca and yanked him briefly in favor of Nardolillo, whose timing had overcome his lack of arm strength. Peg Sacca shook her head in silence. Eleven days to go. Would Tony be ready? Would the team?

Peg Sacca had little reason to worry. With just under two minutes left in the third quarter of the Kickoff Classic, the tens of thousands of Penn State fans in the sellout crowd of 77,409 in the Meadowlands rose in both astonishment and great glee. Down in the corner of the end zone, O. J. McDuffie had made a touchdown catch for the all-time highlight film. He had lost the ball as it hit his fingertips. Then it rolled off his back and, as he and a Georgia Tech defender hit the ground, miraculously came to rest in his hands. Even sweeter, Penn State after the extra point was leading one of the previous season's national champions by 27–3.

Sacca and the team proved that they were more than ready

for the 1991 season. So was the new sleek and slick offense Paterno had worked so hard to keep secret. On the Nittany Lions' first play from scrimmage, they lined up with three wide receivers. That was two more than Paterno usually had showed over the years and one more than expected. Three wide receivers spread the field. That left the middle vulnerable, and Sacca opened with a short pass to a running back near the line of scrimmage. The play had possibilities, but Sacca threw the ball into the turf. Still, an early message had been sent.

Nearly everybody in the class had a part in the early going. Samuels, Cisar, Gethers, and Wright were on the kickoff team. The first Georgia Tech pass of the game was high, but Humphries wrestled the receiver to the turf anyway. Burger, Rucci, and Huntington started on the offensive line. Gerak was second team but established himself as a future force. Sayles at times was one of the wide receivers. Paterno considered him too frail for tight end but wanted to feature his height and speed.

Sacca was better than sensational. From the lackluster performance in that final tune-up scrimmage, he threw two short touchdowns passes before halftime. Then he got better. "I'm looking at Sacca in the huddle and we're laughing," Rucci said. That was after Penn State started the third quarter with a 13–3 lead and ended it with a 27–3 lead.

The onslaught started after back-to-back fumble recoveries by Penn State, one of them by Wright. In short order, Sacca ran for 15 yards and then flipped a pass over the middle to McDuffie from the Yellow Jackets 5 yard line for his third touchdown pass. Number four was a gift from McDuffie, that can-you-believe-it catch.

Incredibly, there was a number five. Sacca got credit for it but did nothing more than toss a short pass to the much-heralded underclass running back Richie Anderson, at Penn State's 48 yard line. Anderson weaved his way 52 yards and into the end zone. The rout was on. In short order, Renkey got a chance to play on defense. So did Cisar, Samuels, and Glocker. Gethers recovered a fumble near the goal line. With ten minutes left, this time in joy rather than frustration, Paterno pulled Sacca for Nardolillo.

For Nardolillo, this was a special thrill, being so close to his home and hearing over the loudspeaker in the stadium that the pro Giants and Jets use: "Matt Nardolillo at quarterback for Penn State."

Not all went smoothly. Georgia Tech rallied, then recovered an onsides kick and made the final score respectable: 34–22. "First couple of series, I get twenty yards in penalties," said Burger, referring to his jumping offsides and drawing a personal foul in his first game at offensive tackle. "Joe pulls me and screams: 'You're not on defense any more.'"

This was Penn State's first victory in a season opener in three years. Sacca's five touchdown passes was a school record. "I can't take [total] credit," he said. "The one to Anderson was practically a handoff; another one O. J. caught off his head. And [the receiver] was so wide open on another one I could have kicked it to him. It's no big deal to me. Really."

During a press conference, Paterno glanced at Sacca, who was in socks and a T-shirt, and said: "My buddy, Tony." That drew a laugh. Seriously, Paterno added: "I've been severe with Tony because I know how good he can be." However, the game ball did not go to Sacca. It was presented by a co-captain to a freshman wideout, Bobby Engram, whose father had been killed a week earlier.

A national television audience had been impressed. So were those who vote in the national championship polls, especially when Paterno said: "We played about the way I thought we would." College football commentator Beano Cook predicted on ESPN: "Tony Sacca will win the Heisman Trophy."

The next game was the home opener against Cincinnati, and Penn State's first appearance in a stadium whose capacity had grown by 10,033. The addition was to the north end, the one opposite the tunnel from which the team entered the field. So large was the north side that no Nittany Lion player could see sky until a few steps from the playing field. With 93,000 seats, Beaver Stadium was second only to Michigan's 101,701 among on-campus stadiums.

Already imposing were the sounds of partisan Penn State fans.

Todd Rucci thought opponents might liken the feeling to "being stuck in a tin can placed in front of a speaker." Whatever, Cincinnati surrendered 17 points the first quarter, 23 points the second quarter, and 27 the third quarter. That's 67–0 with 15 minutes left to play.

By that time, positions were being manned by players unknown to even the most partisan Nittany Lions enthusiasts. The number 56 at one end of the defensive line was Ron Fields. Unless it was Mac Gallagher. Four seasons into Penn State, Fields still was on the foreign team during practice, an academic senior stuck now with freshmen, trusted only in games the team could not possibly lose. So low in esteem was Fields that his number, 56, was also worn by an equally obscure offensive lineman who played a bit more.

Fields was hurt before the last scrimmage and, although completely well ten days later, did not play against Georgia Tech. "They told me I get hurt a lot," he said. "I told 'em I didn't plan on getting hurt." With the score 67–0, a Cincinnati player was tackled behind the line of scrimmage by Eric Renkey and fumbled. Fields recovered the ball and leaped high in celebration. However, the Penn State stat crew credited the good deed to Gallagher. Still, Fields was being noticed, though in a strange way.

Early during most weeks throughout the rest of the season players would find in their lockers a sheet of paper that, from a distance, resembled a wanted notice tacked to the bulletin boards in post offices. Most prominent was a picture and a brief biography. Ron Field's one time, Tony Matesic's another. Close-up inspection revealed that this was a clever way of maintaining team spirit, a reward for having absorbed daily humiliation with grace. The relevant lettering read: "Foreign Team Player of the Week."

This was Bob Daman's idea, his way of contributing to morale as an untitled defensive aide since the back misery that ended his football career two years earlier. Daman figured: "Why not give some recognition to players who almost never get any. Who practice as hard and as long as everyone else, but who almost never play." Because he worked with those white-shirted foreign teamers, Daman was best qualified to recognize the best of the overlooked. He said: "I try to give motivation where there is none to be had."

At most practices Daman held large cards. Each card had a diagram of a defensive formation favored by the upcoming opponent. The players to whom Daman showed the cards were the eleven white shirted scrubs imitating the opposition defense for Penn State's first team offense. The routine for the foreign teamers was to glance at Daman's card and assume the designated alignment as the offense broke its huddle. Boom! Play ends. Everybody back up. Another card. Another set. Boom! Again and again. If the Penn State offense was routinely successful, as it had been in back-to-back routs of Georgia Tech and Cincinnati, the defensive white shirts could take modest pride. It was important, but mostly thankless, until Daman became inspired in the fall of 1991.

Daman would solicit suggestions about deserving foreign team players, but the final decision was his. Once the winner was determined, Daman interviewed him and either got appropriate quotes from teammates or made them up. Daman then cut out a picture of the honoree from the football press guide, fit it with the biography he'd already typed out, and ran off a hundred or so copies.

Of Fields, Daman wrote: "He was hesitant in actually discussing these (pass rush) techniques, but did mention a method of mental imagery of one Vanessa Williams on the other side of the ball. Maybe he isn't so different on and off the field." Fields was quoted as saying of his favorite offensive lineman: "He tries to cuss me out, but can't get the words out."

Matesic had been cleared to practice and was wearing a clear plastic shield across his helmet to protect his eye. He also had been switched back to the defensive line, as a backup at nose tackle because of the uncertainty about Eric Renkey's neck. Almost unnoticed in the glee over Fields recovering that fumble against Cincinnati was the player who caused it, Renkey, heading for the sideline in extreme pain. Another long-lasting burner. His status for the remainder of the season was doubtful.

The coaches loved Daman's weekly product. The players loved the fact that lots of Daman's stuff was a sly knock at the coaches or the squeaky-clean image of the program. If a player of the week indicated a favorite coach, that meant he actually was angry with him. Daman wrote about one of his players of the week: "After a difficult day of preseason practice it was not uncommon for him and his roommate to sit down and study film." Truth is, they were watching porno flicks.

Slightly more than a month after the 81–0 rocket boost to the outer limits of football comprehension that had followed the season-opening rout of a fine Georgia Tech team—five games and thirty-eight days to be exact—morale in the locker room plummeted to what Brett Wright called "pretty much of an all-time low." The mood on Tuesday, October 15, 1991, was quiet but tense, because more than a half-dozen younger players all of a sudden had moved ahead of seemingly established veterans and into starting positions. Penn State had lost two games, and with them any chance at the national championship. Paterno had hit the panic button. Punched it, actually.

To a team that sets its sights on winning a national championship, even one loss is a major disappointment. That can be overcome, however, if the setback is early enough. After all, the first of Penn State's two national titles, in 1982, had come after a twenty-one-point midseason loss at Alabama. So losing at Southern Cal, after winning the first two games by a combined 115–22, could be tolerated. Especially with the strength of the remaining opponents.

The worrisome and risky aspect of the Southern Cal defeat was that it eliminated any cushion. The Nittany Lions had to win all of their next nine games to be invited to the major bowl that would help determine the national champion. The second setback, a six-point road loss to top-ranked Miami, came on October 12. Ironically, the team had played much better against

Miami than it had against Southern Cal. But Miami was vastly superior to the Trojans. Even so, the defeat was devastating. And the more Paterno thought about it the more inclined he became toward change.

Brett Wright saw it all around him as he dressed for practice. Fifth-year starters, one of them a co-captain, now in back-up positions. Greg Huntingdon pulled a green jersey over his shoulder pads instead of blue, demoted to a second-string center behind a walk-on, E. J. Sandusky, son of the defensive coordinator; quarterback Matt Nardolillo was still on the team in name but not really feeling part of it anymore.

"Everyone's pretty much fed up with it," Wright said. "Just fed up."

There had been changes even before the Southern Cal game. In public, Paterno had said, "Nothing bad has happened to us yet. . . . We may be deluding ourselves." So easy had Cincinnati been that Paterno ordered a tough, no pads workout the day after, a Sunday, when all that usually took place were meetings. Two days later, Nardolillo was hit with the gut-wrenching impression that he might never play another significant down for Penn State.

Tuesday is the toughest practice day, when the hardest and longest hitting takes place. Nardolillo sensed nothing unusual about this one as he and redshirt freshman Kerry Collins tossed a ball back and forth while the rest of the players and coaches were walking onto the field outside Holuba Hall. Neither was it out of the ordinary when quarterbacks coach Jim Caldwell asked Nardolillo and Collins to come join him. Then Caldwell dropped his bomb: You two will battle it out for second team now.

That was it. No explanation. No elaboration. Nardolillo was too stunned, too embarrassed to do anything rash just then. He went through practice but realized this was a battle that he was not likely to win. When an underclassman becomes a co-equal, he usually gets the benefit of all doubts. The coaches have made a determination; they want the younger fellow to succeed.

Nardolillo was hit with this just twenty-four days after Paterno had jerked Sacca for him in the final serious preseason scrimmage. It was just seventeen days after he'd run onto the field at Giants Stadium and been thrilled to hear over the public address system: "Matt Nardolillo at quarterback for Penn State." All of that seemed to mean Nardolillo would be second team this season and, with Sacca gone, assume command of the offense next year.

In an instant, in one sentence, all that seemed to have changed. Collins had the stronger arm, by far. His fastball was nearly the equal of Sacca's. Collins also had had a redshirt season to become acquainted with the offense. Collins almost certainly would have to mess up big time for Nardolillo to ever beat him out.

Other players had noticed that. When I mentioned Nardolillo's frustration later to Sacca, Gerak, and Rucci, they responded, almost in unison: "Wrong school."

"We thought he was really good his freshman year," said Gerak. "But he wasn't a dropback quarterback. If he couldn't roll out, he couldn't throw the ball."

"He was first team all-state, ahead of me," said Sacca. "As far as he knew, he was just as good as I was. That's the thing. When you come here, some guys will step on the field, and some guys never will. This is the closest you come to going to work. It's a job. You don't perform, you don't play."

Even so, Nardolillo scheduled a meeting with Paterno later in the week. Paterno said one of the reasons for the change was the chance for Collins to learn the offense. He also told Nardolillo that he'd not been on top of things in games. When Nardolillo disagreed and asked for an example, Paterno recalled that he'd set a formation wrong against Cincinnati.

Nardolillo was incredulous. He'd known that, realized his mistake shortly after breaking the huddle. Because the score was sixty-something to nothing, however, he hadn't bothered to call time and get everything corrected. Besides, the play gained eight yards anyway. "It's hard to understand his reasoning," Nardolillo said.

Sure enough, in the practices that followed, Collins took two snaps for every one of Nardolillo's. Even worse was what Nardolillo had to deal with away from the football field, the depressing fact that every Penn State fan still assumed that he was heir apparent to Sacca. At a gas station once, the attendant pointed to Nardolillo and yelled to several buddies: "Hey, take a look at Penn State's starting quarterback next year." Nardolillo was mortified. Little did they know that he might not even be at Penn State next year.

Penn State entered hallowed Los Angeles Coliseum for its third game of the 1991 season ranked fifth in the country; Southern Cal was unrated, having lost by two touchdowns to lightly regarded Memphis State in its only test. But the Trojans had a week off to prepare for Penn State and used it to concoct every blitz imaginable for Sacca and his inexperienced offensive line. During the Nittany Lions' first series, Sacca was sacked. During the Nittany Lions' second series, Sacca was sacked. During the Nittany Lions' third series, Sacca was sacked. On the sideline, Paterno and his offensive aides were working furiously on blocking assignments.

The fourth series was better. Sacca completed two passes for 19 yards, ran once for another 4, and the Trojans were penalized 15 yards for unnecessary roughness. On third and 5 from the USC 13 yard line, Sacca threw for a touchdown. But the extra point only meant that Penn State had tied the game at 7–7.

Southern Cal took the lead four plays after recovering an O. J. McDuffie fumble and beginning play just twenty yards from the end zone. Its defense protected that 14–7 advantage by keeping Sacca on the run and intercepting him near midfield about a minute before halftime.

Penn State tried to regroup. "We literally changed every pass pattern, just made up everything new," said Todd Rucci. "We finally settled on one pass protection, where we all just stood up and stepped to one side."

Coming from every possible angle, the Trojans continued to chase Sacca and force incompletions. Midway through the third quarter, after yet another hard hit, Sacca arose with a dislocated finger and ran off the field. Because he still had the most experience, Nardolillo was the stopgap replacement for one play, a six-yard keeper on third and ten, while Sacca's finger was pulled into place.

Penn State recovered a Southern Cal fumble at the Trojan 43 yard line. The only first down came on an 11-yard Sacca completion, and the offense had to settle for a 38-yard field goal. When the Trojans quickly converted a Penn State fumble into a 21–10 lead and Sacca kept getting hit hard and throwing incompletions, Paterno went with Nardolillo the final series. He had no chance, either. Nardolillo fumbled the snap on a fourth and 2 play but picked it up and competed a pass for 9 yards. The game ended with him being intercepted. Might that be the last pass he ever threw for Penn State?

Sacca took no snaps during practice before Brigham Young came to Beaver Stadium. To his surprise and delight early in the game, he actually threw a tighter spiral with the injury. Also, BYU and its quarterback, Heisman Trophy winner Ty Detmer, who had thrown for 576 yards against the Nittany Lions in the Holiday Bowl two years earlier, were on a steep downward spiral.

BYU had been beaten in its opening two games, and Detmer had been beaten up. In the first quarter against the Nittany Lions, Detmer misfired on three of his four passes. He was intercepted once and sacked once.

Sacca was surprised by his performance; Rucci, Gerak, Huntington, Burger, and the other blockers were determined to avoid a second straight disaster. By halftime, Penn State's defense had established dominance, and Sacca had completed a 12-yard pass for the touchdown that yielded a 10–7 lead.

Penn State broke the game open with two touchdowns in the third quarter. They were relatively short drives, and Sacca did not throw a pass during either one. In the 33–7 victory, he passed twenty-four times. He'd thrown forty passes against Southern Cal the week before. Nittany Lions backs ran sixty-seven times and controlled the ball for forty-two of the sixty minutes against BYU. There also was victory the next week but little joy.

The fenced-in reception area reserved for parents and friends outside Beaver Stadium was nearly empty after the Boston College game when Todd Rucci hobbled tentatively on crutches toward a dark blue van. He handed the crutches to a trainer, stood on one foot, and then backed his huge body and stiff left leg onto a seat. "My time rolled around," he said.

Rucci was the latest member of the class, and the fourth in all, to be linked with the most dreaded words in football: torn knee ligament. There was sadness and guilt on John Gerak's face as he talked about it with Rucci's mother, because Gerak thought he was the one who had caused his roommate to be in such agony.

He hadn't. In the third quarter against Boston College, Rucci had been pass blocking for Sacca. "I was in a stand-up position, with my knees locked," Rucci said, "and the nose tackle kinda got pushed in the back. He was doing a crab on the ground. I saw him hit the knee. Then I felt two pops and hit the ground. I was whining like a bitch. From what I hear, Joe even came on the field."

The injury was serious. Rucci had torn one ligament and stretched another. The trainers said that only Tommy Wade's injury had been worse. More ominous for Rucci, this was the knee that had required cartilage surgery and caused him to miss his junior year in high school.

As a practical matter, Rucci's injury meant that Penn State was missing the one lineman that it could least afford to lose. And it lost him during a game that should have gone easily but did not. BC actually led at halftime, 7–6, when the extra point that followed Sacca's 42-yard touchdown pass was blocked.

Sacca ran five yards for a touchdown midway through the third quarter, and an underclass runner with a flair for excellence against BC, Shelly Hammonds, soon scooted 56 yards for another. In fourth quarter, Penn State's defense returned an interception 45 yards for a touchdown, then couldn't keep that 28–7 advantage from becoming dramatic.

BC drove 77 yards for one touchdown and narrowed Penn State's lead to 28–21 with a 48-yard scoring pass. With 2:54 still left, the Eagles got the ball on their on 33 yard line and slowly drove it to the Penn State 32. The Nittany Lions were playing soft, willing to trade short passes for the considerable time that they ran off the clock. When BC completed a 15-yard pass, on Leonard Humphries, to the Penn State 17, Bob Daman on the sideline shouted and turned his head in disbelief. After the second of two passes that had little chance of being completed, however, the game ended.

To avoid the crowd, Paterno rides from Beaver Stadium in the small brown pickup truck that also takes some equipment back to the football complex. Even in victory, he looked worried as the truck moved slowly through the reception area. Rucci rode in the van back to the locker room and later joined Sacca and Gerak at the house they were renting. Surgery was scheduled for Monday. "I just got bombed," Rucci said. "Me and Sac just talked. Bitched. I moped around, then went upstairs and passed out."

"Finally. Finally," Rich Rosa said, "I got my start." This was eight days later, 12:30 A.M. on October 6. As Rosa walked across the field in empty Veterans Stadium, he was both pleased and dismayed. Pleased that Paterno had followed through on their meeting of several weeks earlier and given him a chance to open at wide receiver in a game about half an hour from his southern Jersey home. Dismayed that the start, against Temple in place of the slightly injured O. J. McDuffie, had not been more productive.

As had happened against Boston College the week before, the Nittany Lions sputtered and struggled. Distinctive in football pants that seemed to ride higher than most, Rosa caught Sacca's first pass for a modest gain. Later on that opening drive, Sacca scrambled for a 13-yard gain and completed two medium-range passes, the final one for 14 yards and a touchdown.

Then came an all-too-familiar situation: Penn State with a chance to bury an undermanned opponent and finding it difficult. One of those problems was caused by Rosa fumbling the ball, after a 13-yard gain, and Temple recovering at the Penn

State 33. The Nittany Lions held and then pushed more than half the length of the field, only to fail to get the ball into the end zone on six cracks inside the 10 yard line and settle for a 23-yard field goal.

Some Temple trickery, a 46-yard halfback pass for a touchdown, and more ineffectiveness by Penn State on offense led to a 10–7 halftime score staying the same deep into the fourth quarter. The Nittany Lions were ahead but not necessarily in control. The Owls had missed a 35-yard field goal early in the fourth quarter and turned the ball over, on a fumbled snap from center, the next series.

Paterno was trying to establish some run-block consistency with the offensive line. Too often, there were penalties. Holding here. An ineligible receiver there. With 5:15 left in the game, there was enough running and passing for a 51-yard drive to the Temple 22. On third and 12, Sacca connected on a very open pattern for the game-breaking touchdown. Frustrated, Sacca accepted no congratulations when he reached the bench, tossing his helmet and getting a drink.

A few yards away, after the defense quickly intercepted a Temple pass and ran it in for the 24–7 margin of victory, McDuffie fumed: "We're kidding ourselves. We're the worst 5–1 team in the country."

Alone and in small groups, the players walked the length of the field forty-five minutes or so after the game to reach the team buses. "We're not anywhere as good as I'd hoped we'd be," Paterno said. "Right now, we're not playing with a lot of poise."

One of those to whom he was referring was Rosa. The coach during his postgame press conference said Rosa played well "except for that fumble, which should not have happened, obviously." Privately, Paterno had scolded Rosa even more for not being mentally alert a couple of other times. As matters developed, Rosa would never catch another pass for Penn State.

"We'd better get our heads out of our asses," Bob Ceh said, "or we'll be in for a long day in Miami."

During preparations for Miami, the coaches decided to counter the fierce Hurricane pass rush with a trick play. The tight end was to work his way toward the center of the line of scrimmage where Sacca, presumably about to be clobbered, would hit him with what amounted to almost an underhand toss. A shovel pass, it was called, and Paterno decided to help speed the teaching process during practice by becoming a sixty-four-year-old tight end.

At walk-through speed, center Greg Huntington snapped the ball to Sacca, who started to backpeddle. As Huntington, John Gerak, Todd Burger, and the other blockers assumed pass-protection positions, the oldest tight end on the planet threaded his skinny legs down the line. When Sacca seemed at his most desperate, he shoveled the ball to Paterno. See? the old coach said to the real tight ends. You try it.

Over and over the play was run. Slow motion and full speed. At one point, Sacca got bored and flipped the ball behind his back. Made like Magic Johnson on a fast break. He completed the pass anyway. Paterno and the other coaches blanched. Don't do that again, they said. Sacca did it again and completed the pass once more. In fact he felt more comfortable flipping the ball behind his back. The coaches grew more uneasy but felt fairly certain even Sacca would not try such a stunt against the top-ranked team in the country.

Just in case, quarterbacks coach Jim Caldwell came up to Sacca minutes before the kickoff and reminded him once more not to flip the ball behind his back. "But I just had that feeling, you know?" Sacca said later. "I just felt lucky."

Near the end of the first quarter, on third and eleven from the Miami 20, a situation in which the Hurricanes likely would put on a heavy rush to push Penn State out of field goal range, Sacca got the call: shovel pass. And, yes, indeed, he disobeyed orders and flipped the ball behind his back once more. "If I'd banged it off somebody's head," he admitted, "I might have never played again this year." Instead, Troy Drayton, a former walk-on who had beaten out Rick Sayles at tight end, caught the ball and gained exactly enough yardage for the first down.

However, Penn State from inside the 10 yard line had to settle for the field goal that tied the game at 3–3. The half ended at 6–6, with Sacca a sensational 12 for 16 but starting to feel the effects of the 85-degree heat and the pounding from Miami's quick and relentless pass rush. The shovel pass worked, but that was rather like flicking one finger at a swarm of nasty bees.

Sacca was sacked five times in the first half. Run over and thrown to the ground. Five other times in the first thirty minutes, Sacca ran with the ball and also was smacked hard. An offensive line rearranged after the injury to Rucci kept being beaten badly. "The guards are supposed to call the defense," said center Huntington. "A lot of times they were confused. We weren't getting the calls. So we were all off the page, lots of times doing the wrong things. Trying to cover for one another."

Paterno at halftime failed to berate Sacca for whipping the ball behind his back on the shovel pass. Perhaps it was because he had more important matters on his mind, such as trying to get the blocking stabilized. Sacca had another theory: "I don't think Joe could see that far. I don't think he knew I did it." Caldwell knew, and ordered Sacca once more not to do it again. Sacca nodded but made no promises.

On the opening series of the third quarter, Penn State recovered a Miami fumble near midfield. On the first offensive play of the second half, Sacca was sacked for a loss of 6 yards. On second down he bobbled the snap from center but recovered it. On third down he completed a pass but for not nearly enough for the first down. Then came two turnaround plays for Miami. On the first play after Penn State's punt, the Hurricanes beat Leonard Humphries long and connected on an 80-yard touchdown pass. Miami 13, Penn State 6.

On the next series Sacca completed a 21-yard pass to McDuffie while being tackled. But the series fizzled, and about a dozen seconds later the Miami punt returner was dancing in Penn State's end zone, having returned the ball 91 yards. The Hurricanes had touched the ball twice and produced 14 points.

Miami then helped Penn State immensely by getting 30 yards in penalties. The first penalty was for celebrating too excessively after the punt return. That cost 15 yards on the kickoff. A personal foul during the kickoff gave Penn State another 15 yards and the ball on its 43 yard line. Sacca completed two passes to McDuffie for a total of 38 yards during the drive and finished it off with a two-yard scoring pass to redshirt senior Terry Smith. Even quicker, Miami followed with another long touchdown pass and, with the extra point wide right, increased its lead to 26–13.

Sacca kept throwing and kept taking hits. On an incompletion, the Hurricanes were called for a late hit and penalized another 15 yards. Later, on fourth and 1 at the Miami 25 yard line, Sacca kept the ball and got the first down. He was sacked once more, then handed to McDuffie on a reverse for 12 yards. After yet another Miami personal foul the Nittany Lions had a first down on the Miami 9. Smith made a leaping catch in the end zone, and the deficit soon was whittled to just six points.

From their 20 yard line a couple of minutes later, Penn State surged slightly ahead and then was beaten back. One of the calls was for the shovel pass and, yes, Sacca flipped the ball behind his back again. The ball was on target to junior Troy Drayton, but Miami stopped him after a 3-yard gain and Penn State soon punted.

There was one more chance for victory against a team that had won forty straight games at home. With 2:36 left, Penn State got the ball on its 26 yard line. Players threw up their fists on the sideline; Paterno paced. Exhausted, Sacca joined the huddle. His first pass was to McDuffie for 15 yards. His second pass was to McDuffie, for another 15 yards to the Miami 44 yard line.

Sacca by this time had been sacked an astonishing eight times. He also had run eight more times. Officially, he had been tackled sixteen times in heat that sapped the energy of bystanders doing nothing more than clapping. On third and 10 from the Hurricane 44, Sacca was hit hard while throwing an incompletion. He dropped back on fourth down and then failed to realize the situation that quickly unfolded. Miami played loose, leaving what seemed to Penn State players and fans about twenty acres of open space to run. There was plenty of time left and plenty of room for plenty more than a first down. Sacca didn't run. "Just so whipped." he said later. "After looking at the film, I could have crawled down the sideline for a first down. At the time, it didn't even occur to me to run. Being fourth down, I felt: 'Just get the ball up in the air at least. Maybe something'll happen.' " Sacca got the ball to the end zone. What happened was an interception.

The loss to Miami drained all hope of a national championship. In public, Paterno said: "It's tough to gauge what your kids did when you're playing against that much talent.... Miami opted to play us differently than I've seen them play in years. I don't know when I've seen a Miami team do that much blitzing." The coach mentioned some emerging leaders, among them McDuffie and Sacca.

"I wasn't a big Sacca fan when he got here," said Ceh, who was a manager at the time. "He just wasn't a leader. Not real vocal, out for himself, I thought. I see him differently now. My locker's next to his, so I see him and talk to him a lot. It doesn't seem like anything bothers him. If he plays a great game and the media pumps him up, that's great. He plays bad and the media gets on him, he doesn't care. He doesn't let all the outside people bother him. I'm a big fan of his now. He's out there to win and to have fun. Which is what you're here for."

"I enjoy watching Sacca," said Eric Renkey. "First of all, I've never seen him slide. I love that. He runs people over. And he goes downfield and blocks. Sometimes you might get frustrated with him in the past because he wasn't working hard. Then he goes out and blocks on a 48-yard touchdown run. I don't know what's more leadership: hanging out with the guys for five or ten minutes or going downfield in a game and crushing somebody."

Two days after Miami, Paterno was angry and geared for change. Too many foolhardy mistakes, he insisted. He said this fifth-year senior class had accounted for more losses than any other and went about demoting two of them, guard Paul Siever and tight end Al Golden. In all, as the team walked off to practice October 15, four of the six principal offensive line positions, including tight end, had undergone switches. Only tackle Todd Burger and guard John Gerak had kept their blue jerseys.

Greg Huntington before the squad meeting earlier in the afternoon had been stopped in the hallway by his position coach, Dick Anderson. You'll be in green, Anderson said. E. J. Sandusky has been promoted. Because Paterno in the meeting had said he didn't want any whining about position changes, Huntington kept his thoughts mostly to himself.

When he took a seat in an empty meeting room the next day, however, Huntington became so upset that his voice kept rising in pitch and his speech grew more rapid. He sputtered: "I've given everything they could possibly ask of me. Sucked it up. Practiced when I've been sick. And now I'm second string. I would never come to this school if I had to do it all over again. You know the games they're playing, trying to motivate you, but it kills your confidence and pride. The feeling you get around here is you're never good enough."

Last year, Huntington said, he was just getting familiar with guard. Then he was switched to center. Before he could become comfortable at center this season, he had been jerked back to second team. Offensive linemen are rated after each game, and Huntington's grade after Miami had been 69. He'd gotten a 64 in his first game at center, against Georgia Tech, a 90 after the rout of Cincinnati and an 89 after the loss to Southern Cal. The highest grade after Miami been an 80, by Gerak.

Paterno and Anderson had considered the spotty blocking by the offensive line over a longer period than one game. Sacca agreed with the changes, saying: "It just got to the point where they had to do something. Scare 'em into playing better. It got to the point where we just couldn't make any more excuses." Sacca also said Rucci's absence for two-plus games was "like losing my right arm."

Brett Wright became a starter at inside linebacker after the Miami loss because another fifth-year, Mark D'Onofrio, had a shoulder injury too serious to play on. Still, Wright was angry and confused. "We're 5–2 and ranked number 10 in the country," he said, "and Joe in so many words says to us: 'The season is a failure.'"

Wright looked up from his locker. It was the morning after the purge. At the other end of the otherwise empty locker room, out of earshot, defensive coordinator Jerry Sandusky walked toward the small room reserved for coaches. Wright thought about the fifth-year players being benched, humiliated really, and wondered: Is it worth it to come back next year? Wright had been the one member of the class who had never before talked to me about quitting.

"It's so appealing now, two months before the end of the season and thinking I could be done with this," he said. "Then there's the harsh reality of a resume. I look back and I have no work experience to show. Nothing to show a potential employer. I've always done summer school here for football. What do I have to show for it? The Blockbuster Bowl and the Holiday Bowl. I always thought it would be worthwhile if we won the national championship." He laughed. "It hasn't come true."

Paterno was taking a high stakes gamble. He had been able to be so harsh, so authoritative over the years, because Penn State under him had won nearly four of every five games. What if this latest bold move failed? "We could go either way," said assistant coach Tom Bradley. "This way." He pointed his thumb up. "Or this way." He pointed his thumb down.

For most of the first half at home against Rutgers, the verdict was thumbs down. As expected, the only offensive linemen who retained their starting positions after the post-Miami purge were Gerak and Burger. Unfortunately, so spotty was the offense that each of them recovered a teammate's fumble.

Rudy Glocker made his debut as a starter at right end on defense. Brett Wright also assumed the important inside linebacker position called Backer, because the upperclass co-captain who manned it, D'Onofrio, had undergone shoulder surgery. Glocker got a mention from the public-address announcer for a tackle; cornerback Leonard Humphries also drew notice from the overflow crowd of 95,729—for two pass interference penalties in the first quarter, the second of which helped Rutgers gain a 7–7 tie.

O. J. McDuffie reversed the flow, first with a 55-yard punt return for a touchdown and later with an acrobatic 53-yard catch of a Sacca airout. Quickly, Gerak led the blocking on a short touchdown run, and the Nittany Lions took a 21–14 lead into halftime.

Penn State seemed in control during the third quarter, but not to the point where Paterno would have tolerated one scene in the huddle that involved Gerak and Burger. For his switch to guard the year before, Gerak had chosen number 57 for his jersey, because that was his mother's age at the time.

Remembering that his folks were in their late fifties, Gerak once while puffing between plays looked at Burger and said: "Do you think my parents do the wave? . . . It's been bothering me for the last couple of plays."

"Here we are, in the middle of a game," Burger said later, "and I just start laughing hysterically. So when I was walking back to the huddle after the next play, I started thinking: 'I wonder if my parents do the wave.' That whole series, we're on the field wondering if our parents do the wave. Right in the middle of a pretty tight football game. Hey, if you can't have fun, why play?"

After a 20-yard run by Sacca put the game out of reach, Ron Fields charged downfield on the kickoff and made a jarring hit that caused a fumble that Rutgers recovered. At least the announcer got the right number 56 this time, saying for Dolores Fields and everyone else in Beaver Stadium to hear: "Tackle made by Ron Fields."

The next two weeks, against West Virginia at home and Maryland in Baltimore, the Nittany Lions were as consistently powerful as Paterno could hope, winning by a combined score of 98–6. Sacca passed just fifteen times, but completed nine for 172 yards and three touchdowns against the Mountaineers. Two of those scoring passes were to McDuffie. Ivory Gethers had a sack and an interception.

Huntington regained his starting position against Maryland, and the offense moved 80 yards in seven plays for a touchdown on the opening series. Later, McDuffie scored a touchdown that Paterno did not mean for him to get. With the Terrapins down by 33–0, McDuffie "kinda snuck on the field," as he later put it, with the back-up punt return team and broke free for a 60-yard touchdown.

This thumbs-up improvement could not be more timely, for Notre Dame was next. Said Paterno, always cautious in public: "We've got to be our best to even stay with 'em." The added significance this season was that the Notre Dame game would be the final one in Beaver Stadium for Sacca and Leonard Humphries. As they were about to be honored by Penn State fans during pregame ceremonies, others in their class who long ago had said good-bye to Penn State football were scattered about the country.

14

Where Are They Now?

Biemesderfer Stadium is about a two-hour drive and a level of football removed from Penn State. Located just outside Lancaster, it is home to the Millersville University Marauders of the Division II Pennsylvania State Athletic Conference. Trees stand near the scoreboard beyond one end zone; a hillside where fans watch the games on bleachers rises a few steps behind the visitor's bench.

On the foggy evening of October 26, 1991, few in the near-capacity crowd of about 5,000 took special notice of what the public address announcer said after Millersville's third play from scrimmage: "Tackle by Grego."

The tackler was Anthony Grego, the first player of his class to leave Penn State and, ironically, the only one of those who left who was still playing football. Imposing as always at 6 feet 5 inches and 265 pounds, Grego was at defensive tackle for the very competitive Mansfield Mountaineers.

Some at Penn State would have been startled. Offensive co-ordinator Fran Ganter, who recruited Grego out of Bergenfield, New Jersey, had said of him: "He got homesick when he came here in high school for summer camp, and the same thing happened when he came to college." Ganter pointed out a window in his office and said: "He sat out there under that tree bawling his eyes out, waiting for his uncle to come pick him up. We couldn't get him to stay. I don't think he wanted to play football. I don't think he ever liked it."

In this stadium in south central Pennsylvania, in an atmosphere much less tense than the one he'd left more than three years earlier, Grego seemed comfortable. Except during one more moment of irony late in the first quarter. At the exact moment Penn State's 51–6 victory over West Virginia was being announced to the crowd—and to modest applause—Mansfield trainers were carefully removing Grego's shoulder pads and T-shirt.

He'd suffered a slight separation in his left shoulder. Finished for the game. So long gone and so far away, Grego still was part of the class's ever-growing injury list. His left ankle had been bothering him since the spring; his left knee had been bruised the week before; now his left shoulder got knocked loose. On the left side of his body, nothing else was left to hurt.

From a perch on the grassy knoll perhaps fifty yards away, Grego's father leaped to his feet. There had been tension over Anthony's leaving Penn State. Father and son had gone more than a year without speaking, until the Mansfield coach had coaxed them into getting together. Everything had gotten worked out, and the father quickly joined Anthony.

"I was playing good, too," said the son.

"Yeah, got a sack on the first play," the father remembered.

Teammates came by to check Grego's condition. A few minutes later, his left arm was placed in a sling. In black shorts and a gray T-shirt, Grego watched his teammates hold on for a 31–30 victory. Or tried to watch, for the fog was so thick at times during the fourth quarter that the action could not be seen from the sideline.

When the celebration near midfield ended and his teammates headed for the showers under the permanent stands, Grego leaned against a fence.

"Why'd they think I left?" he asked. Meaning Penn State. A girl.

"That wasn't it," he said, although he did join his girlfriend at the time at Mansfield. "I don't know if I had a reason at the time. It just wasn't for me. Call it destiny or fate. I don't regret it at all now."

Mansfield's president, Rod Kelchner, came by and inquired about the injury. Grego was a source of pride for the school, averaging well above a B overall and close to an A in his major, criminal justice administration. He had just missed academic All-American the previous season and was set to graduate on time.

Three years does things to the memory. Grego had some vague recollection about the class. Erie Renkey: "Big kid. I read somewhere he got really heavy." A former roommate, Leonard Humphries: "Quiet." And someone else: "Kid from Clifton [New Jersey], can't remember his name." Mark Graham.

"If he [the Mansfield coach] hadn't given me the opportunity," Grego said, "I don't know what I'd be doing now. Probably wouldn't be in school." It was not all charity on Tom Elsasser's part, for a player such as Grego does not gravitate toward Mansfield.

Grego had met another special girl at Mansfield, Tricia Marrone, and they were planning a June wedding. Naturally, Elsasser wanted him for the 1992 season; Grego wasn't sure. "I've had my time, my chance," he said.

In Berkeley, California, Adam Shinnick had tried spring ball at Cal and suffered another hamstring injury. It was the end of playing football but not the end of football. He was coaching in high school, serving as the offensive coordinator for the Arroyo Dons. This was both fun and unsettling. Fun because he loved working with kids and was planning to try coaching after graduation, set for December 1992. Unsettling because his father, Don, had recently been let go by the NFL Patriots in a staff shakeup. So the son was coaching; the father was not.

Chad Cunningham had stayed at Penn State and gotten involved in several sports that kept him in reasonable shape. Rugby had been nice, until the coach wanted him to concentrate on it more and he dropped out. He made pocket money selling ads for the school paper, the *Daily Collegian*.

"At first," he said about his choosing to quit football, "I wasn't really sure I'd made the correct decision. I was confused. Then it hit me that I'd done the right thing."

How did he know?

"Cause I was happy."

It was awkward going to the games for a while, he said, sitting in the student section, watching Chris Cisar and some other buddies making that grand entrance several minutes before kickoff. The last jolt was seeing someone else with his number, 33.

Cunningham's opinion of Paterno had mellowed. "When I quit," he said, "I was pretty bitter. I felt he kinda got on me too much. Lots of times, I didn't deserve some of the stuff he did. Now, I know he's a pretty good guy. He's just doing what he feels is the right thing to do. I've grown up a little bit, too. Realized he's not just out there to make life miserable for the players."

One moment from his Penn State football experience had been both funny and frightening: a concussion that took about two weeks to get over. It started with a hit to his head during a goal-line scrimmage. After being examined by a trainer, it took him half an hour to untie the same shoe at his locker. Some memory disappeared. He had no clue about the ten-page paper due the next day. Worse, the girl with whom he'd been trying to arrange a date for three months finally called and, because her name meant absolutely nothing just then, he handed the phone to his roommate, Chris Cisar.

"She's picking you up here tomorrow at eight o'clock," said Cisar, having explained Cunningham's peculiar behavior to a baffled Lynn Crane. "You're going to a movie." Later, Cunningham could remember nothing about the date. The trainers took every precaution with Cunningham, and everything returned to normal.

"We didn't have air helmets at the time," Cunningham said. "In high school, we had better helmets than we did here. When I came back, my mom called and talked to the equipment manager, told him I had to have an air helmet. So they got me one. Next year, everyone had air helmets."

Before he'd blown out his knee during his senior season in high school, Cunningham had been among the top few prospects in Michigan. "A good lesson for life," he said, "that things are not gonna come out as you expected all the time. You have to learn how to adapt."

Cunningham thought about that. If he hadn't gotten hurt, he'd have gone to one of the in-state schools, Michigan or Michigan State, that recruited him so heavily and then dropped him. "I wouldn't have been here," he said. "I think I fit in here. The surroundings. The people. I like it here. Being eight hours from home helped me grow up."

The tight end who quit football shortly before he had, and for many of the same reasons, crossed his mind. "I hear Derek Van Nort's engaged," Cunningham said. "Isn't that something?" Van Nort had met Carrie Ellen Mathiott in the summer of 1990 at a church function near where he was completing a work-study project in southern California. He had joined his parents on the West Coast after his father was transferred there, and Van Nort planned on coming back and earning his degree from Penn State before Carrie Ellen entered his life. She was from Palo Alto, in the northern part of the state, and that's where they were to be married on July 11, 1992.

Part of Van Nort's appeal to his buddies in the class had been the ability not to look back once he made a decision. Now, more than three years later, Van Nort rarely even watched football. College or pro. The exceptions were games involving his former classmates, Sacca and McDuffie being the most prominent. Infrequently, his former roommate, Ivory Gethers, would flash on the screen.

Had Van Nort stayed at Penn State, he would have chosen one of the most demanding majors: engineering science. At Cal-

Poly in Pomona, he was involved in chemical engineering and outside work related to his major that might postpone graduation by a year or so. He had the most sophisticated area of study in the recruiting class.

Van Nort took from Penn State football a couple of T-shirts, a headband, and a wristband. He thought about lifting the name-plate over his locker but decided against it. "The memories for me weren't on the field," he said. "They weren't in the equipment. They were in the players. The people." He thought about his first roommate, Gethers, and the odd couple on the other side of the room, John Gerak and Donnie Bunch. Two black; two white. He and Gethers from South Carolina; Gerak from a small town; Bunch from a large city.

"The best times were the four of us sitting around, drinking or just holding a conversation," he said. "There was no pretense. Like where we were from or what our positions on the team were. There were just the four of us talking, relaxed. Very down to earth. Them just as nervous about things as I was. If nothing else can be said for Joe, he does bring in nice guys. What he does once they're here is another story."

One football scene returned: A Monday during the season, the players—wearing smaller-than-usual shoulder pads over their jerseys, helmets, and shorts—gathered on the grass fields outside Holuba. Working up a sweat. Running, throwing, catching. Walking through a few plays. All of the athletic phases of football; none of the harsh parts. The hitting, the insults from Paterno.

"The moon was out," Van Nort said. "Full and bright. I remember it over Mount Nittany. Probably the prettiest sight since I'd been there. That's the clearest memory I have of Penn State football."

And Paterno? Well, there had been a chance meeting between the coach and a business associate of Van Nort's father more than a year after Van Nort left the team. The businessman mentioned that he knew Van Nort, and Van Nort figured Paterno would politely whip off something generic and that would be that. Nice kid. Tried hard. Blah-blah-blah. "He interjected some personal traits," Van Nort said, "some things that I recognized as being specific to me. That impressed me a lot." Joe had noticed after all, and Van Nort confided, "I see him as being a great person."

15

Leaving Their Mark

A record crowd of 96,672 in Beaver Stadium gave farewell ovations to those Nittany Lions making their final home appearance on November 14, 1991, against Notre Dame. Among those trotting to the center of the field were Leonard Humphries, who shook hands with the team mascot, and Tony Sacca, whose gait was I-want-to-savor-this slow.

None of the players was more excited than Ron Fields. From the rock-bottom depths of foreign team white, from barely staying in school, from wanting to leave Penn State and then being talked out of it, he had climbed to this pinnacle: starter at the outside linebacker position called Willie.

This was only because the regular had gotten hurt, but Fields could scarcely contain his joy. Blue jersey. First start. One more year of eligibility. No more doubts about who this number 56 was. No more being mistaken for Mac Gallagher.

Even with this promotion, however, Fields kept his spot on the kickoff team and was among the first Nittany Lions on the field. On the runback, Fields tried to roll block a Notre Dame tackler but hit him head-on. Everything was fine as Fields passed Sacca and the other offensive players coming out for the first play from scrimmage. But when Fields got to the sideline, his neck went numb and he couldn't lift his arm. He'd suffered a burner. A severe one. Gone for the game. Gone for the season. Gone, it later developed, for his career. Football damn-sure can be cruel.

Five of the eleven offensive starters against Notre Dame—Sacca, Gerak, Burger, Huntington, and McDuffie—were members of the class. They put on a show not quickly forgotten. The offense scored on its first possession. And scored again on its second possession, Sacca hitting McDuffie in the end zone from eight yards out. And scored again on its third possession.

On defense, new inside linebacker Brett Wright helped stuff Notre Dame on fourth and 1 from the Penn State 2 yard line just before halftime. Very quickly, it got even better. McDuffie dashed 37 yards on a reverse for a third quarter touchdown and made an over-the-shoulder catch of a 45-yard Sacca pass in the end zone for a fourth quarter touchdown.

During the 35–13 rout, Sacca completed 14 of 20 passes for 151 yards and two touchdowns. Humphries had four tackles and defensed four passes. It was the neatest possible way for both to leave Beaver Stadium.

In the reception area for families after the game, Humphries and O. J. McDuffie posed together for snapshots by O. J.'s mother, Gloria. The Ohio Boys, they called themselves. No telling what might happen, because Paterno's preseason talk was fresh in McDuffie's mind. This might also have been his final home appearance.

As always, Sacca was among the last to leave the dressing room. As always, he joined his parents and other friends and relatives. This time, Peg Sacca did not immediately walk to Tony. She wanted to say something special, and she wanted to do it alone.

Earlier, Sacca's father had said he thought Tony's career had gone quickly. Peg wasn't so sure. The tough times still seemed vivid: Tony being forced to play as a freshman and not doing all that well. Tony being yanked for Tom Bill as a sophomore, and again as a junior. But, oh my, how grand the turnaround had been. As a senior Tony was leaving Penn State with every important single season and career passing record. In a few minutes, Tony was free, and he saw her walk toward him. "Hi, Margaret," he said, still playful as he extended his arms. She hugged him and whispered: "I'm really proud of you."

A few steps away, Glocker's parents were equally proud of Rudy. He hadn't come nearly as far as Sacca, who seemed certain of being a high choice in the upcoming NFL draft. However, he had become a starter, and the odds on that four months earlier would have been about 1,000 to 1.

What no one had seen before when the players walked off the buses for the first preseason practice of 1991 was Rudy Glocker wearing a maroon jersey. Maroon meant defense. And third team defense at that. Glocker his first day at practice since suffering that anterior cruciate ligament injury about eighteen months earlier had been switched from tight end to outside linebacker.

Some of the coaches were uncertain whether Glocker would return from such a serious setback. Many players don't. Or at least ones whose futures seem limited to back-up roles. Some transfer. Some quit college entirely. Some keep their scholarships and continue at Penn State, as Bob Daman had.

Two players in perfectly good health, Brian Dozier and Tom Wade, were gone by the start of fall drills. Neither was a surprise. The perpetually injured Wade had run out of academic cushion and gone back to New Mexico; the vastly overweight Dozier had quit football but remained in school at Penn State.

Wade was the very promising linebacker prospect who never played a single down of official football at Penn State. He'd been redshirted as a freshman. That spring, he tore up his knee and missed his sophomore season. From then on, his grades in agriculture business deteriorated. He was ineligible his third season and gone before his fourth.

The 300-pound Dozier also had been redshirted as a freshman. His next two seasons on the offensive line had brought

him just six plays of action, all during his junior year. Like Ron
Fields, Dozier had not been promoted out of Little Pit until
before that third season. Often, he was first to arrive in the locker
room each day and among the most optimistic about eventually
earning significant time in games.

"I'd been fooling myself," he admitted, "playing for other
people. My mother knew it. She'd been saying that for a couple
of years. I had to face it myself."

For his last meeting with Paterno, shortly after the end of
spring practice, Dozier had shaved off a modest growth of facial
hair and taken off his earring. The session had gone better than
expected, because Paterno said he would help with Dozier's
housing his final few semesters. Because his mother was an official at Swarthmore College near Philadelphia, Dozier qualified
for academic aid at other colleges in the state, including Penn
State. So his education still would be mostly paid for.

Dozier had gotten a part-time job at a resort not far from campus called Toftrees, where the team stayed the night before
home games. He pledged the fraternity Omega Psi Phi, the one
Ivory Gethers had joined as a freshman but devoted less time
to over the years because it conflicted with academics and football.

As he'd stressed all along, Dozier was going to get his degree
in business—and on time, the next May. "Soon as I quit football," he said at the end of the summer session, "my grades
improved. I got As in three courses and Bs in two others."

The departure of Wade and Dozier meant that nine members
of the twenty-eight player scholarship class either were gone or
no longer able to continue football at Penn State going into the
fourth season. Offensive coordinator Fran Ganter figured
Glocker would be the tenth. "I thought when he had the chance
he'd just strut away," Ganter said. "Disappear. He talks about
politics. Says he's gonna be governor of this state some day."

Glocker was going to be the first in his class to graduate, in
January. His goal of getting his degree in three and a half years
was a few months away from being achieved, and he admitted:

"Football has kinda run its course in my life." That notion began forming almost the exact moment the dreadful injury happened. On the turf in Holuba Hall, in pain, his first thought had not been about football. "What went through my mind right away," he said, "was whether I'd be able to ski again. I'd been skiing since I was five; now I'll be able to ski till I'm eighty-five. Or whatever."

So his priorities had changed. Having been redshirted as a freshman, Glocker had counted on starting at tight end his sophomore season. Instead, he hardly played at all. He'd missed his junior season entirely. He also admitted to considerable bitterness that started with getting yanked from the kickoff team for the Alabama game two years earlier. "I just became more cynical from that point on," he said.

After the knee injury, which had happened during a no-contact drill, Glocker had considered a lawsuit against Penn State over the artificial turf in Holuba. So many others had suffered similar no-contact injuries, among them Ivory Gethers. Glocker's father had contributed $500 to a study of the Holuba surface, which was deemed safe.

With all of this in mind—his upcoming graduation, the realization that in the long-run skiing meant more than football, with a two-year buildup of bile, with enough academic and other outside interests to fill every day and with no assurance of a second of playing time at his new position—Glocker still returned. "I'd like to go out on a good note," he said. "I'd like to leave some kind of mark on the field."

At first, the mark was a very small one. Almost no playing time and no tackles. At 230 pounds, Glocker also was among the lightest outside linemen in major college football. But the coaches noticed that Glocker never made a mistake. He was not flashy, rarely did anything that would cause a stir among outsiders. Neither were there any negatives on the charts coaches keep or on the practice tapes that they pore over.

Frequently, fans see occasional style and assume it also means uninterrupted substance. They see a couple of spectacular catches from a highly recruited tight end but fail to notice that the fellow can't block Jell-O. They see a sack from an outside lineman on defense but fail to notice that his being out of position several other times led to huge gains.

Glocker's consistency earned him a great deal of playing time against Miami, and he responded with two tackles against the top-rated Hurricanes, one of them behind the line of scrimmage. That performance in an otherwise morale-sapping defeat elevated him to starter. Rudy Glocker—at last, at long, long last—was in a blue jersey the next Tuesday. Damned if a decent part of his dream wasn't suddenly starting to come true.

Being cautious, he said: "One of the things I learned around here, I think it was Eric Renkey who taught me, is that I don't try and figure out why they do stuff anymore. I just do what they say. I don't make policy; I follow it. But I'm not gonna kick a gift horse in the mouth. When I came here, I thought I'd play a great deal right away. That didn't happen. Now I have the opportunity. I just have to make the best of it."

Glocker proceeded to do just that. In the next game, at home against Rutgers, he had two solo tackles and five assists. Two games later, after a blowout victory over Maryland on the road, Glocker was part of the post-game interview scene. In a gray suit and paisley tie, he was relaxed among reporters. Quick with something quotable. Those who knew Glocker could see a budding politician. When someone asked about his first career sack, he replied: "I've been chasing guys a couple of weeks now and finally got one."

The second sack came the next week, against the team Glocker loved to hate, Notre Dame. It was the play before a Penn State interception that set up a touchdown run by O. J. McDuffie that gave Penn State a 28–7 lead.

There was one slightly embarrassing moment during that rout of Notre Dame. Glocker picked up the ball on a fumbled Penn State kickoff and lost ten yards. "I just kept running backwards," he said. "Got really nailed. Half my helmet was yellow."

Still, could life get any better? Already Glocker was thinking about another change of plans for next season. With the very real possibility of extremely limited playing time this season, Glocker earlier in the fall had all but decided to pass on 1992, his redshirt year. He would graduate on January 9 and wanted to get on with his life.

This also was on Mark Graham's mind late in the 1991 season. So anxious was he to chase money in some sort of high-risk business that he sought me out after a runaway victory over Rutgers. On the final play of the game, he had intercepted a pass and run it back 12 yards for a touchdown. Nevertheless, several minutes later, Graham insisted that whiff of glory would not sway his judgment: "I'm still not coming back next year."

Glocker was coming back. Was he ever. He seemed the one member of his class for whom the dream would come true in every way possible. He had been a scholar from his first step on campus, able to graduate in three and a half years in a difficult major. Now, well into his fourth year, he also was an athlete.

Next season, his fifth, could be close to unique. Glocker was a lay-down cinch to be elected one of the captains by his teammates. No one else would draw such media attention. McDuffie was much more gifted at football but had little inclination for academics.

And Penn State knew how to feature Glocker. As every other high-octane university does when a genuine scholar-athlete emerges, someone capable of thrilling alums and impressing recruits, Penn State pushes its Glockers toward the limelight. Not in an obvious or showy way, of course. An out-of-town reporter might ring up the sports information department and request an interview with a player who typifies Paterno's football program. Anyone fit that mold? Well, you might want to talk with Rudy Glocker. Terrific player for us on defense. A co-captain. Working on his graduate degree. Did research on an associate justice of the Supreme Court. He and Joe even talked about Hemingway one time. Rudy'll call you back.

Renkey was Glocker's intellectual equal. Reporters in search of wit to spice up the Paterno-encouraged diet of bland quotes would seek out Renkey. Rarely were they disappointed. When asked what historical figure he would like to meet, Renkey chose Sir Isaac Newton and explained: "I would give him my Math 140 take-home exam to do." When asked who in the entire world he would most like to trade places with, Renkey passed on the president of the United States and the reigning rock king for Penn State's strength and conditioning coach "so I'd get a chance to weigh all the coaches instead of them always weighing me." Trouble was, Renkey was getting dealt awful football cards. His grades were close to dean's list; his neck was such that he might only be a spot player at nose tackle, if that.

Glocker seemed the anointed one, the one who knew all the possibilities, including football. If he could add twenty or thirty pounds to those considerable football instincts, some NFL team surely would take a draft-choice flier on him. Second best of all, he would be getting his picture on the hallowed walls of the east locker area. His mark at Penn State would be wide and permanent.

Best of all, Glocker would have impressed the people who waited for him after nearly every game of his career: his father and mother. "They were around," he said, knowing that McDuffie's father, Leonard Humphries's and Rick Sayles's father, among others, hadn't been. "It had meant so much for my dad to come to my seventh grade basketball games at three-thirty in the afternoon on a Tuesday. You never get dad-son relationships back."

That was how it kept going: Rudy Glocker in the starting lineup, Penn State victorious, the next success always a bit more impressive than the last. An invitation to the big-deal Fiesta Bowl. One last regular season game, against Pitt on the road.

The shorthand play-by-play account of the opening kickoff of the Pitt-Penn State game read: " . . . Brady returns from L26, 39-yard kick, 12-yard return." That's it. Ball's in the air. Guy catches it and gets tackled. Game goes on. No mention of the accidental collision of two Penn State players during the dash for the ball, or that one of them, Rudy Glocker, didn't get up right away.

Torn anterior cruciate ligament.

Same knee as the one almost two years earlier.

Career over.

That was on Thanksgiving. "I don't cry very often," Glocker said, "but I probably cried every day from then till the day of the operation. Then I cried every day after that till about three days ago. I still get misty-eyed thinking about it now."

This was December 17. Glocker was seated on the bench in front of his locker, crutches propped against a nearby support column. Early on, the worst part was the doctors not knowing the extent of the damage without exploratory surgery. Glocker leaped into denial, saying to his father: "I don't want to hear what the doctor has to say. If I never go to him, I'll be all right."

In his heart, Glocker knew something was terribly wrong. Alone in bed one night, he pulled his leg, and the knee hyperextended. That hadn't happened after the doctor fixed it before. Arthroscopic surgery was performed December 10, the day after his twenty-second birthday.

"Maybe the worst experience of my life," Glocker said. "I sat there and watched the operation. I've always been curious. I'm sitting there, with a spinal. I can see everything. The ligament seems like some kind of mop that's been cut with a saw. The doctor is pulling out fibers. One by one. Ten or twelve of them. I'm waiting for one not to pull. All of a sudden I realized there's no more. I was in disbelief, didn't know what to say."

Even then, close to a month after the injury and a week after the surgery, Glocker got teary. The good news was that there seemed no need for reconstructive surgery. That would have been necessary if he'd wanted to continue football. But the rehab would be at least a year, and Glocker had no more football years to spare.

However, even without major surgery, he would be able to ski. Odd how that news hit him. Two years ago, when he suffered exactly the same injury, Glocker's first concern was whether he'd be able to ski. Now, when football was over but skiing seemed certain, he was sad.

"In terms of emotional stableness," he said, "I just jumped

off the World Trade Center that day and landed in the subway. Just devastated. Literally on my back. The only solace I can take is that I didn't screw myself out of the opportunity. I didn't get arrested. I didn't take steroids or fail a drug test. I didn't get in the doghouse. I made the best of my opportunities.

"I never doubted I could play football here. Never doubted I could come back from the first ACL. Sometimes, I did doubt whether I'd get the chance to show it. You work so hard to get something back. Then—*boom!*—it's taken away again."

Glocker twisted his body, moved his still-stiff leg onto the bench. "It's like the death of the Unknown Soldier," he said. "Basically, I'm dead from Penn State football. And no one even knows you're gone. It's weird.

"I got my fifteen minutes of fame. Then aged four years in ten days. I don't think I ever took on an identity here as a football player. I don't think I ever acted like one. [Rarely had he worn on campus the warm-up suits everyone received for bowl trips or those black high-top Nike shoes that all but brand one a football player.] But the umbilical cord has been cut, so to speak. I kinda got kicked out of the fraternity. Booted. And there wasn't anything I could do about it."

At least, Glocker could rationalize the injury that ended his playing career. He'd gotten it in combat. The others—the finger and the knee, each requiring surgery—had come during offseason practice. "Like the guys from *Spartacus* said: 'Come back with your shield, or on it.' I did that," Glocker said. "And every time I've done something, it's been serious. I couldn't just break a finger. I had to snap a tendon. I couldn't just strain my knee; I had to get about the very worst thing possible. Twice."

Paterno had been shaken by the injury. As he had with the even worse ACL Tom Wade had suffered, the coach had gotten emotional in front of Glocker. "He hasn't looked me in the face since I was hurt," Glocker said. "He sat here the other day, kinda looking at the floor. Said he'd do anything he could for me, that he'd take care of financial aid for grad school."

Glocker accompanied the team to Arizona for the Fiesta Bowl

and participated in parties that included an underclassman spouting Shakespeare to a rather surprised audience at a massive cookout. There was one uncomfortable moment, when a local reporter asked what the best time for an interview would be. Softly, Glocker said: "You can call me during practice."

The Fiesta Bowl trip got off to a rocky start even before the team arrived in Arizona. Several players, among them starting offensive tackle Todd Burger and reserve outside linebacker Ivory Gethers, were left behind because their academic performances for the recently ended semester had been awful.

Burger's and Gethers's grade point averages for the semester were not the worst of those being punished. One fifth-year player, his football career having been cut short by surgery, had flunked every subject. Crashed and burned to a 0.00. Fact is, Burger and Gethers still were eligible to play in the Fiesta Bowl, because it was considered part of the prior semester. But Paterno took a stand.

"Joe told me he wouldn't take me because I'm always on the edge with my grades," Gethers said. "Borderline. Borderline. Always, I guess to him, I'm a gamble. He told me: 'You need to learn a lesson. You need to concentrate on trying to graduate.' Something was taken from me that I really wanted, with nothing really being wrong. I still was eligible, and I told him that. He said: 'I don't care. You're always on the borderline.' "

Burger was beyond borderline. Always on the verge of academic disaster, he had slumped to the point of being off scholarship. He would need a self-financed rally that spring and summer to be eligible for his final season with the Nittany Lions. The embarrassment of it all was immense.

"A very, very, very disappointing Christmas," he said. "I sat at home and did absolutely nothing. To the point that my father finally said: 'You screwed up. This is your fault. But what are you going to do? Sit in the house and vegetate? Here's twenty bucks.' "

Burger and some friends spent most of New Year's Eve at a party in Manhattan. This was less than sixteen hours before the

Penn State-Tennessee kickoff, a fact that hit him hard. "It's twenty to twelve," Burger said. "I'm feeling no pain at the time. Then it comes to me: 'Jesus Christ. I came to Penn State because I wanted to play on New Year's Day. I can't sit here and celebrate. I should be in bed now.' So I left. Jumped on a train at midnight, then took a cab to my house."

In a mid-morning Fiesta Bowl meeting with his offensive linemen at the team hotel outside Phoenix, assistant coach Dick Anderson turned in a room lit only by a videotape player and told Tony Matesic to listen up. There was no response. Anderson hadn't yet heard the news, that Matesic had been booted out of town by Paterno and was at that very moment on a plane headed toward his home in New Jersey.

Matesic said he had made curfew early that morning, that two assistant coaches had checked him in. Then he decided to get some food at a nearby 24-hour restaurant. He dressed in shorts, a sweatsuit jacket, and untied sneakers. As a precaution, he grabbed a plastic cup. If anyone caught him, he would look at the cup and say he was getting some ice.

About fifteen steps out the door, Matesic and two football aides saw each other at about the same time. "I panicked," Matesic said. Later, after another aide said he was being sent home, Matesic called Paterno. And the coach asked the relevant question: "What were you doing hiding behind some bushes?"

"I told him it was a big misunderstanding," Matesic said. "He said not to worry, that they'd get me a nice flight home. Then he hung up."

There was more. Lots more. John Gerak had been drunk in Sacca's room, sloshed to the point of not being able to walk the five or so steps back to his room. His only punishment was being held out for the first three possessions of the game. McDuffie and his roommate, reserve fullback Brian O'Neal, were caught with girls in their room. Nothing at all happened to them. "Brian was going to be sent home," McDuffie said. "I went to Joe. I told him it was partly my fault, and if Brian got sent home, I probably should be too. A lot of people think I threatened Joe.

That's not the case. I didn't say if Brian goes, I'm going; I said if Brian has to go home, I should too."

However long Paterno weighed the matter, his pragmatic side won out. As there had been special circumstances that allowed Ivory Gethers and Bobby Samuels to be admitted to Penn State, as there had been special circumstances that caused Tony Sacca to start as a freshman, there were special circumstances right now. So both offenders stayed, and McDuffie was the game's offensive star, turning momentum Penn State's way with that 39-yard punt return midway through the third quarter and mustering 149 all purpose yards.

That performance helped turn McDuffie's stay-or-go decision toward remaining at Penn State. The victory lifted the team to third in the final polls. Next season seemed even more promising. A fine chance for the national title and a strong-armed quarterback, Kerry Collins, who just might get him the ball enough to challenge for the Heisman Trophy.

None of the players during the rush toward the locker room immediately after the game ended could quite believe the turnaround. From down by ten points early in the third quarter to ahead by eighteen early in the fourth.

"Something happened," said Chris Cisar. "I just don't know what."

"Hey." John Sacca smiled and yelled to brother Tony: "You were horrible. Worst game of the year." Tony was 11 for 28 for 150 yards. But four of those eleven completions were for touchdowns.

"Ever see lightning strike like that?" Tony said.

In the locker room, Paterno mounted a small stool and the players gathered around him. "We beat a classy bunch of kids," he said. "Let's give 'em credit. We hung together, and won going away. That's a credit to you guys ... You proved you can play as well as anyone in the country. The seniors leave with a good taste. Congratulations. Have a good time tonight, but let's not do anything stupid."

Before the team kneeled and recited the Lord's Prayer,

Paterno said there would be a squad meeting the first day the players returned to school. From the back, Sacca piped up. "Can't make it, coach," he said.

Paterno was stupefied. Sacca had been one of those seniors to whom he'd just given a farewell nod. The coach laughed and, with his final words about a tumultuous season for his team and a breakthrough career for his quarterback, said: "Sacca, you're out of here!"

By early spring 1992, Rudy Glocker was in an upbeat mood once more. He'd taken some time to wallow in self-pity about the knee injury that abruptly ended his football career and then gotten on with planning his future. He was very interested in politics.

"I'm not president of the Student Athlete Advisory Board for kicks," he admitted. Where others recoiled from the limelight, from speaking in public, from having their ideas challenged in open forums, Glocker charged in.

What he'd wanted for the summer, an internship with a U.S. senator from Pennsylvania, was coming true. Shortly, he would be going to Washington, D.C., to work in the office of Arlen Spector. His impressive background at Penn State helped make this possible. Equally important, probably more so, had been a phone call from Paterno.

"Joe takes care of his own," said Glocker. "I did well in school, always worked as hard as I could on the practice field [although he lettered just once in four years]. I think he remembered me for those efforts."

Glocker was well aware that Paterno and the football staff had helped Rich Rosa secure summer employment with the NFL Philadelphia Eagles. Earlier, football aide Frank Rocco had guided Glocker along a form-laden path that ended with a $5,000 scholarship from the National Association of Collegiate Directors of Athletics.

Now and then before spring practice, Glocker would pass through the locker room. But most of his time was spent in places other than the football complex and among campus movers and shakers who rarely discussed sports. "They're very enthusiastic about Penn State," he said. "A hundred times more so than I. They're fun people to be around, because of their energy. When I was down, those people lifted me up, just by the energy they gave off."

Glocker had decided to return to Penn State for his fifth year and continue post-graduate work in political science. Through spring drills and the 1992 season, he would be assisting Paterno and his staff for the second time in three years.

Even though his ties to the team would remain tight, Glocker sensed that what he'd come to Penn State for had ended. He thought for a moment and said, "I have a much higher opinion of myself than I ever did before."

Glocker had pushed himself, and hard. Four years earlier, on the back porch of his home, he'd talked about wanting everything grand and meaningful college had to offer. Looking back, damned if he hadn't achieved almost all his academic goals. And football? Who knows what might have happened had his luck not been so lousy.

"While I'm in the process, I always want to do more," he said. "And when I stop and look in retrospect, I'm always pleased with the accomplishments I've achieved. I think I've actually done quite a bit here."

If the playing time and the stats had not been anything special, Glocker still had achieved his primary football goal: He'd made his father proud. That seemed such a sudden realization that it made him close to weepy, and he said of his brief appearance on the grassy center stage: " '91 was enough."

As spring practice came and went, it turned out that 1991 also had been the end of college football for five of Glocker's classmates. Gone to neck injuries were Eric Renkey and Ron Fields. Gone mainly because they did not want to be backups their fifth season were Rich Rosa and Tony Matesic. Gone because he wanted to try his luck with the pros, in Canada, was Bobby Samuels.

This large, though not unexpected, exodus meant that at the

annual spring game, April 25, 1992, the class had reached a watershed. For the first time, more members were not playing football at Penn State than were. Of the twenty-eight scholarship recruits, only eleven were still hopeful of seeing action in the fall. (Among those eleven, Matt Nardolillo had quit the team, and Todd Burger had flunked out of school over the winter. Paterno later coaxed Nardolillo back for quarterback insurance, and Burger regained his eligibility during the spring and summer sessions.)

Renkey had seen the end coming for some time, but the absolute clincher was his neck rebelling even during non-contact drills in the spring. His career had been a swift and downward spiral: letterman as a true freshman, then toe and neck injuries that required no surgery but still caused the decline and end to a career that had seemed so promising.

Looking back, Renkey could remember most of his final plays: against West Virginia for almost the entire last quarter of the 51–6 rout in 1991. "I'd been crushing the center," he said, "and then he did something cheap, grabbed me by the face mask as I went by and pulled me down. Then he stepped on me. I really took it to him. I remember that sequence, but not the final play. My neck acted up the next week, and I didn't play any more."

The last play for Fields had been the opening kickoff of the 35–13 victory over Notre Dame. He went into a roll block, got hit on the head, "and felt fine till I got to the sideline. Then I just dropped. My whole neck went numb. I couldn't lift my arm." He shook his head and said, sadly: "I was supposed to have started."

Renkey, Fields, Rosa, and Matesic remained in school, and all but Fields seemed certain to graduate. In fact, Rosa graduated in May, becoming the first male member of his family to earn a degree.

Renkey had changed his major to psychology and gotten nearly all As in it. Unlike Rosa, he and Matesic would need slightly more than four years to graduate. Fields might not get it done in five. He was walking his usual academic tightrope but finding it more fun.

For one of the high-level classes in his major, broadcast communications, Fields had to produce a story for television. He wrote it, directed it, and shot it. His theme was a familiar one: how colleges recruit players. Ivory Gethers played the hotshot high schooler.

Fields's script included a corrupt college assistant saying to his head coach about the Gethers character: "Yeah, we can get him. Course he'll take the money. His family's not rich. He's lookin' for the pros."

The dilemma for the recruit played on. "The sleazy assistant pulled out an envelope with Ivory's name on it," Fields said, "and I cut away. I picked it back up with Ivory making a decision. He's in the living room, looking at the guy's card and the envelope with the money in it. Tough decision. I had him call the guy and say he'd made up his mind. Then I used a fade-to-black technique."

Fields wanted the other students to draw their own conclusions. Did the poor recruit take the money or didn't he? The professor said Fields should have answered the question himself.

The feedback that John Gerak was getting shortly before kickoff of the 1992 spring game was thrilling. He'd just heard his name over the public address system—"Captain . . . Gerak"—but dismissed the announcement as one of those game-situation things. No big deal in a game that meant more to fans than players.

Gerak was wrong. The announcement that drifted over half-filled Beaver Stadium was huge: Gerak, Brett Wright, O. J. McDuffie, and an underclassman completing his eligibility in four straight years would be co-captains for the 1992 season. Out-front leaders. Very big men on campus.

They had been elected by their teammates a few days earlier, and Paterno had chosen to let them hear about it when the public did. No frills, no hype. Make the announcement, get on with the game.

Shortly after the game started, the players and the fans got equally excited. This Collins kid, Sacca's replacement, not only had an exceptionally strong arm but also an accurate one. When

McDuffie broke open long, Collins hit him. This offense might be even more potent than the one that helped earn a number-three ranking in 1991. This fifth year might bring for the remaining eleven members of the class what all of them had wanted when they arrived: the national championship.

Too bad Sacca and Leonard Humphries wouldn't be around. They were headed toward the NFL, Sacca as the second-round draft choice of the Phoenix Cardinals and Humphries as the eighth-round choice of the Buffalo Bills. Each had said his good-byes.

Sacca and Paterno ended their player-coach relationship in a warm way. On the first day of spring practice, Sacca was watching his suddenly former teammates work out in Holuba Hall, and Paterno joined him on the sideline. Quietly, Paterno mentioned how much frustration Sacca had caused him and also how much he respected Sacca for playing so well under so much pressure. "And," Sacca said, "he thanked me for not complaining about how bad the offensive line was."

Near sunset on July 11 in a crowded room off the chapel of Wesley Methodist Church in Palo Alto, California, Derek Van Nort took the hand of Carrie Ellen Mathiott and they danced together for the first time as husband and wife.

They had been married inside the wooden A-frame church about an hour earlier, and those absent were remembered as fondly as those present. Derek's mother had passed away earlier in the year; his father served as best man. Several former teammates at Penn State had tried to make it, most especially Tom Wade, who lived in New Mexico, but none could.

Van Nort was involved in sophisticated areas of chemistry and engineering, working and going to class in Southern California. So varied were his interests, so often had he meandered during the pursuit of his degree that he might not graduate even in five years. This was in no way bothersome. Van Nort loved everything about his life, most especially the beautiful young woman who had helped devise the modern dance they were performing as the highlight of their reception.

Van Nort had won the respect of Rudy Glocker and his other classmates for never looking back once he had made a decision. Never had he second-guessed himself for leaving the team near the start of his second year. On this lovely night nearly three years later, Van Nort walked away from Carrie Ellen for a few moments. Quietly, he said: "If I'd stayed with football, I wouldn't have this."

PART FIVE

THE CLOCK WINDS DOWN

16

Hurricane Damage

October 10, 1992. One of those dates with destiny that had drawn the class to Penn State—and that was drawing the attention of college football to sun-drenched Beaver Stadium: a game with national championship implications. The number 7 Nittany Lions, unbeaten in five games, versus number 2 Miami, unbeaten in four games. Noon kickoff, to accommodate television. A beyond-capacity crowd of 96,704.

Penn State had been anticipating this for two days shy of a year, ever since the 26–20 loss to the Hurricanes in Miami that had nullified any chance of winning the national title in 1991. Fans so far during the season had thought of little else, what with the lineup of twinkies that preceded the rematch. Even Paterno was uncommonly juiced.

And yet a lot either was missing, seemed out of place, or was downright daffy as kickoff approached. Only ten of the twenty-eight scholarship players who had come to Penn State five years earlier were still playing football. The latest casualty was one of the heroes of the upset of top-ranked Notre Dame two years earlier, Rick Sayles. He and underclassman Bobby Engram had been caught stealing items that included a stereo from a downtown apartment at 2:11 A.M. on August 26. They were kicked off the team.

Sayles admitted the theft, saying: "It was something we did that was stupid, more my fault because Bobby looked to me for advice." Sayles said he had been upset for quite some time, mostly about being demoted to third team wideout and later being told by Paterno that he had "an attitude problem."

"I had a lot of frustration, a lot of anger," Sayles said. "That's why I think I lost my morals that night. Because I was so angry, so tired of being obedient."

This arrest came forty-three days after Sayles and O. J. Mc-Duffie had been charged with disorderly conduct during an early morning incident outside a downtown bar. According to a police report, "Sayles gave verbal and written account and stated that he and McDuffie had too much to drink and their intoxication did not help matters. Sayles apologized for his disorderly behavior."

McDuffie received twelve months' probation. Before Sayles had his hearing, however, he and Engram were arrested. What especially upset Sayles was his impression that Paterno treated Engram more sympathetically than him. Paterno was harsh in his public comments about him, Sayles said, but not Engram. Paterno frequently spoke with Engram after the arrest, Sayles said, but never to him.

"Joe doesn't know me," Sayles said in late September over lunch in a downtown fast food restaurant. "He doesn't know me at all. I was part of the team. I sweat and bled for him for four years. I get in a sticky situation, and he turns his back on me."

Bail for Sayles came from a friend's father, who was a professor at Penn State. The assistant coach who recruited him, Jerry Sandusky, offered the best advice: "It's not what you did so much as how you respond. Okay, what you did was stupid. Deal with it and then get on with your life."

Sayles and Engram remained on scholarship, pending the outcome of the case. Sayles still was living with three teammates in a downtown apartment. He had fallen behind academically and was unlikely to graduate, as planned, in May.

During his four-plus years, Sayles many times had violated minor rules—missing breakfast and skipping summer workouts—and had only been scolded by Paterno. Normally, the punishment also includes early morning runs. That misbehavior had weighed against him, however, when Paterno decided who on the team would be prominent and who would not.

In the public's mind, Sayles may have been misidentified with crimes committed by his younger brother. Rick's name is Lyle Richard; his younger brother is Elrick, and he sometimes lived with Rick while working around town. In 1991, Elrick spent four months in Centre County jail after pleading guilty to twenty counts of simple assault.

"The law won't punish me as much as I've punished myself," Rick said. "I almost had a nervous breakdown. I was embarrassed to show my face at first. I never went to jail. But that is a very real possibility."

In addition to Sayles, seven who either quit the team or were forced off by injuries had stayed in school. So eighteen of the twenty-eight still were enrolled at Penn State five seasons later, after the four-years-and-out departures of Tony Sacca and Leonard Humphries.

Rudy Glocker, Bob Daman, and Rich Rosa were working with the coaching staff, their uniforms on this keenly anticipated day being blue slacks and blue pullover knit shirts. Eric Renkey and Tony Matesic also were working in the football program, sometimes in ways hilariously ironic given their freshman and sophomore years. Could anyone, including Paterno, have imagined that Renkey would be helping academic advisor Don Ferrell? It was Renkey, after all, who had gotten a 1.31 his first semester at Penn State; Renkey who had locked his door and refused to answer his phone during class-cutting sleepathons in order to elude Ferrell.

That was 1988 and 1989. This was the fall of 1992, and Renkey could be seen monitoring study hall, showing freshman players how to use the computers. And Matesic, who had constant weight problems, was weighing in players before practice.

"We've gotten some good chuckles over that," said Renkey, who added that the only thing more ironic would be Tony in academics with Ferrell and him weighing in people. Ferrell once had caught Matesic sleeping through class his freshman year; Renkey had sailed over 300 pounds at the end of his sophomore season.

One more slice of irony involved none of the players who dropped off the team but two who stayed—Chris Cisar and Mark Graham. For years, both had vowed not to return for their fifth season. No way, each kept saying. Yet here they were, pulling on the pads for one more crack at glory. Graham was a starter, at right cornerback, and Cisar was recovering from minor knee surgery but figured to log lots of time on kick teams.

"Mark and I are the two most pessimistic people on the team," Cisar admitted. "We gripe, complain. Even if practice were only five minutes long, we're gonna complain. But it does seem as though things are working out."

Cisar had graduated in May, had even accepted a job with an insurance company. When Paterno called and wanted him back, however, when the coach said starting was a possibility, Cisar retreated from the real world. He took graduate-level courses in business and was especially looking forward to the spring and another shot at baseball.

Graham was five credits from graduation. The lure for him was finally getting a chance to start, after trailing so long behind his former roommate, Leonard Humphries, who recently had been cut by the Bills and was shopping himself around the NFL. "I look out there during games or in practice," Graham said, "and there's Cisar near me. He's marketing; I'm finance. We've had a lot of classes together. We've started games together. Neat."

As to the overall ambience in Beaver Stadium an hour before kickoff against Miami, "neat" might be an appropriate description. But only to an outsider, someone unfamiliar with Penn

State and, most especially, with Joe Paterno. The stands were filling; the excitement was building; the confidence level among teams was high.

But what was that sound! That incessant cascade of unfamiliar music spewing from the south end of the field. Yes, it was the anthem of the hip "Takin' Care of Business," coming through, loud and clear, and no one had ever heard anything remotely like it at a Penn State football game.

Oh, one of the fraternities might let loose during a pregame tailgate party outside. But the games themselves were solemn occasions where buttondown folks paid homage to traditional football and to traditional football themes. The wildest excitement was when the drum major tried that front flip as the Blue Band marched in precise lines down the field during pregame.

Heads turned. Words of wonderment were exchanged. The elderly consulted the young as to just what the name of that tune was. "Takin' Care of Business" greeted the earliest arrivals, freshmen scurrying for the choicest lousy seats. "Takin' Care of Business" greeted every startled alum and all the fat-cat conuibutors seated near midfield.

Once the bedazzled faithful determined what this strange noise was, they soon fingered the person responsible for it: Joseph Vincent Paterno. Who else could do something so radical? Conservative, cautious, sixty-five-year-old JoePa had gone out of his everlovin' mind.

Paterno had a plan. He wanted to intimidate the Hurricanes. He wanted as much noise as possible, and he thought a $3,000 sound system blaring out "Takin' Care of Business" would help take care of the business at hand. In theory, the idea seemed sound: Get the joint rockin' before the game, get 90,000-plus voices primed to create a nerve-jangling reception.

Usually, Paterno intimidated through silence. Let the other guys prance and talk trash, wear little do-dads on their helmets and emotions on their sleeves. We are Penn State. Stoic in public. Tough and basic in no-frills uniforms and black hightops. That had gotten the job done against the struttin' 'Canes in the

Fiesta Bowl after the 1986 season, when the Nittany Lions had won the national championship.

Penn State players took their hats off inside buildings and ripped helmets off during games. The 1992 co-captains—Mc-Duffie, John Gerak, Brett Wright, and fourth-year senior Reggie Givens—had been driven to their introductory press conference at the start of fall practice in a light brown pickup.

All of a sudden, Paterno had jumped way out of character. Which might have been fine in any other setting. Trouble is, Paterno picked the wrong opponent to pick on in this way. Was Miami unsettled by this flurry of flash? Were the players cowering during pregame warmups? Absolutely not. They were loving every second of it. Given the chance, they would have turned on the stereo themselves.

Many Hurricanes waved their helmets in a can't-rattle-us gesture during warmups. Wide receiver Lamar Thomas pranced by the Penn State student section at the east side of the field, laughing while being pelted with marshmallows.

Penn State's players were sober faced but enthusiastic. The fifth-year players were a small but determined lot: Gerak, Greg Huntington, and McDuffie on offense; Wright and Graham on defense. Rucci, still not fully recovered from reconstructive knee surgery, was a backup at tackle on offense; Todd Burger and Cisar were reserves on defense; Cisar and Ivory Gethers were prominent on kick teams; Bob Ceh was the snapper on punts and placekicks. Matt Nardolillo was seldom-seen quarterback insurance.

For McDuffie, there were high personal stakes. A big game would vault him into contention for the Heisman Trophy. He went through what over the last two years had become a ritual: rising about 3 A.M. and taking a bubble bath while listening to a Walkman.

A Sacca would be at quarterback: Tony's younger brother, John. This was contrary to all the forecasts and Paterno's maneuvering in the spring. Hard-throwing Kerry Collins was supposed to assume command of the offense when Tony Sacca

ascended to the NFL. Collins's arm was one of the reasons Mc-
Duffie had opted to postpone the pros and return for a fifth year.

However, Collins had hurt a finger on his passing hand during
a volleyball game at a family picnic, and it was slow healing. So
Sacca played most of the five previous games and threw well,
not once being intercepted in eighty-three passes.

Still, Penn State fans had their doubts about Sacca under extreme pressure with such limited experience. Even more unsettling was something the fans were unaware of: Placekicker Craig
Fayak's back was acting up. He was not even close to full
strength.

Sacca and the rest of the offense were strong early on the first
series. He completed his first two passes, and a draw play fetched
15 more yards, to the Miami 41. However, three plays netted
just 3 yards, and Fayak tried a 48-yard field goal that was
blocked.

From midfield, the Hurricanes stayed on the ground all but
twice during nine plays, fullback Donnell Bennett running the
final 10 yards up the middle for the touchdown and a quick 7–
0 lead.

McDuffie slipped a bit on the kickoff, but still returned it 28
yards. Then the offensive pattern continued, a nice combination
of passing and running moving the ball to the Miami 12 yard
line. From there, Fayak was wide left from 20 yards. Two good
scoring chances; zero points. This also was contrary to the Penn
State Way.

Midway through the second quarter, the Hurricanes kept the
ball for five and a half minutes and gained 84 yards before kicking a 26-yard field goal that lifted their lead to 10–0. That's how
the half ended, with Penn State having an edge in yards gained
but hampered by those two missed field goals.

On the first series of the second half, Gerak, Huntington, and
the other blockers continued their good work. The first three
running plays produced 39 yards, to the Miami 33 yard line. The
offense stayed on the ground and, five plays later, Richie Anderson followed a Gerak block and scored from 10 yards out.

Neither team could muster any sustained offense, and the Nittany Lions took over on their 36-yard line near the end of the third quarter after an 18-yard punt return by McDuffie. On first down, Sacca dropped back for a screen pass, and an instant after he launched it 90,000-plus fans and everyone on the Penn State sideline went limp.

Under pressure, Sacca had thrown his first interception at the worst possible time. His hundredth pass of the season was directly into the hands of Miami defensive end Darren Krien, who ran 28 yards into the end zone. Soon, Miami was ahead by 17–7.

Disaster, hope, and more disaster quickly followed for the Nittany Lions. Once more, the offense moved into position for a Fayak field goal. Once more, this time from 36 yards, he missed. Luckily, Miami was offsides and the drive continued.

On fourth and one from the Hurricane 5 yard line, Paterno decided to go for it. Anderson swung wide right, and Miami middle linebacker Michael Barrow sliced in and wrapped him up for a one-yard loss. Huntington and McDuffie later thought Paterno should have called for an Anderson dive up the middle.

With nearly nine minutes left in the game, Penn State had come away from three very promising drives with absolutely no points. The next possession, however, the combination of Sacca-to-McDuffie worked as though Tony still were throwing.

From near midfield, Sacca hit McDuffie down the middle for 19 yards. A running play netted 9 yards, to the Miami 14. Then, in the face of a big rush from Miami's left defensive end, Sacca let fly for McDuffie. He caught it over a smallish defensive back, and Penn State was down by just 17–14.

There still were more than six minutes left, but the Hurricanes controlled the ball for nearly three before having to punt. Then Penn State went three downs and out on offense and needed to use all three time-outs on defense before forcing Miami to punt.

That punt was excellent. McDuffie tried to return it, but could get just 8 yards before being pushed out of bounds at the Penn State 19 yard line. The situation soon became totally hopeless, when two penalties created third-and-25 from the 4 yard line. Predictably, Sacca's desperate pass was intercepted.

And then it was over. The first reaction was shock. McDuffie and the other survivors in the class had been so confident, so sure fate would be kind in this fifth year that for several moments they couldn't believe time had run out on them. To *Sports Illustrated* earlier in the week, Gerak had predicted a 28–7 victory. "I'd never been so focused coming out of the tunnel before the game," McDuffie said. "Eyeballing what it would be like after we won. I saw us going crazy. Saw fans on the field. Everything."

Statistically, Penn State had almost every edge: four more first downs, 62 more yards rushing, 90 more yards passing, nearly seven more time-of-possession minutes. Miami was celebrating.

"Right after it ended," McDuffie said, "I shook some hands and then went over to the student section and applauded them. Going back through the tunnel, the tears came, and I said to myself: 'That was it.'"

Reality kept coming in stages.

"I was just sitting in the locker room, a couple of tears running down my face, nothing major," said Todd Burger. "Then I looked at Brett Wright, who was hysterical. He looked at me. I went over to him, and we were like two little kids crying. Fifth year. One game. That's what you play for."

"Why can't it be our turn?" Huntington said.

The next morning was even worse, for everyone in the class, most after a long night of serious drinking, finally sensed they had played their last Cosmic Game. Notre Dame would be big, of course. So would the last home game, against Pitt. There was still a chance at the national title, but it was razor-thin at best.

That was because months earlier, Penn State had locked itself into the Blockbuster Bowl. Because it was committed to the Big Ten, but not yet a football-playing participant, Penn State was out of the conference-oriented loop for all the major bowls except the Blockbuster.

Gerak put the situation for the 5–1 Nittany Lions most

bluntly: "There is nothing really to play for. Whether we're 6 and 5 or 10 and 1 doesn't matter. We go to the same place."

Most of the players filed into breakfast individually and either picked at their food or walked out after signing in and being officially present. Sacca sat alone, reading about himself in the paper.

"We had the perfect opportunity to leave our mark," Burger said, "but we came up short, again," He was joined by Ivory Gethers, who four years earlier had predicted not one national championship but two.

"Have to move on," Gethers said.

Nearby, Gerak said: "I remember how we thought as freshmen, when we went 5–6, that the seniors just quit [about midseason]. We can lose five of the next six or win five of the next six and it won't make much difference around here. If you don't win a national championship, it's a bad season."

Rudy Glocker was the last to arrive. He ate alone. "As I walked across the field," he said of his pregame routine as an undergraduate aide, "the sun was starting to come through the clouds. The student section was starting to fill. This is what I always wanted to play in. It just never happened."

Glocker had helped the defensive coaches in the press box, and Penn State's defense had effectively locked into Miami's passing game quite early. He also recalled the Penn State-dominated stats and said: "It's so frustrating when you know you've lost, as opposed to Miami winning."

Gerak, McDuffie, and the others in his class who played the day before had come and gone. As their it's-all-over sadness was relayed to him, Glocker listened. Then he thought for a moment, about his own experience, and said: "They got to live the dream a little longer."

Sometimes, dreamland is a hallway. Or so it seemed to Rich Rosa as he scurried toward the squad room in midafternoon of September 23. He rounded a corner and there, squarely in his path, was a figure that might have caused anyone else to melt on the spot. Socially, Rosa was the quickest thinker in his class, and so he said the proper thing: "How are you, Mr. President?"

"Nice to see you," George Bush replied. "Going the same place I'm going?"

Yes, the president of the United States also was going to the squad room, but his escort, Paterno, had gotten temporarily sidetracked. So for several awkward and wonderful moments there were just the two of them, Rosa and President Bush, chatting each other up. (Not that they were alone. Near the Secret Service agents was Penn State's videotape man, recording everything for posterity.)

"What's your name?" the president asked.

"Richard Rosa."

If his face or his voice offered no hint of nerves colliding inside Rosa, that formal introduction did. To no one but his mother was he Richard. Ever. Regardless of the circumstances, his smile would be wide and genuine and his greeting a casual: "Rich Rosa."

For President Bush, Rosa was formal and uncommonly flustered. Rosa could have said that he'd helped swell the crowd for Bush's speech on campus an hour or so earlier. He'd met a friend two days earlier who worked with the local Republicans and been given about a hundred up-close passes, which he handed out to teammates and football-office staffers.

But Rosa was not his usual glib self just now. Fortunately, that wasn't necessary, because joining him and Bush was a nonplussed Eric Renkey, also on his way to the meeting room and with no clue about who he might bump into along the way.

After shaking hands with Bush, Renkey asked how the president was getting along. "All right," Bush said. "Having a good time here. Looking for that coach."

Paterno still was not in sight. No matter. Bush, Rosa, and Renkey exchanged pleasantries. The excited young men said they were in grad school, Rosa in industrial relations and Renkey in psychology. Rosa said he worked with the wide receivers. Nothing dramatic, nothing that might linger even for an instant in a president's mind.

Yet Bush mentioned specifics about Rosa and Renkey when

Paterno arrived a few minutes later and led him into the squad room. There, with every player in his assigned seat, Bush was in comfortable territory. Paterno, who had been friends with Bush for years and had given one of the seconding speeches for him at the 1988 Republican National Convention, beamed from a nearby chair.

"Discount about 90 percent of what Joe said," Bush told the players, referring to Paterno's flattering introduction. Interrupting, Paterno snapped: "They do that anyway."

Bush was brief. He talked about teamwork and used as an illustration his experiences as a World War II fighter pilot: "Don't pull away from a wing man." He ended by saying: "We [Yale] always kicked the hell out of Joe's team [Brown]." That got a big laugh, and Bush paused for some autographs as he walked out of the room. By now, Rosa had developed an even fuller appreciation for Paterno. The old coach could deliver some mighty fine perks—the president of the United States—and pretty much on command. The old coach and his program also could produce fine summer work, that internship with the Eagles. As a semi-coach himself, Rosa saw still another side to Paterno.

"If a guy could coach a year and then go back and play, it would be the best thing he ever did," Rosa said. "You do see things from a different light."

Practice, for instance.

"Not going after passes, not being aggressive," he said, mentioning two of his own weaknesses Paterno had harped on. "He was right. It frustrated me, but he was trying to make it as realistic as it was going to be in a game situation.

"I'm doing that as a coach. I can see what he's talking about." Here Rosa raised the pitch of his voice and mimicked Paterno: " 'Hey. Gotta reach out and catch that ball.' " As himself once more, Rosa admitted: "It's the truth."

Rosa and everyone else had complained about a lack of communication between the coaches and themselves, especially the assistants. In his new role, Rosa never had to face such situations, but he said: "It's tough to sit down and look a guy in the face.

You want to be totally honest with him and yet you don't want to hurt his feelings. You've got to be careful what you say." As a fifth-year senior, he had hoped to be a starter as a defensive back. That was before Paterno had coaxed him into switching to wideout three years earlier. "I realized I would never be a star after my sophomore year," he said. "I knew I would always be a role player. And a little role. Maybe a guest starter [as he had been the year before, against Temple, when his buddy McDuffie was hurt]."

In his new role, Rosa only lingered in the dressing room he'd once helped define. Rarely did he even glance at freshman-dominated Little Pit. Someone else occupied his locker in the main room, the one upon which he had stuck a decal of the bumbling television character Homer Simpson.

"I used to have regrets," he said, drawing an imaginary line between himself and the active players. "There was a time when I thought I could still be playing out there, if three or four guys went down. This is their chapter now. My chapter's over here."

Ron Fields thought the appropriate end to the final chapter of his football career at Penn State could be found inside an unfamiliar locker in the dressing room. No longer a player, he nevertheless was conducting a locker-by-locker search on an early morning in late September. He wanted to find his helmet and then buy it.

The helmet was distinctive, Fields said, because of the unusually large gouge on the top. He had put his head down too far once on a tackle during practice, missed the runner, and then jammed his helmet against a rock. The gouge was deep and about an inch long. Even the periodic reconditioning of helmets would not get this mark patched over, he said.

As a freshman, Fields had bought a football and gotten Paterno to autograph it. He now wanted something more personal and did not realize during his hunt that others also had purchased their helmets, Tony Sacca getting his for $35.

Fields carefully looked at dozens of helmets, even climbed onto a table in the equipment room and examined several spares perched on a top shelf. No luck. The helmet had probably gotten too worn to repair.

Like Eric Renkey, Fields had been forced from football by a neck injury that did not require surgery. Unlike Renkey, Fields when healthy had not been a featured player, although he did letter in 1991. He remembered being hurt once during practice and smiled while recounting it: "Deep gouge near my left knee. Needed one stitch. One stitch. All the time I'd been bounced around on the field, the doctor stuck a little needle in me and I fainted."

Fields, Renkey, and many others in the class had, without consciously realizing when, crossed a sort of academic boundary. They cared about schoolwork now, actually looked forward to going to class. This was mostly because they were firmly planted in majors of their choosing, no longer stuck with courses needed for graduation but of little interest.

Whether Fields would graduate, even in five years, still was in doubt. As academic advisor Ferrell had predicted, Fields could survive with just nine credits a semester. Any more was a stretch. With 12.5 credits in the spring of 1991, for instance, he had gotten a 1.91. With nine credits in the summer, he had gotten a 3.11. With fifteen credits in the fall, he had gotten a 1.73.

But Fields's eyes sparkled as he talked about a particular class in his broadcast major: ethics in journalism. He wanted to be a producer someday, and some of the important daily questions he might have to answer were troubling.

His professor posed this situation: A man calls the television station, complains about being unemployed and says he's going to set himself on fire in protest. You send a camera crew, which films the scene in all its shocking detail. The question: Why didn't the crew stop the guy? Should they have been an active participant in the story?

"I would have stopped him," Fields said.

Renkey always had the ability academically, and he excelled in whatever excited him. He cared about psychology and had gotten close to an A-average in it. Grad school also was enjoyable, even though the work load in his three courses, 200 pages of reading each week in each class, plus papers and tests, could be enormous. "I've learned that I can handle grad school," he said. "More important, I learned I also will enjoy it."

Renkey knew he had changed, but couldn't explain exactly how: "Meeting different people. Different circumstances. I think vastly different about a lot of things. Stuff you don't get in suburban America. When I came to college, I listened to only one kind of music. I've learned to get along with different people. Tolerate more.

"You never realize how set in your thinking you were until you meet people who don't think the same way. You've got to try and argue your point. That's what college is about, particularly what grad school is all about."

Playing baseball had given Chris Cisar a greater appreciation for football. "You bust your ass," he said, "but you get a lot of things. Stuff you take for granted. The baseball players, for instance, have to get the field ready, and they put the tarp on the field after practice. Those guys have to clean Beaver Stadium after a football game to make money to go away on a baseball trip."

Still, baseball wasn't so dangerous, and Cisar said: "I'm a 22-year-old in a 40-year-old body."

As his buddies 2,000-plus miles away were dealing with losing their last chance at a national championship with more than half a season still ahead, Tony Sacca could not have been more content. He had one of the best jobs in sports: rookie back-up quarterback on a bad NFL team, the Phoenix Cardinals. So much with Sacca had changed. Ironically, he was getting with the Cardinals what he'd been denied at Penn State—a redshirt season, a chance as a first-year player to grasp the system without having to lead unfamiliar teammates during win-or-else games.

"This is so easy," he said in early October. "Training camp is hard, of course, but now you show up for practice [which, with meetings, lasts from about 9 A.M. until late afternoon]. No classes to worry about. And they're paying you. Amazing."

Sacca had treated himself to a dark green Corvette, which did not stand out in the Cardinals' parking lot but drew stares of envy from customers in his restaurant of choice this warm evening: the Red Robin. He could afford more but still preferred a family-oriented ambience. Soup and salad would be fine, he told the waitress.

First to arrive in the booth, however, was a small revelation: Half a season removed from Penn State, Sacca was showing great concern for the Nittany Lions' coaching staff. A few weeks earlier, he'd sent some play suggestions to quarterbacks coach Jim Caldwell.

How incredibly lucky he'd been rarely entered Sacca's mind. And only lingered a little while when it did. Quarterbacks always expect the best. On third and long, they assume something good will happen. With tacklers seventy-five pounds larger bearing down on them, with defensive backs trying to bump receivers off balance and otherwise disrupt pass patterns, they are cocky-confident their arms will deliver first downs. So when Sacca was reminded that he was the first in his class for whom the dream of pro glory had come true, he was quiet for several moments and then said: "I guess in the back of my mind I always knew I was gonna make it."

He had witnessed all the injuries, many from within inches of the scene. One of the worst had been the knee injury suffered by his roommate, Todd Rucci, against Boston College his last season and which now, a year later, still had not fully mended.

First-hand and up close, Sacca also had seen that talent did not guarantee success. Bobby Samuels had as much ability as anyone in his class. But he was hurt some, then seemed to drift away. At the start of fall practice in Sacca's next-to-last season, the locker next to him was occupied by Samuels. Then Samuels was banished to Little Pit, because academic problems limited his practice time to twice a week. Incredibly, Samuels's place was taken by the manager-turned-starter Bob Ceh.

So Sacca had seen it all. He'd also played through nearly everything possible on the emotional spectrum: being yelled at by Paterno, being adored by the masses at Penn State—and also second-guessed by them quite a lot. He'd been the one who gambled on football and, at least temporarily, won. "We didn't worry too much about school," Sacca said. "All the guys I hung out with did what we had to do to stay eligible. Tried to get good grades, but if we didn't it didn't bother us too much."

Sacca said he was fourteen credits shy of his degree. Eight were language requirements he'd kept pushing aside. In the spring of 1993, he said, after the NFL season, he was going to return to Penn State and make up at least some of those credits. His closest friends, Rucci and Gerak, still would be there. This spring, they would be the ones sweating out their NFL draft fate.

Sacca had heard about Leonard Humphries being cut. The defending AFC champion Buffalo Bills had taken nine corner-backs to training camp but only kept four. And did not keep a corner on their developmental squad. Coach Marv Levy told Humphries the bad news over the phone near the end of training camp, but he did it politely.

"I always will keep going," said Humphries, who returned to Penn State and frequently could be seen during the fall working out by himself in Holuba Hall. "If I get cut again, I'll keep after it." As backups, he had planned to take his tests for law school or a real estate license.

Humphries was another reminder to Sacca about his immense good fortune. Then the young headstrong quarterback thought about his old headstrong coach, Paterno, and said: "One night a grad assistant ratted on me for not taking my hat off in the cafeteria, and Joe wouldn't let me go to dinner for two nights.

"But as my senior year went on, I could sense he was starting to feel bad for what he'd done to me. Things he'd say in the papers, about how tough I was. My whole senior year he never said one word [of sarcasm] to me. I'd skip one in the ground, and the year before he'd be running and screaming and ready to throw me out of practice. Last year he'd look away. Not say a thing."

Although he and Paterno had parted on good terms, Sacca said: "Joe probably cost me $5 million [the difference, he estimated, between his contract as a second-round draft choice and what he could have commanded as an early first-rounder]." He was serious, but quickly added: "I have no complaints."

Back at Penn State, the crowd for the game after Miami had settled into Beaver Stadium earlier than usual. October 17, 1992, was homecoming, and there were lots of reasons for optimism. Penn State had won the previous twenty-one affairs under Paterno. Also, the Nittany Lions had lost just once in twenty games to the opponent this balmy day, Boston College. "Remember what Tom Bradley said a year ago?" Rudy Glocker asked as he walked the field during pregame. Indeed, after the 1991 loss to Miami, assistant coach Bradley had said of the remainder of the season: "We could go either way." He pointed his thumb up. "Or this way." He pointed his thumb down.

Immediately, Penn State had gone the way Bradley had hoped. Up. Stating with homecoming, against Rutgers, the Nittany Lions kept winning right through the Fiesta Bowl. Six games; six victories. A major bowl. Third in the country.

The winning could happen again, because none of the five remaining regular-season opponents, including Notre Dame in South Bend, was awesome. In addition to the 19–1 record against Boston College, Kerry Collins seemed ready to assume command of the offense if John Sacca faltered. And O. J. McDuffie was just ten yards from becoming only the ninth Penn State player to amass 3,000 all-purpose yards. His numbers: 1,499 receiving, 252 rushing, 969 on punt returns, and 270 on kickoff returns.

But Glocker and many others also knew there were valid reasons for worry, the main one being motivation. The Nittany Lions were going to the Blockbuster Bowl, no matter what happened the rest of the season. And the chance of any sort of matchup that could vault them into the top five was remote.

McDuffie's hopes of winning the Heisman had been dashed. But he, Gerak, Huntington, Rucci, and a former walk-on coming on strong at tight end, Tony Drayton, were motivated by NFL scouts preparing for the late-April draft. Their fortunes also could go either way.

Like Sacca, McDuffie had concentrated on little else but football. He would graduate, however, needing only to sail through a leisurely eight and a half credits in the fall. Also, he was taking no chances that a career-threatening injury might keep him from being rich. As many other potential first-round draftees around the country had been doing for years, he had borrowed $12,500 and insured himself for $1 million.

Much of the fall had gone well for McDuffie. Some had not. Because of the injury to Collins, he had not been involved as much as he had hoped. And the Miami game dashed his team-oriented goal.

"At times, I'm glad I came back," McDuffie said. "At times, I'm not." Co-captain was not quite what he'd imagined, because Paterno still made all the critical decisions. He could have intervened more forcefully with Paterno on behalf of his good friend Rick Sayles, but had chosen not to. "At this point," he said, "it's like opening an old wound. I told Rick he should make the first move. He didn't want to."

Two offensive plays into the Boston College game, McDuffie got the 10 yards he needed to move up in the record books. The completion from John Sacca totaled 25 yards in all, to the Eagle 33 yard line. But the Nittany Lions could muster nothing out of that drive and little else the first quarter, trailing by 7–3. This was not unusual, but it was worrisome because Boston College entered the game unbeaten and ranked twentieth in the country. Penn State had fallen two notches, to ninth.

Penn State got a break early in the second quarter when the Eagle punter accidentally touched the ground while fielding a punt at his own 30. The Lions took over there and gained a 14–10 lead almost immediately. This was the sort of emotion-sapping turnaround that had knocked plenty of opponents out in the past, including BC.

Fists were flying among Nittany Lions players in confident anticipation. Fans also sensed some sort of quick spurt. On the next series, however, Penn State handed the momentum right back to BC. On fourth down at BC's 35 yard line, the Nittany Lions were called for roughing the punter. So instead of giving the ball to Penn State, the Eagles retained it and were fifteen yards closer to the end zone. On third down, the Penn State secondary allowed a receiver to break free and produce the wide-open 48-yard touchdown that gave BC the lead once more.

The next time BC got the ball it passed Penn State dizzy for another touchdown. Same thing the next time, and at halftime the Eagles had a 28–10 advantage. Midway through the third quarter, matters worsened when BC scored on yet another long pass and took a 35–10 lead.

Part of the stunned crowd started to leave, so dismal did the chance of a comeback seem. When McDuffie gained 43 yards on a reverse and Penn State scored, the Eagles still held a 35–16 lead with 10:27 left in the fourth quarter.

Then Sacca and McDuffie helped lead an 80-yard drive that ended, thirteen plays later, with them combining on a 7-yard touchdown pass. Sacca completed a pass for the two-point conversion, and Penn State pulled within 35–24.

Boston College held the ball for nearly five minutes before punting with 2:42 left. Two plays later, Sacca was out with a shoulder injury, and Kerry Collins trotted onto the field. What followed was storybook stuff: a 24-yard completion with his first pass, a 41-yard completion to McDuffie with his second pass, and a 20-yard completion to McDuffie with his fourth pass. On the sideline, Tony Matesic waved a towel to keep the suddenly aroused crowd cheering. McDuffie caught a break on the sideline, sweat dripping from his nose as he sank to his knees. Soon, a 2-yard run produced a touchdown, and McDuffie was back on the field. Collins then hit him for the two-point conversion, and BC led by just 35–32.

All Penn State could do was try a seldom successful onsides kick. Even in practice, these desperate gimmicks rarely worked. In street clothes on the sideline, the injured place kicker, Craig Fayak, predicted success: "Gonna get it! Gonna get it!" Moments later, the ball took a huge hop and miraculously a 6-foot-

5-inch tight end caught it. Eric Renkey threw his fists in the air and shouted: "Yes! Yes!"

There were ninety-nine seconds left and Penn State was forty-six yards from the end zone. Collins retreated. Everybody in the stadium knew that he eventually would try and find McDuffie long. One of those certain of it was a BC cornerback, who played off McDuffie just enough to con Collins into thinking his favorite receiver was open near the sideline.

Collins threw a 30-yarder across the field to his left. McDuffie had no chance, because the BC defender stepped in front of him and made the catch. The pop the ball made against his pads signalled the end of the comeback. Exhausted, McDuffie lay a while before pulling himself off the ground. He'd been brilliant, with 212 yards on eleven receptions, 43 yards on one run, and 25 more yards on three returns.

Publicly, McDuffie said: "We were flat. Nobody was ready to go."

Privately, Greg Huntington said: "We thought we could win just because we're Penn State."

Because they were Penn State and because Notre Dame was Notre Dame, everyone hit an emotional high four weeks later. November 14 turned snowy, and the field in Notre Dame Stadium was a white blanket cluttered with cleat marks early in the first quarter.

The Nittany Lions came into the game 6–4. They had rallied with an 89-yard drive in the fourth quarter to beat West Virginia in Morgantown; they had fallen too far behind too quickly and lost to Brigham Young in Provo, Utah, before a much-needed off week.

"You've got to rise to the occasion," McDuffie said after the BYU loss. "The Miami game we should have won. The Boston College game we came out flat and got our butts kicked. West Virginia almost surprised us. And BYU? We weren't ready for them, either. It's been downhill ever since the Miami game.

"It just comes with Penn State's nature to set your goals once in a while."

Co-captain and inside linebacker Brett Wright was out of the

Notre Dame game with a knee injury that would end his career three games short of the finish line. Nevertheless, the defense played exceptionally well early on, and Penn State took a 6–3 lead on a 1-yard run. Nothing was automatic this raw day, and the low extra-point kick got blocked. Memories of the place-kicking problems against Miami immediately resurfaced on the Penn State sideline.

Collins had been elevated to starter after his strong performance in relief against Boston College. He directed the comeback against West Virginia; he was spotty against BYU, completing 28 of 54 passes but not producing points when the offense twice advanced to the 7 yard line.

In the cold and with a wet football against Notre Dame, Collins was wild high. Also, he was hampered by the improbable, O. J. McDuffie missing two tough but catchable long passes. About the miserable conditions, McDuffie observed, "What happened was everybody's gloves and cleats froze up."

The teams traded field goals through the second and third quarters, Penn State settling for one from the 12 yard line after failing to get a touchdown on first and goal from the one.

There was one scene late in the third quarter that remained vivid to the few who witnessed it. Paterno ordered a running play called 43 Slice and then said: "If we don't make this, we'll go for a field goal."

What could Paterno be thinking? It already was fourth down. Fourth and 12 from the Notre Dame 32 yard line, to be exact. Third and 12 had been a long pass batted down near the end zone.

Going for it on fourth down from the 32 seemed wise enough, because a 50-yard field goal was out of range and a punt might sail into the end zone and net only 12 yards. But a run? Well, maybe. But Paterno had said: "If we don't make this, we'll go for a field goal."

That eliminated any doubts. Paterno had lost track of the downs. Whether it was being sixty-five years old, being cold, being tense, or a combination of all three, the brilliant old coach had blown it. No one was prepared for any such thing. No one bucked the coach, told him he'd gotten confused. The doomed play lost three yards. Fortunately for Penn State, Notre Dame failed on a fake punt from the Penn State 34 after it gained possession.

However, midway through the fourth quarter, the Nittany Lions recovered a fumble on the Notre Dame 44 yard line. This time, John Gerak, Greg Huntington, and the other blockers cleared the way on a six-play drive that ended with a 13-yard touchdown run and a 16–9 lead. Had the earlier extra-point try been successful, Penn State would have led by a virtually out-of-reach nine points with 4:25 left.

When it got the ball back, Notre Dame called a pass play to the tight end, but the fullback broke free over the middle and Rick Mirer hit him for the touchdown. Still, Notre Dame needed a two-point conversion to win. Mirer rolled to his right, and a Nittany Lions rusher broke free and bore down on him. At the last possible moment, Mirer flipped the ball toward the right side of the end zone, and many a Notre Dame heart started to pound even harder.

A slippery ball on a cold day with the game on the line was headed for the player least likely to catch it—Reggie Brooks. Coach Lou Holtz later admitted, "Reggie Brooks has bad hands. I don't want to mess up his future, but he's not the first guy I'd want to throw to."

Reggie Brooks caught it—in the opposite end zone that Rick Sayles had caught an important pass in Penn State's dramatic victory two years earlier. Same place; similar drama; different result.

Gerak was proud of the effort, saying: "There is no team in the country with any better talent or character, but you need that inner confidence. I think we had that today."

And then, seven days later, the survivors were lined up in the tunnel inside Beaver Stadium, getting ready for their good-bye game at Penn State. Rain pounded outside. They had not gotten all of what they'd come to Penn State for, but there had been achievements and achievers.

A full-color action shot of McDuffie had been on the cover of the student paper that morning. In deference to his considerable skills in baseball and football, the caption read: "Bo. J." Inside was a profile that included the Heisman pitch Paterno had made for McDuffie after the BYU game: "He goes in and plays tough. He plays hurt. He can literally win a game by himself. There can't be anybody who deserves recognition more than O. J."

"I'm sure I will shed quite a few tears before and after the game," McDuffie had said. The tears started to swell just prior to being introduced during pregame. In truth, the class had been totally together for less than two weeks out of five years. Seventeen of the twenty-eight who arrived on scholarship still were in school. About half showed up for the pregame individual recognition.

Remembered by the nine active players were moments everyone in the stadium had shared and moments no one but they could understand.

Some wore a piece of tape wrapped around a finger as an unobtrusive reminder that Rick Sayles was no longer on the team. Sayles was still in town, still in school, still awaiting judgment on the late August burglary and theft charges, still without any reconciliation with Paterno. "Joe would have a fit if they did anything flamboyant," Sayles had said that morning.

Sayles was in a breakfast hideaway off the main street downtown, preparing to attend what he called a "mini-party" of ten or so friends that included watching the regular season finale against Pitt on television. He was smiling, but admitted: "Of course I want to be there [in uniform with his buddies]. I'm kinda sulking today."

About three weeks earlier his path had crossed Paterno's. Sayles was going to a field hockey game. Paterno was going to the office, or so Sayles thought. They passed within a few feet of each other, Sayles said, and their eyes connected briefly. Then each looked down and silently went his separate way.

The cheering that greeted each of the seniors got going again midway through the first quarter, when the offense quickly ground out 47 yards and took a 7–0 lead over Pitt. The offensive line, led by Gerak, Rucci, and Huntington, continued to dominate, and the Nittany Lions had a 23–6 lead at halftime.

Early in the fourth quarter, McDuffie capped his Beaver Stadium career with a 6-yard touchdown pass from Collins. That increased the margin to 43–6, and Paterno poured in the reserves, among them back-up quarterback Matt Nardolillo.

On the sideline, Gerak, Rucci, and Huntington, the three key fifth-year blockers, stood together. They were caked with mud. Their hair was matted. At least, they were going out with a bang. "Ten kegs waitin' at home," Gerak yelled. "Biggest party ever."

The biggest official party of the year was the annual football dinner held in the indoor facility adjacent to the football office. The crowd of a thousand or so included players and their families, faculty, alumni, and boosters. Underclass players wore their jerseys; seniors were in suit and tie and walked with their parents about fifty yards to front row tables as Paterno made the introductions.

McDuffie won the major awards. He'd barely gotten a mention for the Heisman, but made all the important All-American teams. He also was judged the outstanding senior player, as Tony Sacca had been the year before. He wasn't able to stay for the entire program, scooting off to tape a Bob Hope special. There were two surprises, at least to the players involved. Greg Huntington was judged the outstanding offensive lineman, beating out the more heralded Gerak and Rucci. Chris Cisar was voted best special teams player and broke up with emotion during his acceptance remarks. Staying the extra year really had been worthwhile.

Bob Daman said he was going to ask Paterno about getting a varsity letter for helping the staff during his last two years. A letter would be tangible evidence, in the media guide and elsewhere, that he'd actually existed in the football program. Otherwise, he said, who would know?

Huntington and Cisar posed for pictures after the ceremonies. This was about 8 P.M., purposely early to give parents a chance to arrive home at a decent hour. What the two celebrants had planned for the rest of the evening was a quiet session in a computer room. Cisar looked sheepish and said, "Guess this is what they mean by student-athlete."

To many in the audience, Paterno's remarks had seemed odd, more like a pep talk for the upcoming Blockbuster Bowl instead of the genial and general theme that the evening seemed to call for. He knew this season, and this class, should have been more successful. He was almost desperate in challenging the team to go out, against Stanford, with a victory.

As always, the Penn State players for the Blockbuster Bowl January 1, 1993, came out for pregame warm-ups in waves. Kickers and holders first, then the returners, then the backs and receivers and then, last, the linemen. Their jerseys had distinctive patches to signify Penn State's admission to the Big Ten Conference. This would be its last game as an independent.

For the class, this last-ever game had an appropriate twist: Two more players, Ivory Gethers and Mark Graham, were not going to see action. Gethers had missed too many practices, he said, and Paterno had benched him. This after Gethers had made ten unassisted tackles in the final regular season game against Pitt.

"I've had it with dressing and not playing," he said shortly after the team arrived at the stadium. "This is the last game I know I'm not going to play. I'm just trying to move on [as a free agent with someone in the NFL], to become a football player again and be looked at as a football player. Not because I have low grades, or I didn't make a breakfast, or came last to a meeting. This is Joe's house, you know?" More than anyone in the class, Gethers maneuvered for five years along some unseen and shaky wire. He was hurt a lot, and seriously. Also there seemed no position for which his body was ideally suited. He was too light for linebacker, possibly not quick enough for safety. And mediocre grades kept his eligibility in doubt.

Yes, Gethers said, Paterno during that first meeting with the class more than five years earlier had said academics and other non-football issues would be factors in allotting playing time. But

Gethers had seen friends from back home prosper at other major schools and was angry that he had not. Some in the class thought that Gethers had been the one most misused by Paterno, Eric Renkey saying: "Ivory can play. They look for excuses not to put him in there."

Paterno had known that Gethers would have a difficult time balancing academics and football. He'd convinced admissions to take a chance on him and Bobby Samuels, who had left school during his fourth year for a tryout with a pro team in Canada.

Gethers said he was being hit from both sides, from the coaches when he arrived late for practice and from his professors when he left early for football. And then on this extremely warm first day of 1993, he did what came naturally. Knowing that he would not play against Stanford, he still suited up.

Graham wore his jersey, slacks, and loafers into Joe Robbie Stadium. At 170 pounds, he sensed there would be no more football for him. Not even the sort of free agent tryout Gethers might arrange. He had delayed graduation and returned for his fifth year for the chance to finally start and be part of a team that won the national title. He had started the first seven games, then hurt his shoulder; the team had won its first five games, then dropped four of its next six.

As Graham walked toward the Penn State dressing room during early warm-ups, he passed John Gerak walking in the other direction. This was symbolic, because Gerak had much more football left. At 6 feet 5 inches and 280 pounds, he figured to be one of the top guards chosen in the NFL draft in late April.

Like Graham, most of the class had left football at various times and for various reasons before this final game. Of the original class, most were still in the football program in some capacity. Rudy Glocker, Rich Rosa, and Bob Daman served as aides to the assistant coaches. However, only seven of the twenty-eight would play: Gerak, Huntington, Rucci, and McDuffie on offense; Burger and Cisar on defense. Nardolillo would hold for placekicks. The wondrous walk-on, Bob Ceh, still was the snapper for punts and placekicks.

Moments before kickoff, there was one more dropout. Because he would not be playing, co-captain Brett Wright felt out of place and decided not to participate in the coin toss. So Gerak, McDuffie, and underclassman Reggie Givens walked hand in hand toward midfield to meet their Stanford counterparts.

Many Penn State players, among them Gerak and McDuffie, had wanted to turn down the Blockbuster bid, because of the 7–4 record lots of schools around the country would consider admirable. Judging by the half-filled stadium at kickoff, customers not deeply connected to Penn State and Stanford felt similarly.

Emotionally, Stanford and new coach Bill Walsh had the advantage. Walsh had left the San Francisco 49ers as one of the best coaches in NFL history, and he wanted to reaffirm his genius against Paterno, the coach with the fourth-highest victory total ever in college football.

Stanford started with a no-huddle offense and quickly gained a 7–0 lead. Penn State missed some chances, among them a dropped pass by McDuffie at midfield and a fourth-down run that failed, and trailed by 14–3 at halftime.

Quickly, it became 24–3. Stanford cornerback Darrien Gordon was surprised by more than the result. "After the first half," Gordon said, "I didn't see the fire in his [McDuffie's] eyes. I don't know if he quit, but I think the whole team quit. I never thought a team with so much tradition would quit." McDuffie was angry after that 24–3 score held to the finish, looking at some underclassmen in the dressing room and snapping: "We had different players last year, players with heart."

"It's not the ending I expected," Ceh said.

After this embarrassing defeat, Paterno was as brief as he'd been after the thrilling victory over Tennessee in the Fiesta Bowl the year before. He told the seniors he felt badly about their leaving "on a note like this." He told everyone to "stick together" and wished assistant Jim Caldwell success as the new head coach at Wake Forest. And one more thing before the prayer: squad meeting in ten days, at 5 P.M.

Gerak helped Huntington off with his jersey and pads. Huntington did the same for Gerak, then walked up to a few underclass buddies and hugged them. Rucci sat with an ice pack on his neck. Gethers spoke quietly with some underclassmen and left.

"If you'd said these five years would have gone by that fast," said Cisar, "I wouldn't have believed it. But they're gone." He smiled and repeated a question: "What will I look forward to? Sixty-hour work weeks."

Gerak offered two summations. Of the season, he said: "We played well against Miami. In reality, Miami was the best game we'd played to date. But we lost. We could have used that as a positive note, instead of looking at it as the season's over."

Numbers were a bit tricky over the five-year life of the football class. There were sixty games in all, but no player had more than four full years of eligibility. (Huntington actually played during all five years, having been hurt early enough as a true freshman to get a medical redshirt.) Even so, Gerak said of his class: "We came in with a 5–6 season five years ago. We're leaving 7–5. We never really made our mark, so to say, as some of the other classes did. Some great individual performers, O. J. and Tony Sacca. But in five years we really didn't have that great season. Number three was the best we did. We all know number three is not Penn State."

Those were the final words after the final game. Gerak picked some things from his locker and started walking toward the dressing room door. He was the last player out.

Afterword

The charm and the frustration of this book is the near-constant change among those involved. And because none of the characters had precisely the same experience, either with college or with college football, few broad conclusions are possible about the sport, about the eager young men who play it, or about the driven adults who coach it, especially that grand collection of contradictions at Penn State, Joe Paterno.

I do think that the closer you look at college football, the more you think the world could get along quite nicely without it. Or, at the least, with a decidedly smaller dose of it. From what distance should we first focus our lens? How about the drive to the game. Autumn. So many magnificent colors as you snake along the car parade to State College, Pennsylvania, to Norman, Oklahoma, to Ann Arbor, Michigan, or to whatever other college towns, large and small, football draws us.

You arrive at the game. You almost always know someone, for football sells itself on providing a magnetic sense of community. But even if you don't know a soul, you look around the parking areas and see people having a magnificent time: tailgate parties, odd and creative costumes, an occasional band playing its way through the merriment.

You go into the arena. There is no lovelier September scene than the University of Washington's Husky Stadium, where from a perch not too far from the home team's bench you can also see Mount Rainier and the lake from which the well-to-do arrive by boat. What serious follower of sport would pass up the chance for two on the 50 yard line at Notre Dame Stadium? Or to get even a faraway glimpse at some of the sidelines that Bear Bryant trod?

You watch the games: fast and furious, occasionally balletic, a celebration of youth. You often see someone hurt, limping or carried off the field, but his face either is hidden under a helmet or is too far away for its contortions to show. Besides, another player whose face also is hidden under a helmet takes his place and plays well. Or so you think, because the actions of twenty-two men going hell-bent for a few seconds at a time are too swift to grasp immediately.

Now let's zoom in a little closer, to the place mostly off limits: the sideline. The sounds of pads and helmets crashing together a few yards away is frightening. That player you saw leaving the field and quickly forgot is wincing to a trainer's touch. Soon he may be reaching for his helmet, getting ready to return to action. Or he may be headed for the dressing room and, later, for surgery.

There are other expressions under the helmets on the sideline: hopeful and yet resigned. They are the majority of the players, who will play very little that game, very little that season, or very little their entire college football life. The sad reality about college football is that most players don't make it. The competition is so fierce and the sport so dangerous that the majority of players in all football classes fail to succeed at this level, or at least in the way they'd dreamed.

Why they try is the title of this book, *For the Glory*, which also happens to be the first three words of the Penn State alma mater. So infatuated with football had they become in high school, so much had they seen it either as a near-constant part of their environment and an important part of their self-worth that they had to take the risky next step.

Which is why college football is not going to go away. You look at some numbers and shake your head in dismay: twenty-eight scholarship players arrived at Penn State in late summer of 1988; twelve of them had an injury serious enough to require surgery. Some of those twelve were operated on twice. Rudy Glocker had three operations. Eric Renkey (neck), Ron Fields (neck), and Bob Daman (back) never needed surgery; nonetheless, they were forced out of football by their injuries.

None of these players was crippled for life, although football-related injuries kept Chris Cisar from pursuing baseball. But even the worst injuries, the torn anterior cruciate ligaments that required reconstructive surgery, eventually mended to the point where every player returned to action. Todd Rucci was drafted by the New England Patriots after his. Even so, how can anyone glorify any exercise that puts a warning label on a major part of its equipment, in this case the helmet? Football parents know about this. But their view often is too narrow, riveted as it is on one player. With twenty-nine players, including the ultimate walk-on, Bob Ceh, I kept getting jolted by the sights and sounds of misery. Rarely did I walk into the locker room before or after practice and find that one of my guys wasn't limping badly or carefully placing his arm in a sling or fingering a cast or grabbing for a set of crutches.

"They should insert something in the letter of intent you sign," Eric Renkey said. "It should say something like: 'Warning. This will not get you directly into the pros. It will, most likely, be five years of pure hell. Or tough work at the very least. Be prepared.' Do I realize how dangerous football is? I feel it every day."

Football's true believers may well be looking at me in an odd way. Over that five-year period I had surgery, though minor, on each of my knees. In all, I've had three operations on my right knee and may have had it replaced with something artificial by the time you read this. But the culprit was basketball.

So that's the first troublesome issue: injuries. How can a gee-
zer who might be worse off than any of the wounded he chron-
icled go off on college football for being chancy? Walking to the
store is an adventure in some neighborhoods. And the notion of
football being combat without guns is, after all, a considerable
part of the allure.

Even so, I would like to see every thread of artificial turf torn
up and replaced by God's grass. This is personal, without basis
in scientific study. But nearly every player I have spoken with—
before, during, and after the research for this book—hates the
stuff. So I join them, this being a players' book.

With that in mind, with a decided prejudice toward players, I
have one other proposal for the pooh-bahs of college football:
Reduce the number of scholarships, and reduce it dramatically.
This may seem out of whack, what with the alarming number
of injuries the sport produces, but I don't think so. Football
scholarships should be reduced because too many scholarship
athletes play too little football.

When my class was finished at Penn State, the total number
of scholarships a school could grant was eighty-five. Even with
nineteen players hurt at any one time, coaches still could field
three teams on offense and three teams on defense with scholarship material. And that ready-to-play squad would be about
twenty more than NFL teams used each week. From a player's
perspective, that's way too large. It means, quite simply, that
there is not even close to enough playing time for everybody
capable of playing.

Penn State says it only recruits players it feels could start for
two years. Yet of the twenty-eight scholarship players in the class
of 1988, only six—Tony Sacca, Leonard Humphries, O. J. Mc-
Duffie, John Gerak, Greg Huntington, and Todd Burger—actually fulfilled that noble goal. Lots of the rest were hurt too
seriously to play. Tommy Wade played for only two of his four
years as a Nittany Lion. Two of the twenty-eight, Anthony
Grego and Eric Lewandowski, dropped out before the first serious scrimmage of their first year.

Others rarely played. Rich Rosa was heavily recruited out of high school but almost never got into games at Penn State. He was almost always behind two or three superior players at wide-out on offense and in the secondary on defense. Brian Dozier, Rick Sayles, Matt Nardolillo, Mark Graham, Ivory Gethers, and some others had similar experiences. Very good players coming into college; very little playing time once they got there.

The reason was the coach's cushion, an inordinately large squad. There do not need to be five high-school All-Americans lined up against each other at many positions. Reduce the schol-arship limit to, say, sixty, and that won't happen. Sixty scholar-ships means everyone has a chance to play. Sixty scholarships encourages versatility, which is fine because only a small per-centage of college players ever advance to the NFL anyway.

Also, sixty scholarships would keep Paterno and lots of other coaches from working their players too hard during practice each week. Bloody Tuesday, that full-contact, all-out practice that leads to injuries and tires the players to the point of making them less alert academically than they should be, will be tamer. The pros almost never scrimmage during the week; why should the colleges?

This book has caused me to change my mind about why a recruit should consider a particular college. At one time, I bought the academics-first line, that a player's decision ought to be weighted most heavily on the quality of education he might get. And that his chances of playing should be given secondary con-sideration. Now I think that it ought to be the other way around. Unless he has some special discipline in mind, a player ought to go to the school where he can get on the field the quickest. With a couple of exceptions, I don't think the quality of education varies greatly at any of the schools that routinely populate the top-25 polls within Division 1-A.

So if Penn State and Notre Dame, Texas, Southern Cal, Miami, Washington, and the rest of the big-time gang from all the geographic locations in the country come calling, examine the roster carefully. Ask yourself: How deep are they at my po-sition? Then try and find someone bright enough to evaluate your ability and honest enough to be straight with you. Ask him: At what level can I play? Many players shoot too high and never get off the bench.

The current admissions rules for scholarship athletes seem to be moving in the right direction, which is away from near-total reliance on the culturally biased Scholastic Aptitude Test. This leads to the sort of mix I saw at Penn State: Rudy Glocker, who scored 1260 on his SAT and graduated in three and a half years, and Ron Fields, who didn't crack 700 until his third try and took more than five years to graduate. Yes, Fields made it after all, getting his degree in broadcast communications in August 1993. So did Sayles, in psychology. And after all his worrying, he had gotten probation for his theft arrest.

In fact, my class fared quite well academically. Of the twenty-nine who arrived in the fall of 1988, only six had not gotten their degrees, at Penn State or somewhere else, by the winter of 1993. One of those who had not graduated, Bobby Samuels (whose tryouts with Canadian and NFL teams had not gone well) was enrolled at Penn State. There was also an excited phone call only a few weeks before publication when Ivory Gethers called to say, "I'm an alum!"

Officially, Derek Van Nort had not graduated. But his education may well have been superior to most others in his class. In California, Van Nort kept adding minors to his chemistry-related major and joining sophisticated work-study programs. Tony Sacca had taken three courses at Penn State after his first season with the Phoenix Cardinals but still was about a semester shy of graduation. Todd Burger stopped going to class after his final season and remained seven credits short of his degree.

Burger was an immense frustration to Paterno, always on the borderline academically and sometimes below it. The coach could not scare Burger, as he had some others. To Greg Huntington, for instance, Paterno in the spring of 1992 issued this ultimatum: Take enough credits during the summer to be able to graduate by the upcoming December or you won't play your final season. Huntington reacted by taking fifteen credits during the summer and missed dean's list by six-tenths of a point. That left him with just seven credits for the fall. He graduated when Paterno wanted and played well enough that final season to be drafted on the fifth round by the Washington Redskins. Burger was too far behind for that sort of pressure. He could have mixed passing seven credits and trying out for NFL scouts in the spring of 1993. Instead, he chose to step off the track a few yards from his academic finish line.

Football does make academic excellence very tough to achieve. If credits were given for practice time and classroom work, it would be worth about twenty-five in the fall, eleven in the winter, and twenty in the spring. Think about that: A football player in the fall carries about a thirty-seven-credit course load, including the twelve officially on his transcript. Mostly, a player is weary before he even walks into a classroom in the fall. That's because of those energy-sapping two-a-days, plus scrimmages, that begin in early August. A player is physically drained and mentally uneasy because of the keen competition for positions, and then he has to go to class.

College even without football takes a good deal of discipline. College with football almost requires the sort of forced time management that Paterno uses at Penn State: study hall each night for freshmen and upperclassmen with grade-point problems. For at least the first two years, players tend to see football and academics as an either/or situation. Eric Renkey slept through most of his classes his first semester, to be energized and thus maintain the considerable playing time he was getting as a freshman. Chris Cisar said during his second season: "I don't know what to concentrate on, football or the books." By his fourth year, Cisar knew that he could manage both.

As to freshman eligibility, I'm not sure that the few who can handle it should be hampered by the many who can't. My class was almost perfectly balanced after its second semester. Eight players had a cumulative average of at least 2.60; seven players had a cumulative average of less than a 2.0.

Ideally, a freshman would spend his entire first year totally away from football, getting used to the jump from high school.

Some think that's what redshirting already does. It does not. Redshirts practice and attend meetings with everyone else. All they don't get involved in is the fun part, the games. Redshirting mostly is a hedge against injuries, and most of my class needed it. As usual, economics probably would tip the balance in any arguments about not throwing freshmen into college football too soon.

Let's now zoom into Penn State and to Paterno. Did the school and its coach live up to their part of the bargain with this class? Looking back five years later, after he'd gotten his degree and become a second-round draft choice with the Minnesota Vikings, John Gerak described life with Paterno as "like playing for your dad in a bad mood." That hits it square on. Paterno is demanding. He always seems to want a little more than your best and gets loudly personal when that doesn't happen. Throw out the most positive virtues—passion, loyalty, wit, warmth, tenacity, a brilliant mind, and a work ethic second to none—and they all fit Paterno. Yet he also can be abrasive, sarcastic, judgmental, unbending. Not to mention that hair-trigger temper that frequently erupts on the sideline and sometimes gets captured on television. Usually, Sue gives the matter a good airing at home, and Joe apologizes.

Do the positives outweigh the negatives? I think that they do. And once they could see beyond Joe the Screamer, which was difficult, so did nearly everyone in the class. However, I do think he failed in one regard: not giving himself enough to them. Extended up-close glimpses of Paterno were rare. The class saw him often, but almost always in the same ways: as the loud taskmaster at practice, as the father-figure being stern about discipline and academics during team meetings and one-on-one sessions in his office, as the author of he-can-do-better notes to their parents. They wanted the man they called Joe to act like an ordinary Joe now and then.

Deep down, each of the 100-plus members of the squad knew that was impossible. Others also were tugging at Paterno for a moment of his time. More influential others. University officials. College football big shots. Television personalities. Governors.

The president of the United States, George Bush.

Still, Joe *had* made time for them when they were being recruited, had come into most of their living rooms, even. That suggested an intimacy that almost never happened once they got to campus. There wasn't much time in Paterno's life for chitchat, let alone the sort of relatively close relationship nearly every player had enjoyed with his high-school coach.

Except for year-ending evaluations each spring, which mostly were formal anyway, if you didn't do something wrong, you were not invited to Paterno's office. Some of the straight shooters, such as Greg Huntington, wondered why Paterno had more time for someone frequently in trouble, such as Donnie Bunch. Midway through his freshman year, Huntington had a bout with pneumonia that forced him to spend about a week in the campus health center. That he no longer was in high school hit him when nobody from the football office bothered to visit.

"Joe could do better with communications with the players," Eric Renkey said. "A lot of guys don't know where they stand. That leads to a lot of frustration. He talks about this being a family. I sometimes think it's a dysfunctional family, because there's not much communication."

Rudy Glocker and some others had occasional looks at Paterno with his guard down. Tommy Wade had heard Paterno mention how much a speed-reading course he'd taken growing up had helped. But even that took place when Wade was squiring a recruit.

Paterno knew about his players, often more than they wanted him to, but he frequently would breeze past them in an otherwise empty locker room. He wasn't cold or impolite, simply an unimaginably busy man in a hurry.

The assistant coaches were impossible to categorize in more than a superficial way, because each player had a unique experience with them and, therefore, a different opinion. Offensive coordinator Fran Ganter seemed to some a bit anxious to report everything to Paterno; to Wade, however, Ganter was the aide with whom he could be the most open. Eric Renkey thought defensive coordinator Jerry Sandusky put too much stock on how overweight he was and not enough on his performance; Glocker found Sandusky the easiest to joke with. And so on.

There was one universal opinion about the assistants: None of them would buck Paterno. Or at least not when they were around. Who knew what happened in meetings. "I would see an assistant compliment a player during practice," said Wade. "Then Joe would come up and chew the player out. And the assistant would say: 'Joe's right.' I saw that with all of them."

As a counter to his dark side, Paterno had a sports psychologist, Dr. David Yukelson, who was a confidant to many players but whose office was about a mile away from the football complex. Yukelson provided a comfortable shoulder for players uneasy about going to Paterno and his aides, even the ones who recruited them. Players would brighten when I mentioned Yukelson. "Good man," they would say. He would keep quiet about their doubts and anger, show them ways to improve their concentration, sometimes simply let them talk. Nothing got back to Paterno, unless the player needed serious psychological help.

There was a secret that Paterno chose not to share with his players: how strongly he also was tied to the fraternity of football. He confided in the spring of 1990, "I'm scared to death to retire, to be frank with you. I don't know what I'd do." Not know what to do? Of all the easily recognizable coaches in all of sport, college or professional, Paterno outwardly seemed the one who might actually look forward to life after football. He seemed the best read, the most thoughtful, the one whose mind might even be anxious for more than Xs and Os and coaxing teenagers to play a game for him. "I have absolutely no hobbies," he said. "I see some of these guys just get out of it before they're ready. I'm not just talking about coaches. They get old fast."

Only once did I break the ground rule for this book: that nothing any player said about Paterno would become known to Paterno before their experience was over. That time was in the late summer of 1992, when Rick Sayles thought Paterno had abandoned him after his arrest for theft. I went to Paterno just before practice began and said Sayles deserved better from him. Paterno was gruff, offering vague reasons for his lack of support.

That very day, Paterno and assistant Tom Bradley had gotten notes from Marilyn Renkey, thanking them for helping Eric. The one to Paterno read in part: "Even though Eric's football career didn't turn out the way we wanted it, it's been a great experience." She underlined great. Twice. One day. Two dramatically divergent opinions about the coach.

Later, there was a warm letter from Adam Shinnick, who when he'd transferred to Cal-Berkeley four years earlier had been bitter about a lack of concern for his injuries. The significant part of Shinnick's letter was this: "I deeply regret what happened at Penn State between myself, you, and the training staff. I want you to know that I have always stood by what you told us in a team meeting. You once told us that 'the people in this room are the greatest people you will ever be associated with.' Coach, I want to thank you for the positive influences you had on my life."

Rudy Glocker offered this about Paterno after the team went from a 5–0 start in 1992 to a 7–5 finish: "I think he got soft. I think maybe he's gotten away from some of the things that made winning possible. If being stern and a disciplinarian got you this far, keep it up. He may be obsessed with winning a national championship but maybe he's forgotten what it takes to win it." Glocker thought about what appeared to be inconsistencies, such as sending a back-up (Tony Matesic) home prior to the Fiesta Bowl and allowing a star (O. J. McDuffie) to remain after a more serious offense. "I think Joe has a sense of urgency," Glocker said. "The Fiesta Bowl turned our way because of O. J. But that might have cost Joe down the road, because maybe not enough guys were scared of him."

Five seasons later, in early August 1993, the class was completely split. In truth, they had been totally together only briefly at Penn State. Gradually, each had taken a separate path away. Sacca was in his second training camp with the Phoenix Cardinals. O. J. McDuffie (Miami Dolphins), John Gerak (Minnesota Vikings), Todd Rucci (New England Patriots), Greg Huntington (Washington Redskins), and Todd Burger (Chicago Bears) were in their first and seemed likely to survive. A walk-on who had arrived with them at Penn State, Troy Drayton, had grown into a terrific tight end and was making an impact with the Los Angeles Rams.

Huntington's first meeting as a professional was in one regard similar to his first with Paterno. All the Redskins rookies were told to look around them, that many in the room wouldn't make it. After the attrition of his class at Penn State, he didn't need to be reminded. Like all rookies, Huntington had been poked and prodded by NFL medics and subjected to a variety of tests prior to the draft. Especially puzzling to him was the 480-question exam given by the New York Giants. Among the questions he recalled were: Do you occasionally tease small animals? Do you ever think about being a nurse? Do parts of your body ever go numb? Huntington was unfazed. "I'm a lot more confident of myself here than I was coming out of high school," he said. "I guess you do grow up."

Being drafted by the Miami Dolphins gave McDuffie a chance to be reunited with his father, Terry White. They saw each other for the first time when O. J. came to Florida with his high school baseball team, and again when Penn State played in its two Blockbuster Bowls. So the excitement for O. J. beyond the esteem of being a first-round draft pick in the NFL was placing a phone call and saying, "Pops, I'm coming to Florida." They lived thirty miles apart during his rookie season and his father, a chef, often came by and prepared dinner.

Back in Pittsburgh, Eric Renkey had stopped work on his graduate degree and was working with troubled youngsters. He had come around to Paterno's way of thinking in one major regard, always arriving for meetings at least several minutes early.

Many in the class had gone back to their roots for jobs. Tony Matesic had an entry-level position on Wall Street, observing, "Who could have imagined that?" Tommy Wade returned to New Mexico and, surprisingly, to football. He was admitted to

New Mexico State and, because his knee injury had been so serious, was allowed to play a year after his eligibility would have otherwise expired. He was expected to graduate in the spring of 1994. Donnie Bunch also returned home. He had left Camden with his girlfriend, Audrey, for a couple of years and done odd jobs in Oklahoma. He was looking for steady work.

Rudy Glocker had accepted a summer fellowship in Sweden, where after a speech he'd gotten close enough to be caught in the same snapshot frame as the former head of the Soviet Union, Mikhail Gorbachev. As many of his teammates had expected, Mark Graham was involved in his own small business: marketing sporting apparel. Rich Rosa had a chance to stay in football, as a grad assistant to Jim Caldwell at Wake Forest, but decided to accept a job in finance. As usual, he knew where nearly everyone else was and what they were doing. He would be keeping in touch.

As will I, whenever and wherever possible, for their lives are really just getting started. And I'd like to see how they play out. Knowing these kids over six years, I've retired hundreds of memories and twenty-nine jerseys. Penn State can put whomever into its football suits, but number 24 will always be O. J. McDuffie, number 88 Eric Renkey, number 56 Ron Fields, number 48 Chris Cisar. And so on. Because of these kids, I can walk into any college football squad room in the country, look at the hundred or so unfamiliar faces and say: "We've never met, but I know who you are."

Acknowledgments

I have had two concerns above all others: that I would never get to the acknowledgments, because this unique effort wouldn't fly, or that when I did, I would forget someone magnificently helpful. So I apologize to anyone whose kindness I may have forgotten. There have been so many.

This book would not have happened without two people: Faith Hamlin, my agent, and Pete Wolverton, my editor. Faith often had more faith than I did in a project that spanned three administrations: Reagan's, Bush's, and Clinton's. She is fabulous. And any writer could feel comfortable handing his prose to Pete.

Those who also have encouraged and tolerated me the entire time include my son, Scott (who once said, "Dad, it's only a book"); my daughter, Lauri; my sister, Margy, and her family (Roger, Chrissy, and Alex); Carol and her mother, Marge Reilly; my daughter-in-law, Heidi, and her parents, Bill and Hansi Wardlaw; my grandson, Wayne; Gloria Folker, Kathy Blumenstock, Ben Marlin, Len Shapiro, Bill Gildea, Chuck and Ann Boohar, Jim and Brenda McKelvey, Marge Walls, and Peggy Hockersmith.

And: George Solomon, Bob Kaiser, Len Downie, Don Graham,

Christine Brennan, Steve Berkowitz, Michael Wilbon, Judy Mann, Anthony Cotton, Tony Reid, Jeanne McManus, Frank Ahrens, Ben Gieser, Mark Asher, Tony Kornheiser, Tom Boswell, Don White, Bill Brubaker, Sushant Sagar, Gail Shapiro, Joel Richardson, Pat McLaughlin, Neil Greenberger, and at least a half-dozen others at the *Washington Post* who pushed the proper keys to keep thousands of words from vanishing.

And: Joe Paterno and my twenty-nine favorite Nittany Lions, who get a dedication and also a nod. Plus Joe's assistants and his support staff, most especially academic advisor Don Ferrell, administrative aide Cheryl Norman, and staff assistant Mel Copobianco. Communications director L. Budd Thalman was gracious and generous as were his aides: Mary Jo Haverbeck, Jeff Brewer, and Jim Caltagirone. Former athletic director Jim Tarman was a major reason I chose journalism thirty-some years ago and remains a source of inspiration.

And: Elisabeth Jakob, David Black, Ally Finkel, Marlin Mackenzie, Joyce Greene, and Susan O'Malley. Writer pals Bill Fisher, Bill Carroll, Gordie Jones, Ron Christ, Ron Bracken, Rich Scarcella, Ray Parillo, Neil Rudel, Phil Grosz and his staff, Ira Miller, Dick Weiss, and John Feinstein, who helped make books such as this one possible.

And: my mother, Elizabeth, who didn't leave until the finish line was in sight.